Also by Ulrich Steger

CORPORATE DIPLOMACY: The Strategy for a Volatile Fragmented Business Environment

THE STRATEGIC DIMENSIONS OF ENVIRONMENTAL MANAGEMENT: Sustaining the Corporation during the Age of Ecological Discovery (*with Ralph Meima*)

The Business of Sustainability

The Business of Sustainability

Building Industry Cases for Corporate Sustainability

Edited by

Ulrich Steger

First published 2004 by
PALGRAVE MACMILLAN
Houndmills, Basingstoke, Hampshire RG21 6XS and
175 Fifth Avenue, New York, N.Y. 10010
Companies and representatives throughout the world

PALGRAVE MACMILLAN is the global academic imprint of the Palgrave Macmillan division of St. Martin's Press, LLC and of Palgrave Macmillan Ltd. Macmillan® is a registered trademark in the United States, United Kingdom and other countries. Palgrave is a registered trademark in the European Union and other countries.

ISBN 1–4039–3396–0

This book is printed on paper suitable for recycling and made from fully managed and sustained forest sources.

A catalogue record for this book is available from the British Library.

Library of Congress Cataloging-in-Publication Data
The business of sustainability: building industry cases for corporate sustainability/edited by Ulrich Steger.
    p.   cm.
Includes bibliographical references and index.
ISBN 1–4039–3396–0 (cloth)
1. Sustainable development.   2. Social responsibility of business.
3. Corporations—Environmental aspects.   4. Economic development—Environmental aspects.   I. Steger, Ulrich.
HC79.E5B8665 2004
658.4'08—dc22   2003068963

10   9   8   7   6   5   4   3   2   1
13   12   11   10   09   08   07   06   05   04

Printed and bound in Great Britain by
Antony Rowe Ltd, Chippenham and Eastbourne

Contents

Part I Building a Business Case: General Findings, Observations and Lessons Learned

Part II Industry Reports

List of Tables

List of Figures

List of Boxes

Acknowledgements

It is not an easy task to address the economic logic of corporate sustainability within a strictly empirical framework. Too much is clouded by propaganda and meaningless correlations that rarely aid understanding of what companies are doing and why. The methodological challenges are well known and difficult to tackle in practical field research: politically correct answers, few hard measures, widely differing perceptions of the same issue among executives, even those in the same company, and a certain though understandable weariness by executives when asked to fill out yet another research questionnaire. In fact it is probable that few spheres of activity are as over-researched by academics, consultants, ethical investment funds, journalists and so on. As one sustainability officer noted, 'Sometimes I have the feeling that my colleagues and I are confronted by an army of researchers who outnumber us 10 to 1.'

Therefore first and foremost we would like to thank the member companies of the Forum for Corporate Sustainability Management (CSM) at the International Institute for Management Development (IMD), which pushed us to go for the 'big splash' rather than carrying out yet another case study on the subject. Teresa Presas (formerly of Tetra Pak), Peter Hughes (Philip Morris International), Ruth Blumer (Sulzer), Paul Mudde (ABN-AMRO), Armi Temmes (M-real Corporation), Hans Jöhr and Tim Wolfe (Nestlé), Thomas Scheiwiller and Amanda Pingree (PricewaterhouseCoopers), Michael Schemmer (Bombardier) and others encouraged us by putting forward compelling arguments for embarking on the journey.

Secondly, we would like to thank our 'reference companies' and our key contacts at those companies. These were mostly members of the Forum for Corporate Sustainability Management (CSM) and the Learning Network at (IMD). They gave us special access either to company information or to senior management staff, which enabled us to conduct numerous in-depth interviews and delve into the reality of their corporate sustainability actions. Our thanks go to Daimler Chrysler (Ulrich Müller), Lufthansa (Karlheinz Haag), Du Pont (Pierre Trauffler), Shell (Marc Weintraub), Swiss Re (Thomas Streiff), Unilever (Jeroen Bordewijk and Jan-Kees Vis), Hoffmann-La Roche (Pierre Jaccoud and Hans Künzi) and ABB (Christian Kornevall and Michael Robertson).

Special thanks are due to George Jaksch of Chiquita, Martina Priebe of ATAG, Heiko Hünsch of Siemens, Stefanie Held of the International Finance Corporation, Hans-Peter Meurer and Marita Hilgenstock of RWE, and Georges Dupont-Roc of Total. Unfortunately we cannot give the full list of interviewees here – there were simply too many – but we are grateful to each and every one of them because without their contributions we would not have been able to present a complete picture. The same is true of those who helped us to collect over 1000 completed questionnaires, and in particular the programme directors at the IMD.

Our partnership with the Business and Industry Unit of the World Wide Fund for Nature (WWF) invaluably enhanced our endeavours and will also facilitate the application of our results through the many dialogues the WWF has with the business community. We are especially grateful to Paul Steele and Chris Hails, and are particularly appreciative of the support we received from Jean-Paul Jeanrenaud and Maria Boulos.

The unique composition of our Advisory Council made it an extremely effective sounding board, comprising as it did NGOs (the WWF and the World Business Council for Sustainable Development, represented respectively by Jean-Paul Jeanrenaud and Margaret Flaherty), industry representatives (Thomas Streiff from Swiss Re, and Jeroen Bordewijk and Jan-Kees Vis from Unilever) and two external experts, Heike Leitschuh-Fecht and Reinier de Man. They challenged us all along the way, thereby contributing significantly to our understanding and framing of the results, and enabling us confidently to present the interim results to our members at our biannual forums, which further enriched our understanding and helped us to make sense of often contradictory data.

We would like to dedicate our research results to the European Academy of Business in Society, and hope we have laid a foundation for further work in this area by both companies and academics, thus allowing regulators to draw a more precise line between placing parameters on company behaviour and allowing them a greater degree of flexibility.

Last but not least, such extensive research could not have been accomplished in such a short time without the substantial support of the IMD and its stimulating research culture. Few projects of this size – over 350 interviews in 16 countries and analysis of more than 1000 completed survey questionnaires – could have been completed in 16 months. We started hiring our research team in May 2002, commenced the research in June 2002 and sent the final manuscript to the publisher at the end of September 2003. We thank IMD leaders Peter Lorange, Jim Ellert and John Walsh, and we are grateful for the management and administrative support provided by Philip Koehli and Petri Lehtivaara and their teams, all of whom showed more interest in furthering the research than in enforcing budgetary restrictions. Their support committed us to delivering results that would be relevant not only to the IMD's Learning Network but also to the wider business community and the public at large. Our research is evidence in itself of the necessity of meeting the highest standards of academic conduct, as will also be seen in a number of forthcoming PhD theses.

Finally, we enjoyed great teamwork: while each researcher was responsible for the research in his or her industry, we had to use a common framework and methodology so that we could compare the results and present them as an integrated whole. In theory this sounds simple, but in reality – given the broad variety of issues, logistical difficulties and so on – it required many lively debates to come up with solutions that met with common accord. Innovative solutions are the outcome not of preconceived ideas but of the challenges and conflicts that arise in open and free discussions. All this did not prevent us from having great fun both on 'the battlefield' and during a good dinner afterwards.

Thanks are also due to Henri Bourgeois and Claudia Schindel who carried out the research on the technology and chemical sectors respectively, but whose conclusions could not be included in this book due to space considerations.

I am especially grateful to the core CSM team, Aileen Ionescu-Somers, Kay Richiger and Oliver Salzmann, who shouldered a great deal of additional work. In addition to her own research, Aileen kept a watchful eye on project management and the meeting of deadlines, as well as taking care of the hundreds of details that, if not properly supervised, could easily have derailed the project. Oliver patiently and tirelessly oversaw the 'number crunching' and the development of websites to present the results of the project, and without Kay's outstanding administrative skills we would definitely have ended up in chaos. Finally, I greatly appreciate the help of Nancy Lane for data analysis, Blandine Milliot-Louché for data entry and Lindsay McTeague for editing, as well as the support of Sue Gordon and Michelle Perrinjaquet in the preparation of the final text. While each researcher is accountable for the results presented in his or her chapter, I take full responsibility for any flaws, errors and omissions.

ULRICH STEGER

The editor and publishers are grateful to Scottish Power for permission to reproduce Figure 7.5 (p. 142) from its Scottish Power Environmental Sustainability Report, 2001/02.

Foreword

According to research by the Institute of Policy Studies, in 1999 the top 200 corporations' combined sales exceeded the combined economies of all the world's countries minus the top 10. This is only one of the many statistics that point clearly to the fact that active corporate engagement is essential if the world is to achieve the changes in production and consumption patterns and international and domestic law that will be required to put us and our planet on the path to sustainability. Recent trends have led to higher expectations of companies' environmental and social performance. Corporations are expected to take responsibility for the social and environmental consequences of their operations, to understand and address the interests and demands of their stakeholders, and to demonstrate through greater transparency that they are behaving responsibly. Recent trends have also led to general acceptance that social, environmental and economic goals do not conflict but are integrally connected to long-term competitiveness.

The path to sustainability will not be an easy one, not least because it will involve behavioural change both at the level of corporate strategy and by the people who drive corporations. This will require tremendous courage as well as strategic vision and the knowledge and tools to act on both.

The WWF believes that the customized tools that have resulted from the research reported in this book will be applicable to a wide range of industries and will help forward-looking companies to bring sustainability into the mainstream of their business.

This book is the result of an unusual research partnership between a leading business school, the IMD, and the WWF, one of the world's largest conservation organizations. Both institutions were interested in deepening their understanding of the economic rationale behind the business case for sustainability. The WWF's involvement built on prior work[1] that aimed to encourage wider adoption of sustainability principles into business practice by focusing on potential business benefits as key drivers of improved company performance in ethical, environmental and social areas. The IMD, with its access to global companies through its corporate sustainability research initiative (the Forum for Corporate

Sustainability Management – CSM), was in a good position to identify the research topics that are most relevant to companies today.

The result is a constructive step forward in the discussion on the business case for sustainability. It attempts to grasp company-specific perspectives and suggests tools to assist companies to develop their own business case, to maintain or create value in areas of strategic business concern.

The next step will depend on companies themselves, with the support and encouragement of organizations such as the WWF and learning centres such as the IMD. It is encouraging that the idea for the research was generated by industry itself through the CSM.

CLAUDE MARTIN
Director General, WWF International

1. WWF, *To Whose Profit? Building a Business Case for Sustainability* (WWF in partnership with Cable and Wireless plc, 2001).

Preface

This book presents the results of the IMD Forum for Corporate Sustainability Management's research on 'Building a Business Case for Corporate Sustainability'. The aim was to reveal the economic logic behind the sustainability strategies of globally active companies. We worked on the central assumption that companies, as predominantly economic entities, will make significant efforts only if they have a business reason for so doing and are able to build and communicate a business case. As business cases are industry-specific, and in many instances company-specific, our research was conducted in nine industries, ranging from oil and gas and utilities in the energy sector, automotive and chemical industries to 'front-line' industries such as food and beverages and aviation, and 'modern' industries such as pharmaceuticals, financial services and technology.

The research also aimed to help companies to build their own company-specific business cases for corporate sustainability. More detailed research will appear in a series of PhD studies, where the industry data will be more extensively analyzed, processed and compared in detail with the overall research results. We have designed a 'diagnostic tool' for each sector that enables company teams to use the empirical findings for their industry as a template. The tools, as well as the industry reports, can be downloaded free of charge from http://www.imd.ch/research/projects/bcs. A full description of the research methodology can also be found on the website. In this book, for the readers' convenience we have integrated the oil and gas and electricity industries into a single chapter on the energy industry, as well as greatly condensing the original industry reports. Due to space considerations we have been unable to include chapters on the chemical and technology industries, but these can be found on the website.

The book is organized as follows. Part I consists of four chapters. Chapters 1 and 2 describe the conceptual framework and goals of our research, the hypotheses tested and the methodology used. Chapter 3 presents the general and cross-industry findings, with particular emphasis on the sustainability issues with which companies are confronted, and their economic relevance. All too often the focus is on tools, but the logic of what companies are doing is fundamentally based on the economic relationship between sustainability actions and their business.

We review the specific value drivers that link sustainability issues to economic performance, and the methods companies use to manage sustainability issues.

Finally, in Chapter 4 we assess the business case and put our findings into a broader perspective, especially with regard to the strategic mismatch between the articulated expectations of NGOs and politicians on the one hand and what can reasonably be expected from companies on the other. We conclude with some of the surprises and nagging questions with which we were confronted during our research.

Part II contains the results of the industry studies. All the chapters have a similar format and address the same questions: what is the industry's current economic situation, what are the pertinant sustainability issues and their economic relevance, what are the value drivers, who are the main stakeholders, and how are important sustainability issues being integrated into business strategies? Hence readers can easily make cross-comparisons of industries and themes.

Research at the IMD is aimed not only at meeting global academic standards, it also has to be relevant for the IMD's Learning Network and the participants in its various programmes. This governed the presentation of our research and our desire to transform the empirical evidence into a usable set of diagnostic tools. The next step will be to evaluate what companies have learned by means of these tools (a number of pilot projects are currently underway). In this respect our research is an invitation for companies to take action – and for us to take part in the process. The bottom line of our project on building a business case for corporate sustainability was put in a nutshell by one of our Advisory Council members: 'If you want to, you can!' And we certainly hope you will.

Part I

Building a Business Case: General Findings, Observations and Lessons Learned

1
Corporate Sustainability: The New Catch Phrase?

If you are a follower of current political debates you will not have missed the rhetoric devoted to sustainable development, with government papers by the score (the exception perhaps being the Bush administration) and innumerable statements on the subject by companies and industry associations. Nobody wants to be the 'odd man out', be they British nuclear power companies, Brazilian pulp and paper companies or Danish cleaning service providers; all pay tribute to the slogan 'Doing well by doing good'. Environmentalists and social activists are uneasy with this trend, with officials muttering about 'greenwash' while at the same time considering how they can jump on the bandwagon and cooperate with companies.

Only economists, and perhaps historians ask themselves about the logic of all this. Since mediaeval times, when religious, economic and political power was often combined, these institutions have evolved to take on differing roles in society. Today the purpose of companies, which are now social institutions in their own right, is not to promote the common good but to meet market needs while making a profit (as an indicator that they have added more value than the resources they have used). Or at least this is what economists have believed since the time of Adam Smith. Put simply, if there is no economic logic behind what companies are doing, they are violating their basic mission. This does not mean that companies do not care about the social or ecological impact of their operations, but simply that they will do nothing voluntarily in these areas that will serve to damage their profits. After all, society has developed (democratic) governments to see to the common good and if taxpayers expect companies to behave in a way that will not benefit them economically, governments will have to legislate to force them to comply. Therefore if companies are to embark on the road to corporate sustainability – which is shorthand for the myriad of environmental and social actions that go beyond regulatory compliance – they must have an economic reason, a business case, for doing so.

This book is all about discovering the economic logic of corporate sustainability. For a variety of reasons research on this topic has been very inconclusive (for a detailed discussion of the relevant literature see Salzmann *et al.*, 2003). This is due not only to limited empirical evidence, an obstacle that we have tried to overcome in our research, but also to the basic, often overly generic, approach of these studies. Furthermore they rarely address the question of whether the business case is the same across industries. Therefore in this book we approach the issue on an industry-specific basis in order to provide more detailed and representative insights.

Reference

Salzmann, Oliver, Ionescu-Somers, Aileen and Steger, Ulrich (2003) *The Business Case for Sustainability – Establishing a Sound Research Base for The Development of a Case-Building Tool* (Lausanne, Switzerland: IMD).

2
Searching for and Building a Business Case

Objectives, methodology and empirical basis

The objective of our research was to detect whether an industry-specific business case exists to demonstrate the economic logic behind the actions that make up companies' sustainability strategies, that is, the principal economic reasons for and drivers of the business case. Based on the empirical evidence gathered during the research we developed a set of sector-specific diagnostic tools to help managers build their company-specific business case (as a member of our Advisory Board put it, 'You have to build your business case, you do not just simply find it'). The reason for adopting this approach was to avoid lecturing managers from the safe haven of an academic institution about where and how to fight their battles.

To test our hypotheses empirically we chose – together with a review of previous empirical research in the area – two methodological approaches. The first consisted of 418 interviews in 16 countries with general and functional managers and sustainability officers (or whatever title the companies gave to the latter function) in 104 different companies from nine industrial sectors based on a fixed interview guideline. These companies included a number of what we refer to as 'reference' companies – at least one company in each sector with which we collaborated very closely. The second methodological approach was to carry out two questionnaire surveys, one for sustainability officers and the other for managers in other departments (referred to as 'general managers' throughout this book). A total of 1068 executives completed the surveys (945 general managers and 123 sustainability officers).

We focused on large, globally active, companies with more than 10 000 employees and with activities in Europe, the Americas and Asia and a home base in one of the OECD countries. This was not only because such companies were in the public spotlight, but also because this is the type of company that is a member of the Forum for Corporate Sustainability Management (CSM), a research initiative at the IMD and that selected this research topic amongst others through an open and democratic selection process. The research started in June 2002, the preliminary results were presented to the CSM member companies in April 2003, and the project was concluded in June 2003 with the publication of the nine sectoral reports and proposed diagnostic tools.[1]

The conceptual framework

Companies (together with consumers and others) create external effects through their operations or actions. These effects can be positive – for example spill-over effects from research and income multiplier effects in local communities – or negative, a classical example being pollution. It is expected that governments or other entities that are external to the market process will internalize the externalities into market-relevant costs if the impact of the externalities is not acceptable to important stakeholders, for example the investment and operational costs of pollution-control equipment to protect people living near a plant.

However not all externalities are internalized as this would result in a static rather than a Pareto optimal equilibrium. The externalities created by innovation are a telling example; so far nobody has claimed compensation from the fossil fuel industry for job losses and stranded assets resulting from the growth of renewable energy sources, assuming the latter can create such externalities when they are in a position to compete. Sustainability issues often emerge when important stakeholders press for the internalization of externalities and reduction of the negative impact of corporate operations. In the past the pressure was primarily directed at governments because they were expected to do the job. Companies did not do so voluntarily because the increased costs would reduce their profits.

The tables have now turned and companies have become the targets of stakeholder claims, for two reasons. First, national states have lost the power to internalize externalities because of the need to consider the global competitiveness of their economies. A more coordinated approach appears to be necessary (see Steger, 2002, chs 2 and 3). Second, although in many cases internalization is economically disadvantageous, companies have three means of internalizing externalities without endangering their economic goals:

- Through technological innovation, which is often advantageous in all three dimensions of sustainability.
- By applying management concepts to reduce (negative) externalities or generate positive externalities.
- By influencing customers to demand more sustainable goods and services.

The array of clean technologies that have emerged in recent decades is an example of the first of the above. These often exceed the required legal standards but at the same time can be more cost effective. An example of the second is supply chain management and outsourcing to replace capital-intensive production at home with more labour-intensive production in developing countries, and an example of the third is the introduction of eco-labels to attract buyers for more environmentally friendly products. The corporate business case for sustainability is therefore dependent on three preconditions:

- An insufficiently internalized externality becoming a sustainability issue as a result of demands by important stakeholders.
- The relevance of the sustainability issue for the company in terms of the effect on value drivers such as turnover and brand reputation.
- The possibility of using one of the above measures without incurring negative economic consequences.

However even if a business case exists, which is our central research hypothesis, the specific way in which companies are exhausting this potential is significant. As mentioned above, the business case may very considerably across sectors and countries. In addition there are many potential barriers, as well as promotional factors. Included in the former are the mind-set of managers, knowledge gaps, regulatory barriers, investor behaviour and so on, while the latter include public or market pressures, new business opportunities, top management leadership and the nurturing of a corporate culture. In our research methodology, all this was formulated as hypotheses and translated into an interview guideline and questionnaire.[2]

The diagnostic tools, which should help sustainability officers to develop a company-specific business case, mirror the results of the empirical investigation in both structure and findings. The key paradigm of · the diagnostic tools can be visualized as a 'smart zone' (Figure 2.1),[3] the business case area or zone in which the company creates additional

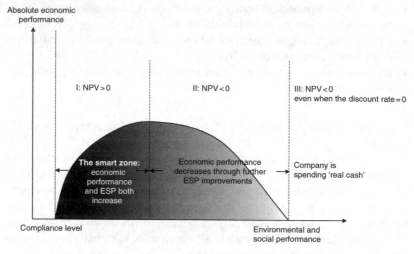

Figure 2.1   The relationship between economic performance and environmental and social performance (ESP) beyond compliance

economic value by improving its environmental and social perform-ance beyond that required by the legal standards that manifest the internalization of externalities by governments. As countries differ in their level of internalization, so too does the business case in these countries.

Lankowski (2000), Wagner (2001) and Salzmann *et al.* (2002) propose an inverse U-shaped curve to describe the relationship between corporate economic and environmental and social performance (ESP). Figure 2.1 portrays the possible relationship between absolute economic perform-ance and beyond-compliance ESP, that is, how economic performance is affected when companies voluntarily internalize external environ-mental and/or social effects. The curve defines three 'intuitive' phases of the impact of ESP improvements on corporate economic performance, in which all corporate sustainability initiatives are benchmarked against the risk-weighted average cost of capital (WACC) or another internal company- or project-specific cut-off rate. Of course real life is never as smooth and clear-cut as the curve might suggest, but it gives an idea of how we frame the basic relation.

Compliance with legal requirements is beyond the economic consid-eration of a company – all entities have to do it and what matters is how efficiently companies manage it (in our framework, legal require-ments are already internalized externalities). The business case starts when a company is voluntarily doing something that improves not only its economic performance in absolute terms, but also its environmental and social performance. The net present value – the revenue stream discounted with the risk-weighted cost of capital, or the internal hurdle rate – is positive (NPV > 0), meaning that the firm would make this investment even if it did not improve ESP.

Zone I represents the 'smart zone'. We can plausibly assume that the most profitable projects are the first to be carried out, so that the curve is steep at the beginning (representing high NPVs) and then flattens out (at this point the NPV is zero) before turning downwards. In Zone II the NPV is negative; therefore the overall economic performance is declining. But if the discount factor were lowered this might change (the lower the discount factor the more extensive the smart zone). It is therefore, plausible to assume that a company might not actually loose cash, but simply allocate capital to subprofitable projects. This recognition is important because projects in Zone II might be carried out because there are potential synergies that are difficult to quantify. But the requirements are tough because normally there are more profitable projects that are competing for finance. These projects have opportunity costs in terms of profitability.

Zone III illustrates a 'philanthropic' level of ESP performance. Even at zero cost of capital, expenditure on better ESP does not add economic value and therefore negatively affects economic performance in absolute terms; in other words the company is losing cash (note that at the intersection between the curve and the abscissa the company is economically in the same position as with full compliance).

The smart zone illustrates a concept rather than establishing a mathematical or quantitative model against which to measure the business case for sustainability. We have chosen this concept because it should be easily understood by managers and engender curiosity about where a company is positioned on the curve.

Notes

1. Available at http://www.imd.ch/research/projects/bcs.
2. See ibid.
3. Expression attributed to J.-P. Jeanrenaud, head of the Business and Industry Unit of WWF International.

References

Lankowski, Lecna (2000) *Determinants of environmental profit: An analysis of the firm-level relationship between environmental performance and economic performance* (Helsinki: Helsinki University of Technology).

Salzmann, Oliver, Ionescu-Somers, Aileen and Steger, Ulrich (2003) *The Business Case for Sustainability: Establishing a sound research base for development of a case-building tool* (Lausanne, Switzerland: IMD).

Steger, Ulrich (2002) *Corporate Diplomacy* (London: Wiley).

Wagner, Marcus, Schaltegger Stefan (2001). 'The relationship between environmental and economic performance of firms', *Sreener Management International*, (34) 95–108.

3
Cross-Industry Research Findings

The economic industry dynamic and the business case for sustainability

Our investigation of the economic situation of the eight selected industries has revealed both similarities and differences. With the exception of the oil and gas industry, which is enjoying windfall profits from (relatively) high oil prices, most of the industries are operating in a tough economic environment. However we feel that this is better for our research, given that the 'do-good' rhetoric of better times tends to disappear rapidly when the going gets tough. A point in common among the industries is that globalization has led to boundary erosion, a blurring of industry segmentation and an increase in competition, resulting in increased rivalry and often overcapacity. Companies try to avoid profit-depressing factors by massively differentiating their production, which makes it difficult to reap economies of scale. Linked to this is their ambition to move beyond commodity products, with their low rates of profitability and correspondingly low stock prices. Whether it is asset management in financial services, the increase of generic products in the pharmaceutical industry or car production that can no longer use technology and quality as a differentiator, all industries are struggling to maintain a difference and thus a price mark-up, mostly through their brands.

However the specific economic circumstances of the various industries differ widely. The pharmaceutical industry is falling from grace after a long period of profitable growth driven by an aging but health-conscious population. Nowadays profit margins are being squeezed by regulatory pressure and the aggregation of demand by health management organizations. Another round of industry consolidation is now looming.

The airlines are currently facing what is probably their worst crisis since World War II, but this has always been a high-growth, low-profit industry. Although the airlines predominantly drive the extensive system of airports, travel agencies, logistic companies and so on, they have never earned their cost of capital over a business cycle. Today the new low-cost carriers are presenting a great challenge to network airlines, with their global reach and high fixed costs.

The financial services industry is also in the doldrums. While trying to help others recover from the economic (and sometimes immoral) excesses of the last boom, its own financial picture does not look much better. Basically the industry is in search of a viable business model; the global 'integrated financial service provider' model (Bancassurance) came up with mixed results and therefore lost its appeal. Depressed stock markets and high provision for credit defaults took a huge toll on profitability, as did excess capacity in investment banking. Cross-border mergers and acquisitions are still an exception – despite the liberalization of capital markets – even within the European Union. A characteristic of the financial services industry is that its customers mainly create risk and potential damage, ranging from bankruptcy to liability compensation. The industry only has an indirect influence, which makes early risk detection a priority.

The automotive industry has found itself in a similar profitability position. In spite of its glamorous public image, financial analysts have long rated it as one of the least attractive industries in which to invest, due to its capital-intensiveness, highly specific assets and persistent overcapacity. As one of the most global industries, in which six large players account for approximately 85 per cent of the market, rivalry is intense – and as all economists know, a narrow oligopoly is the most competitive market structure. All manufacturers follow the same strategy: they offer a full range of models covering every niche, including top of the market models ('that's where the money is'), but also reaping economies of scale through platform strategies. Any competitive advantage is at best temporary.

The food and beverage industry, on the other hand, is less glamorous but despite slow growth it is blessed with fairly stable profitability. Its main problem is the influence of strong retailers that push industry consolidation and drive down prices. Growth in developing countries and market leadership via strong brands appear to offer global players a way out from profit squeezes. Supply chain management helps to control costs and provide interesting services for retailers, such as automatic replenishment of shelf stock.

The technology industry is similar in its non-glamorous robustness, although it is more cyclical than food, particularly in the case of IT hardware providers, which have gone through a rapid boom and bust cycle, thus setting a new benchmark for cyclicality. It comes as no surprise that performance innovation and price competitiveness drive global competition in this very segmented industry, with the exception of mobile phone manufacturers, assuming that these can be counted part of the technology sector in that the mobile phone has become as much a trendy toy as a technology carrier.

The situation is different again in the chemical industry, which is very differentiated and much of its supply goes back into the industry. Since the separation of 'life science' products (pharmaceuticals and agrochemicals, based on the biotechnology platform), fine and speciality chemicals have become a focus of development for global players to avoid low margin, highly cyclical commodity business. Obviously this has brought more stability to the industry. In the more extensive industry-serving sector, performance innovation and price competitiveness drive business. The consumer product sector (light chemicals such as washing powder and lotions) has become more brand-driven and has many economic similarities to the food industry.

Finally, the energy industry can be split into the oil and gas industry (exploration, production, refining) and utilities (electricity generation and distribution, gas distribution, often complemented by water or environmental services). The first is a classic example of a cyclical commodity industry: highly vertically integrated to cushion the impact of the business cycle, and reaping economics of scale and scope by means of mergers and acquisitions. As mentioned earlier, the industry is currently enjoying increased profitability, but there is global awareness of the fragility of the situation.

The utilities sector, long accustomed to the happy life of a regulated natural monopoly, is still reeling from the competitive forces that overwhelmed it after deregulation. Although many rearguard battles are still being fought – France, with its huge national monopolies in electricity and gas, is notorious for this, as are most of the developed Asian countries – it seems inevitable that monopolized electricity grids and pipelines will be transformed into an open access network in which different suppliers compete. The rules of the new game are just emerging.

Sustainability issues

Where do sustainability issues come in?

The reader might wonder that sustainability issues, which are discussed in detail in the following subsections, are omitted from this brief cross-sector analysis of the economic situation. Is this not against the paradigm of integrating sustainable development criteria into corporate strategy? The answer that has emerged from our research is that none of the current sustainability issues are so strategically important as to be 'make it or break it' factors for the industries researched, perhaps with the exception of the 'no resource equals no business' argument in the food and beverage industry. While climate change is an important issue for the energy industry in the long term, at the moment it is enough to invest on a relatively small scale, say a couple of hundred millions, in renewable energy pilot projects. The nightmare of cities being choked by traffic jams would clearly derail the business model of the automotive industry. But this worst-case scenario has been under discussion for more than 30 years and does not seem overly to perturb the industry. No company is investing even on a small scale in new business models for individualized mobility. The chemical industry was purged in the 1980s and has cleaned up its product portfolio and eliminated the 'dirty dozen' – chemicals that are bio-accumulative, toxic and persistent. The food industry has been rocked by scandals, but these have barely dented the strong trend towards convenience food. And it is hard to believe that the crisis in the airline industry can be resolved by transforming the industry into a more environmentally and socially benign one as it faces up to the economic fundamentals that pushed it into its current crisis. Nor has a single global player put sustainability at the core of its business model.

DuPont has come closest to 'sustainable transformation', even shedding its traditional nylon business and focusing on knowledge-intensive, high value-added chemical, biotechnological and material solutions. Based on five growth platforms, DuPont aims to exploit its impressive and extensive science base by creating more knowledge-intensive products and services, thus avoiding common traps. First and foremost DuPont has an economically sensible innovation strategy to reduce environmental damage and/or increase social benefits, depending on the market in which it is operating. However the sustainability aspects of this strategy will continue to be challenged by stakeholders; for example DuPont's use of genetically modified crops has already come under scrutiny. (The reason for the risk-averse, even cautious, drive towards sustainability by the majority of companies will be discussed in Chapter 4.)

We should not be surprised that sustainability issues are not a top priority for global corporations. First, by definition sustainability in a market economy means dealing with externalities – in other words, non-market factors – that have not been internalized in the past. Internalization is often required by government regulations, which shape market standards or structures and provide framework conditions that are relevant to all players in an industry, but rarely do they feature large in the supply and demand equation that drives business. In the food industry, where environmental risks are rapidly translated into individual health risks, the potential for greater sustainability is obvious. However as none of the global players can rely on niche markets, such as that for organic products, a global standard for sustainability in the supply chain is required. Otherwise the potential to gain competitive advantage and differentiation in terms of more sustainable products will be limited. Secondly, although the fashionable rhetoric of sustainability is relatively new, since the industrial revolution there has been a need for companies to respond to non-market issues. Either this has been imposed on them by law, demanded by a countervailing power (for example unions) or internalized voluntarily because it makes good business sense, for example introducing more ergonomic working conditions to improve productivity. Companies have come a long way since 'Manchester capitalism'.

Thirdly, the demand for externalities to be internalized is extremely fragmented. There is no single issue *per se*, but an extremely broad range of issues of differing relevance to companies, starting with the simple example of a local branch of the Royal Society for the Protection of Birds objecting to the construction of a bypass, which is of relevance to the construction company concerned and virtually nobody else. At the other end of the spectrum are global issues such as climate change through the emission of greenhouse gases, which affects nearly all companies, and for which numerous players – governments and many NGOs – do not necessarily agree on the steps to be taken. At the very least, approaches differ by region. For instance what is considered an example of corporate social responsibility in the USA might be something that has long been dealt with by law or agreements with workers' councils in Northern Europe. In addition, issues are sometimes only relevant in a home country, and in other instances only in far-away developing countries.

An indication of the fragmentation of sustainability issues (remember these are external effects that stakeholders can demand to be internalized) can be found in the survey we carried out amongst sustainability officers. When asked to list the sustainability issues that were relevant to their companies, there were nearly as many different responses as possible responses (of the total number of responses received (350), it was possible to create 225 answer categories in an effort to cluster the responses). Only a few issues came up repeatedly, for example climate change/ global warming (27 times), access to medicine/treatment/healthcare (10 times) and energy supply/usage/shortage (7 times). Our research revealed that it is not an easy task for corporations to identify sustainability issues that are relevant for them. In another of our projects we counted more than 120 relevant issues for Shell, ranging from climate change, biodiversity, political involvement (for example in Nigeria) to threatened boycotts in the Midwest of the USA against Shell petrol stations because they (legally) sold pornographic magazines. As Shell has learned, many issues can flare up, hit the headlines and have a major impact on the company.

Before engaging in a more detailed cross-industry analysis of such issues we shall look at the overall picture and ask ourselves how managers perceive sustainability and its relevance to their corporation.

How do managers perceive corporate sustainability?

When asked 'How familiar is your company with the concept of sustainable development (also known as corporate social responsibility in the USA)?', at least 40 per cent of the general managers who responded to our questionnaire revealed a relative degree of ignorance ('not at all', 'a little', 'fairly'), whereas around 30 per cent claimed that their companies were 'familiar' and 25 per cent 'very familiar' with the concept. If we had questioned the respondents directly, the answers would have probably tended more towards the 'very familiar' end of the spectrum. Interpretation depended on what the respondents understood as 'familiar', and our subjective interpretation is that it applied to those who understood the basics and had recently read something on the topic, whereas 'fairly' probably implied that the respondents had heard the expression in the course of their work. The sustainability officers were more positive, claiming that almost half of companies were very familiar and a third familiar with the concept.

When asked whether the importance of sustainability would increase in their companies, 75 per cent of respondents in management functions other than sustainability expected it to increase; only 2 per cent thought that it would decrease. Once again sustainability officers were more upbeat, with 85 per cent assuming that it would increase. We took this result with a pinch of salt as this type of social desirability bias can be found in all manner of surveys and opinion polls. However a survey that was first conducted 30 years ago and repeated recently with a similar questionnaire revealed that the importance of 'society' to managers had declined. Shareholders were ranked in first place on both occasions, while 'society' dropped from fourth to fifth or even the last place (Kinard *et al.*, 2003). If the managers in our survey had really believed that sustainable development would increase in importance, then it could be expected that more than 16 per cent of respondents would have indicated that their companies were 'very much' aiming to integrate environmental and social criteria into their business strategies and operations. As we discovered during our interviews, few of the companies that made this claim could back it up with demonstratable action. Twenty per cent of sustainability officers even claimed that their companies were 'very much' on the way to integrating sustainable development and more than 50 per cent declared 'much' integration. But as approximately 60 per cent of general managers assumed that capital markets would reduce their tendency to neglect sustainability issues 'only a little' (let alone the 23 per cent who expected no change), it is unlikely that such a push would actually occur. Our scepticism is supported by the findings outlined in the following section with regard to the degree to which managers felt that their business units were influenced by social and environmental issues.

Relevance of sustainability issues

In our questionnaire survey of general managers (GM survey, n = 945) and sustainability officers (SO survey, n = 123) we asked how much their business unit/functions (GM survey) and companies (SO survey) were influenced by social and environmental issues. (Figure 3.1) For both social and environmental issues the answers in the GM survey show a Gaussian distribution (normal probability curve) around the middle category 'fairly'. If the ordinal answer categories were transferred into a proportional scale – 'not at all' (1), 'a little' (2), 'fairly' (3), 'much' (4) and 'very much' (5) – the average would be about 3.1 for both areas. Interestingly, for the GM survey the standard derivation for answers in the environmental area (1.3) is higher than in the social area (1.1), implying that the answers are more differentiated in the former than in the latter. Such response distributions are typically observed in surveys in which a question has not been well understood or the participants have not had a clear opinion.

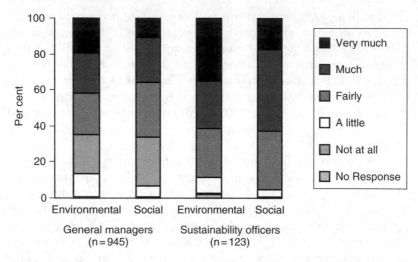

Figure 3.1   The degree of influence of social and environmental issues on business units/companies

The SO survey produced a different picture, with sustainability officers giving a higher ranking to the effect of social and environmental issues – the rankings 'much' and 'very much' account for more than 60 per cent all responses. On the proportional scale described above, the average answer would be 3.9 for environmental issues and 3.7 for social issues. The effect of environmental issues is not only ranked slightly higher than social issues, but also the responses are even more differentiated (higher standard derivation).

In the following paragraphs sectoral differences will only be discussed for the GM survey, given that the total number of SO responses (n = 123) does not allow us to demonstrate clear differences among the eight industries, general managers in the finance and technology industries perceived their business units/functions to be least influenced by sustainability issues, while their counterparts in the energy and chemical industries claimed to be very influenced by these issues (Figure 3.2). The industries with the greatest differences between the influence of social versus environmental issues were the chemical, energy (both with a higher environmental influence) and financial services (higher social influence) industries. The reason for these differences will become clearer when we look in detail at the relevant issues in a later section. These responses were also in line with the results of the qualitative interviews outlined in the reports.

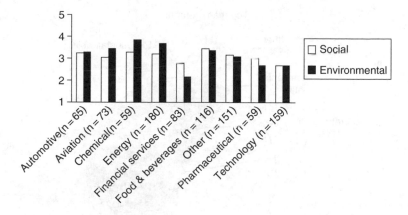

Figure 3.2 General managers survey: influence of social and environmental issues on business unit/function (1 = not at all, 5 = very much)

In an attempt to shed light on the attitudes of general managers we asked them to agree or disagree (on a scale of 1 to 5) with certain statements, ranging from Milton Friedmann's more radical market approach of 'The business of business is business' to a moderate or pragmatic view and finally to a more altruistic attitude. Again the majority of the respondents walked the middle line by opting for the following statement: 'Companies should consider social and environmental issues/ expectations and try to integrate them into their strategies, because by doing so they gain long-term competitive advantages' (more than a third opted for 'very much' and nearly half for 'much').

Barriers to and promoters of social progress and environmental performance

When asked which business function could most effectively promote social progress or improve environmental performance, the largest percentage of general managers chose human resources and corporate staff, followed by R&D and manufacturing (Figure 3.3). The responses of the sustainability officers were quite similar, except they placed significantly less emphasis on R&D, presumably realizing that technological innovation is only one necessary step (and is not in itself sufficient) towards corporate sustainability.

In line with our hypothesis we also asked which departments presented the greatest barriers to these aims (remember that one of the purposes of the diagnostic tool is to help corporate sustainability officers to identify opponents to and allies for their work). While it is not

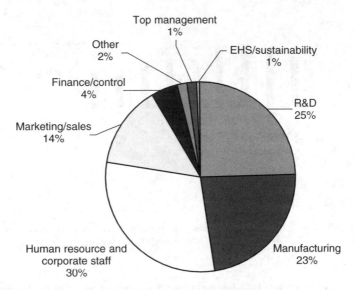

Figure 3.3   General managers survey: the share of business functions in promoting social progress or environmental performance (n = 2068)

surprising that finance and control were considered to be the main villains, it is astonishing that manufacturing and marketing and sales were perceived both as significant potential supporters/enablers and as opponents to greater corporate sustainability action (Figure 3.4). The experience of respondents had probably been very varied: more positive in industries with a longer tradition of sustainability management (for example the chemical industry) and more negative in industries only recently exposed to the question of sustainability (for example airlines).

The bad news is that general managers seemed little inclined to cooperate more intensively with the company's sustainability/environmental officer: less than a quarter believed that this would contribute 'very much' or 'much' to more sustainable business practices. And they had good reason to be relaxed: neither their customers, nor their shareholders (as mentioned earlier) nor governments (with the exception of the utility and pharmaceutical sectors, which face the specific issues of emission trading and drug pricing) seem to be leaning too hard on them. General managers considered the government to be the second most proactive stakeholder (behind public pressure groups, as shown in Figure 3.5), while sustainability officers thought that pressure from the industry itself took second place, again behind public pressure groups (Figure 3.6). However it should be noted that the latter's influence is

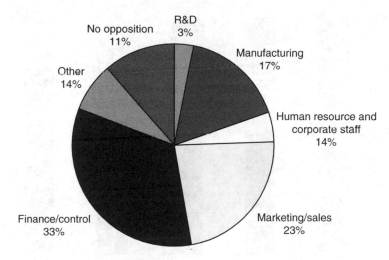

Figure 3.4 Sustainability officers survey: sources of opposition to corporate sustainability actions

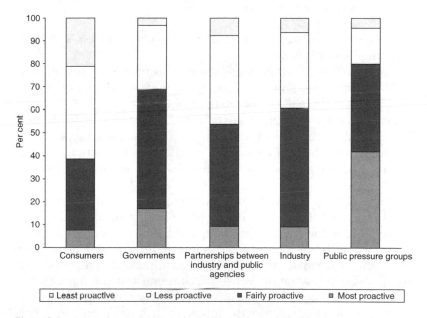

Figure 3.5 General managers survey: pressure by stakeholders

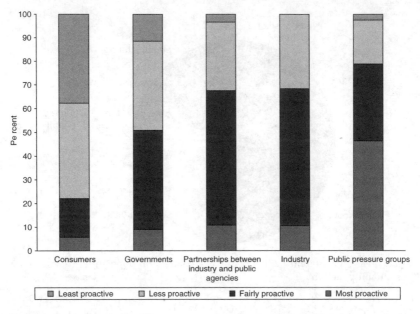

Figure 3.6   Sustainability officers survey: pressure by stakeholders

generally minor in terms of economic impact. Consumers are clearly the least proactive group.

In most sectors general managers saw the role of industry slightly more negatively and the role of consumers and governments slightly more positively than did sustainability officers. We suggest that sustainability officers have a more positive view of corporate activities because as the standard bearers in their companies they have to appear to be optimistic, and they are more aware of the proactive activities of the sector's sustainability leaders and the reactive attitudes of external stakeholders.

Managers were well aware of their companies' environmental and social initiatives (Figure 3.7): only 1 per cent of general managers did not respond to the relevant question, and another 1 per cent were not aware of any initiatives. However there is little reason to be over-optimistic; when asked how successful the initiatives were, 44 per cent gave a 'more or less' rating (which is not promising in terms of future sustainable development), and just 4 per cent gave the rating 'very successful'. When asked why the initiatives had not been particularly successful, 36 per cent chose not to respond. One third considered that they themselves were the problem (because of reactive thinking

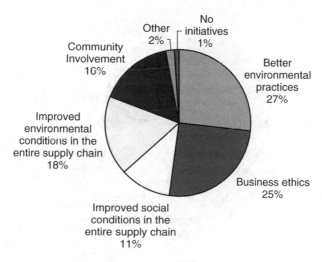

Figure 3.7 General managers survey: awareness of corporate sustainability initiatives

and lack of knowledge), followed by their companies' organizational culture (to which they obviously contributed). Only 7 per cent mentioned regulations as a barrier (this is managers' usual 'whipping boy'). It should be noted that 12 per cent listed the lack of appropriate tools and processes as a barrier, although this is mainly of interest to academics and consultants as the matter can be dealt with relatively easily.

The importance of brands and reputation

One specific aspect that is often given as a reason for corporate sustainability action is the importance of brands and company reputation/ image. Not surprisingly, 90 per cent of managers rated these factors as important or very important. Sixty per cent had experienced brand-related attacks from different sources in the past three years (Figure 3.8). However only 57 per cent rated the incidents in terms of significance, of whom almost two thirds said that the brand name or company reputation had not been affected or had only been slightly affected – in other words, roughly two out of three managers believed that there had been no lasting negative impact on their brand or reputation even when stakeholder clashes had occurred, which is another explanation for the limited priority attached to sustainability issues.

This is the general picture that emerged from our data. The differences between the results of the interviews and survey questionnaires were

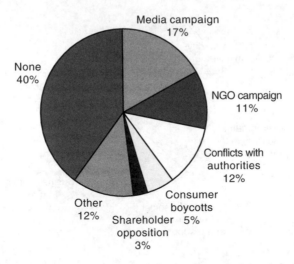

Figure 3.8 General managers survey: brand-related attacks by stakeholders

insignificant, but the interviews did help us to interpret some of the quantitative data.

In specific industries and for specific issues we need to take account of the fact that the picture may vary. When looking at sustainability issues it is important to keep the big picture in mind. But generally speaking, these are considered by companies to be second-level issues, and not, as already mentioned, key corporate make or break it issues. It is nevertheless important to deal with them in a structured and professional way.

What specific sustainability issues do companies perceive?

In this subsection, based on the picture drawn in the previous subsection we shall consider the environmental and social issues that emerged during our research and explain some of our observations.

Environmental issues

The many issues that emerged during our research on the environmental aspects of corporate sustainability can be grouped into seven categories (see Appendix 1 for details of the issues covered in the surveys).

The first group consists of issues with a general environmental impact that confront companies in a specific – and from their point of view mostly negative – way. Environmental aspects of products and labelling are examples of this, for example, the automotive industry is confronted with new regulations on fuel efficiency labelling. Others relate to the ecological footprint left by companies, where often the heavy weight of mining can be felt, even in the technology sector. In some cases, however, the impact can be positive, such as when companies contribute to reforestation or biodiversity, as in the chemical industry, where there are best practice examples of large industrial complexes being converted into wildlife sanctuaries.

The second group consists of broader biological issues: the use of pesticides in agriculture and their potential effects on health, biodegradable products as market opportunities, and the controversy over biotechnology. The food industry is the biggest player in this case.

The third group comprises a wide variety of issues related to soil, water and air. Involving all industrial producers, this has been the most strictly regulated area in many countries for more than 30 years. Companies are normally well acquainted with the issues and the battles are about conforming to regulations in a cost-effective manner, local conflicts of interest (for example industrial odours permeating residential areas), tighter emission standards and so on. The airline industry has an issue that is very industry-specific: noise.

The fourth group consists of all waste issues. These are not as prominent as they used to be, but include the use of waste for industrial incineration (for example cement kilns) and the packaging issue, both of which provide plenty of scope for action by regulators, local communities or NGOs.

The fifth group mostly applies to the chemical and pharmaceutical industries, but also has implications for the technology and food industries. One example is the controversial matter of the long-term effects of specific substances, even in minute quantities ('one atom is enough') – chlorinated hydrocarbons, for example, are suspected of being endocrine disrupters and of affecting regenerative functions such as sperm production. Nuclear radiation is another example.

The sixth group relates to resource consumption, notably energy but also water. Issues in this area offer a wide variety of new business or efficiency options to corporations. Finally, there are issues related to transportation and spatial development.

All in all, environmental issues seem to be well understood by managers and in most sectors they appear to have a clear picture of the environmental issues that affect their companies. These are often broadly discussed (for example emissions in the automotive industry) and are easy to classify and structure. Well-elaborated checklists are included in established environmental management systems (EMAS, ISO).

Social issues

The picture for social issues is less clear than that for environmental issues, not least because such issues can be highly culture-dependent. For example grants from companies for employee pilgrimages to Mecca are in great demand in Egypt but not in Northern Europe. For more than 150 years now, companies have been confronted with social issues that have powerful spokespersons (employees or their representatives), in contrast to the environment, which cannot speak for itself.

Occupational health and safety issues dominate the social agenda of companies in some industries: they are most important in the chemical and technology industries and least important in white-collar industries such as financial services. Grouping other issues has presented us with a considerable challenge (for details see Appendix 2). A substantial group of issues that are particularly pertinent in Anglo-Saxon countries can be placed under the heading of 'ethics' – which in contrast to the more philosophical connotation of this word in Northern Europe, simply means 'don't lie, don't steal, don't cheat' in the Anglo-Saxon cultural context. Corruption, tax evasion and money laundering are included here, as well as child labour, which also falls into the second group: the social dimensions of globalization. This miscellaneous set of issues ranges from protest group extremism to poverty and security.

There is some overlap between the above and the third group: developing country issues such as the global divide in the provision of telecommunications, healthcare, electricity and so on, the plight of indigenous people, and what is sometimes referred to as the 'race to the bottom' of environmental and social standards.

The fourth group consists of health-related social issues that mainly affect the food and pharmaceutical industries, including the connection between obesity and the fast-food industry, access to and the cost of drugs, tobacco marketing and so on.

The fifth group comprises a broad range of issues related to working conditions (mainly in the supply chain). And here there is some overlap with corporate health and safety issues. The sixth group, which falls under the heading 'General social issues, including local community issues' is of an equally imprecise and abstract nature.

The final set of issues come into the category of global human resources. These issues, which are particularly relevant to companies that operate globally, include cultural diversity, labour relations in various contexts, equal opportunities and so on (it is notable here that companies give some weight to these issues whereas public debates on sustainable development tend to exclude them).

During our study, most of the interviewees conceded that they lacked a clear picture of social issues and felt that they were working on an intangible concept. In the opinion of most managers, social issues are illusive and difficult to grasp, which explains their reluctance to get involved in them if there is not an urgent need to do so. Other reasons may be that many of the interviewees worked in their companies' environmental departments, the sheer complexity of social issues, and that many issues were deemed to have been dealt with during the past century or so and therefore did not warrant further attention.

Whereas environmental issues are often discussed in an overall context and are quite tangible and/or visible, social issues are often discussed quite separately from their overall context. The interviewees frequently referred to just one or two general issues, mainly health and safety, business ethics and impacts on developing countries.

Sustainability management issues[1]

In our study, responses in this area tended to relate to how to manage, not what to manage (for details see Appendix 3). The first group of issues relate to stakeholders and stakeholder management, which pose a variety of challenges (these will be dealt with separately in the next main section), the second to 'awareness' (the issues cited here focus on senior management attention and employee involvement), and the third to goals. The issues in the latter group are extremely diverse but are often driven by the question 'How can one ensure that corporate sustainability management is contributing to economic performance?' (for example via eco-efficiency, CSR marketing, sustainability-driven innovations).

The fourth group comprises sustainability management issues along the value chain: ensuring that suppliers meet certain standards, production-related issues such as safety, and the product dimension, for example product stewardship. The fifth group consists of all issues related to communication (for example how to manage reporting requirements), and the sixth of tools, systems and measurement. The seventh and final group includes all environmental compliance issues, of which there are a surprisingly large number given that companies are familiar with environmental issues and have experience of managing them. The many regulations and ongoing political activities, however, are obviously generating management concern. The sheer diversity of sustainability issues makes it difficult to formulate a compelling, easy to communicate strategy response that is relevant to all managers. Attempts to aggregate these issues often leads to discussions that appear to be 'up in the clouds' to business-unit managers – they can only work on a case-by-case basis. However even dealing with them one by one can easily overwhelm those who have to make the myriad daily operational decisions of which corporate leaders and the general public are barely aware.

Our analysis has also shown that even those involved vary considerably in their understanding of what sustainability issues actually are – there is no common language. It is important to be aware of this as a general phenomenon, and it also imposes a limitation the discussion that follows on the importance of sustainability issues and cross-industry differences, even more so because in our study some sustainability management issues were classified as social issues by those charged with dealing with them.

Sector-specific issues and issue conduits

How do the many issues mentioned above affect companies? Before we go on to draw some general conclusions, Table 3.1 presents a preliminary summary for eight industries

Table 3.1   Main sustainability issues, by industry

Automotive	Aviation
Issues arise along the entire value chain, from suppliers and production to products. The related issues are well known and widely discussed in public, but to date there has been no customer demand for solutions.	Issues are mainly related to flight operations. Whilst the relative impact per passenger is decreasing, the absolute impact (for example of greenhouse emissions) will increase due to high traffic growth.
Main issue groups: • Mobility • Energy use and emissions • Recycling • Safety	*Main issue groups*: • Noise and local air pollution • In-flight emissions
Chemicals	**Oil and gas**
Issues arise along the entire value chain, from suppliers and production to products. Environmental and social issues related to the supply chain and production are localized, but chemicals are used in all man-made products and therefore most issues are widely spread.	The use of the product (a non-Renewable Resource) is in itself a key issue that leads, long term, to fundamental questions on sustainability of the business as a whole. In the short to medium term, there are several social and environmental issues involved in prospecting, extraction, production, refining and sales.

Main issue groups:
- Various environmental and safety issues connected to the production process, including spills and accidents
- Effects of chemical products on health and wealth

Financial services
Business operations have only a minor direct impact, but the activities of customers of financial products and services may have an enormous impact. Hence financial firms, and especially the big global ones, are indirectly confronted with the whole range of sustainability issues

Main issue group:
- The entire range of indirect issues related to product portfolio and customer base (role in society)

Pharmaceuticals
The industry considers that its business model already contributes to sustainability. The main sustainability issues relate to social responsibility.

Main issue groups:
- Access to healthcare
- R&D
- Intellectual property
- Health economics in developing countries

Main issue groups:
- Climate change
- Health and safety
- Biodiversity and protection of nature

Food and beverages
The supply chain is closely connected to the food chain and other areas of ecological importance; hence the industry is confronted with countless issues even if there is no direct responsibility. Issues to do with products are critical if they have a direct impact on consumers' health.

Main issue groups:
- Supply of raw ingredients and water (environmental and social effects)
- Health and safety (obesity, dietary deficiencies, allergies)

Technology
The industry considers that its business model already contributes to sustainability. The main sustainability issues are associated with environmental heath and safety aspects of its operations and final products.

Main issue groups:
- Eco-efficiency of products and services
- Life-cycle management
- Environmental production issues

- Remanufacturing

As can be seen from Table 3.1, sectoral issues differ widely in terms of environmental or social implications:

- There can be a direct impact from core business operations (noise in aviation) or it can occur down- or upstream in the supply chain (quality of supply in the food chain).
- Companies can either manage issues directly (in technical decisions about fuel consumption in the automotive industry), only indirectly (deeply ingrained car-use habits) or not at all (for example by ignoring the increase in food allergies).

- The issue can be long term (climate change in the energy industry) or require short-term crisis management (violation of intellectual property rights in the pharmaceutical industry).
- An industry may either be held directly responsible for an issue (problems to do with chemical products) or declared responsible by public perception (the financial service industry for activities by clients).

This diversity creates a complicated picture that is often difficult for managers to understand. In addition there are various conduits through which sustainability issues are attached to companies:

- Direct action (chimney climbing, gate blockades): while this remains part of protesters' 'toolset' it has lost the prominence it had in earlier years, largely because of its limited impact in most cases.
- Lobbying: NGOs and other interest groups have become skilful at influencing the political process. Although outnumbered in personnel and resources by industry associations, they are often able to compensate for this by speedier action, more skilful and understandable communications, their ability to focus on single issues and their greater credibility as not-for-profit organizations.
- Media campaigns: in today's world these influence not only governments and regulators but also consumers, not so much by telling people what to think, but what to think about. The battle for hearts and minds is shaped by 30-second sound bites, the visualization of issues and dramatic effects.
- Boycotts (which often require media support): These hit the 'soft underbelly' of companies – their dependence on consumer demand – because customers can change products and services at the drop of a hat. The failure of the attempt to introduce genetically modified food ingredients into Europe was due to the high probability of consumer boycotts after activists had established a negative image for what came to be called 'Frankenfood'.

Thus companies have also to try to understand the factors that motivate various stakeholders because their high profile, leverage and needs can affect economic value.

Which stakeholders are important?

This section discusses the stakeholders that, in the view of managers, have the potential to affect the economic value of their business and are either promoters or deterrers of sustainability action by corporations.

Shareholders

The managers in our study almost unanimously referred to the deterring role of shareholders (who were generally regarded as the most important stakeholders) and to increasing pressure by them on certain issues. For example the Carbon Disclosure Project, set up by a group of institutional investors, is currently scrutinizing the corporate sector in terms of its CO_2 portfolio. European shareholders appear to exert more pressure over issues such as climate change than do their US counterparts. Although ethical investors were mentioned by various interviewees, they are clearly still considered to be of marginal importance in the sustainability arena.

Our survey results indicate that sustainability officers expect a more positive reaction by shareholders to improved environmental and social performance in the future. Positive expectations are greatest in the food and beverage industry and lowest in the pharmaceutical industry. General managers' views on the future attitude of financial markets are generally negative, and significantly differ from those of sustainability officers in the same sector. Whereas managers in the food and beverage and oil and gas industries expect the most positive trend, their counterparts in the technology and utility industries are most sceptical. Overall it appears that the 'usual suspects' anticipate increased scrutiny by their shareholders.

Customers

In general customers appear to be least proactive in pressing for sustainability. In particular, our interviews revealed that customers of the aviation, chemical, food and beverage, pharmaceutical and oil and gas industries are mainly concerned with getting the best quality at the lowest price and most are not willing to pay a sustainability premium or switch to another product for reasons of sustainability. Customers in developing countries tend to focus even more strongly on products' core functions and affordability, and sustainability criteria such as low energy consumption and recycling potential are largely ignored. Conversely customers of the financial, utility and technology industries are relatively proactive. Overall, customers are least proactive about oil and gas issues and most proactive about issues related to the technology industry.

Regulators

The utility, chemical, pharmaceutical and aviation industries are traditionally strongly regulated, although much less so in developing countries, which tend to be more concerned with constant and adequate revenue flows. Hence environmental and social issues are only slowly gaining significance in these parts of the world. The consequences of this are twofold: NGOs are taking on the role of watchdogs in developing countries, and in the face of global scrutiny some companies are moving beyond regulatory compliance, for example through joint ventures in the oil and gas industry and responsible care in the chemical industry.

In our study, sustainability officers in the food and beverage, technology, and particularly the oil and gas and utility industries considered regulators to be relatively proactive on the question of sustainability, probably because of the many regulations there are on food safety and climate-changing emissions. Their counterparts in the pharmaceutical industry rated them extremely negatively in terms of their contribution to sustainable development, presumably because the industry is under increasing pressure to lower its drug prices to reduce the cost of national healthcare. The general managers' responses showed fewer variations across the various industries. On average our interviewees saw governments as more proactive stakeholders, but far less so in the case of the food and beverage and pharmaceutical industries.

On the basis of our study we conclude that managers' perception of the degree of proactivity exhibited by regulators may depend on the level and type of regulation concerned (market-oriented versus administrative measures). There appears to be a perceived optimum between a lack of regulatory standards (associated with cost advantages for laggards) and overregulation, which restrains companies' flexibility and requires significant changes to corporate activities (moving away from 'business as usual').

Civil society

Local and global NGOs launch campaigns against the negative effects of corporate activities and lobby policy makers for more stringent regulations. Small local pressure groups play a significant role in addressing specific local issues (for example noise near airports or activities that damage biodiversity). Their global counterparts scrutinize companies in terms of both the local and the global effects of their activities. The media play a similar role, although they primarily serve as a catalyst.

Whereas managers in the chemical and utility industries do not perceive NGOs as an active threat, their counterparts in the pharmaceutical, food and beverage, technology and oil and gas industries consider that they and regulators are their most significant pressure groups, focusing as they do on broader issues such as food safety, climate change and access to drugs, rather than just local social or environmental problems. In all but the technology and pharmaceutical industries, sustainability officers rate public pressure groups as the most proactive stakeholders.[2] The general managers surveyed basically confirmed this view.[3] The degree of pressure exerted by NGOs depends on the following:

- The visibility of the industry's products and operations – 'front-line' industries with well-known brands, such as the food and beverage industry, are more vulnerable. Public scrutiny of broader issues, particularly when related to developing countries, is also seen as significant.
- The perceived power of sectors relative to that of regulators. Both the oil and gas and the utility industries face NGO pressure on the issue of climate change. The electricity industry appears to be less targeted by public pressure groups as it is strongly regulated and subject to a gradual reduction in subsidies for domestic mining activities, leading to lay-offs and closures.

Industry

For all industries our study suggests that the activities of leaders in sustainability often stir laggards into action (the 'pull' effect). They usually point to external barriers such as regulations, lack of customer demand and technological uncertainty when confronted with the question of why their industries do not improve their environmental and social performance.

The most positive (self-) assessments by sustainability officers on their industries' contribution to sustainability have been provided by those in the oil and gas and electricity industries. Although their responses may have been significantly affected by a social-desirability bias, both industries have committed themselves to curbing greenhouse emissions and improving their social performance in developing countries (the latter is obviously more relevant for the oil and gas industry). Also, in the pharmaceutical and oil and gas industries competition plays a considerable part in the promotion of sustainable business practices.

Compared with sustainability officers, general managers responded more similarly across sectors with regard to the contribution of their industries to sustainable development. Most striking is the chemical sector's highly positive self-assessment. It can be concluded that greater competition (on licence to operate) and intra-industry cooperation – as in the chemical industry through Responsible Care and the oil and gas industry through upstream joint ventures – are associated with more positive self-assessments.

Employees

Employees are becoming increasingly important stakeholders. Their attitude towards sustainability issues often depends on age. In the oil and gas and food and beverage industries, younger managers, though often less involved and less influential, are generally regarded as more proactive than the 'old guard'. In the chemical industry, older managers have a relatively proactive attitude towards environmental issues, presumably because of the industry's traditionally strong commitment to environmental health and safety (as part of responsible care), whereas younger managers appear to be more concerned about social issues.

The increasing importance of employees as stakeholders can also be deduced from sustainability officers' responses to questions about value drivers. Attracting talented employees and increasing employee satisfaction appears to be particularly important in the R&D-intensive pharmaceutical industry.

Public–private partnerships

In all but the food and beverage and pharmaceutical industries, sustainability officers perceive that public–private partnerships (PPPs) are less proactive about sustainability issues than the industry norm. However general managers from the oil and gas, food and beverage and pharmaceutical industries consider that the opposite is true. These industries face significant problems in developing countries with regard to people's access to drugs, damage to biodiversity and revenue sharing, and see partnerships with public agencies such as the World Bank, WHO and FAO as an important means of resolving these.

Stakeholders' responses: the uncertain trumpet

There are considerable industry-specific differences between managers' perceptions of the roles stakeholders play in the sustainability arena. Among other things there are different expectations about the future reaction of shareholders to corporate sustainability, and varying perceptions of the role of regulators and industry, which can be attributed to specific issues (for example climate change and safety) and industry dynamics (such as regulations). However general managers in all industries see the role of consumers more positively than do sustainability officers. This may reflect asymmetrical information, different expertise and different thinking between the two groups.

Managers' experiences with stakeholder interactions differ more amongst issues and stakeholders than across industries. They are frustrated that stakeholders and the public at large are clearly more interested in bad news than in the positive things that are accomplished. Anecdotes abound about stakeholders' poor response to environmental or sustainability reports, even when the latter are accompanied by prepaid envelopes for feedback purposes. The internal impact of such reports is clearly greater than the external one. Since the introduction of the Global Reporting Initiative (GRI), comprehensive and strict standards have been imposed on sustainability reporting. Some companies are concerned not only about the extra work this involves, but also that the standards get in the way of producing a report that is 'user-friendly'. One solution would be to print a summary for worldwide distribution, produce tailor-made versions for specific target groups such as local communities, and post the complete version on the company website.

There have also been mixed experiences with stakeholder dialogues. There is some consternation in corporate circles about reaching out to traditional adversaries such as environmentalists and human- and workers' rights groups, not only because of communication barriers and dubious returns, but also because it is time-consuming and inherently risky. Companies that have tried have had mixed responses. Whereas community groups and local authorities have generally been responsive, regulators and NGOs have either been cautious or simply refused to participate. In the case of regulators the reason for this is clear: they do not want to be seen in bed with the industries they are regulating. For NGOs it is sometimes a question of workload (as one NGO leader complained, 'I am overwhelmed with the sheer number of invitations from industry to have a dialogue – if I were to follow up even half of them, I would have to completely stop my campaigning work'), but also of the questionable benefits of such dialogues in promoting their goals.

From previous research (Steger, 2002) we know that only approximately 5 per cent of all industry–NGO interactions are oriented towards problem solving or even cooperation. Another 20 per cent involve open dialogue and scientific discourse, while approximately 50 per cent are clashes during public debates and lobbying efforts in which industry associations and individual companies are pitched against various NGOs in an attempt to influence legislation/regulation or public opinion.

The remaining 25 per cent are made up of various campaigns, including the US-based Jewish World Congress campaign for compensation from the European companies that employed slave labour during World War II; the numerous activities of Greenpeace; the Friends of the Earth and others' 'Stop Esso' campaign in the UK and Scandinavia; and Oxfam's campaign against Nestlé on the matter of small coffee growers' rights. Even more is happening at the local level: protests against the extension of airports and quarries, the destruction of GMO trial crops (especially in France and the UK), campaigns against companies that test their products on animals, and so on. Sometimes even corporate sustainability front-runners are attacked, even though their claim to be 'whiter than white' means that they cannot reject NGOs' demands off-hand (unlike companies with a more hard-line stance such as Exxon).

Whatever the situation in question, there is a general attitude of ambivalence towards corporate sustainability efforts among pressure groups (with the exception of the more hard-line, ideologically motivated ones, which tend to fight on regardless). On the other hand there is deep suspicion of 'greenwash'.

NGOs often have a rather poor understanding of how companies work and find it difficult to read the actions and intentions of organizations that are so different from their own. While they see some companies as potential allies in their cause, companies do not regard NGOs as the most important stakeholders. This mismatch in perceptions explains a great deal of the frustration that arises in NGO–company interactions.

In the case of regulators too, when it comes to sustainability issues there may be support, ambivalence or ignorance. Regulators of the pharmaceutical industry, for example, are more interested in prices than sustainability activities, whereas regulators of the utility industry support such activities as long as they are broadly in line with official government strategy. In the financial services industry, regulators are often barely aware of such activities. Customers and the financial market/investors are seen as constituting the biggest barrier to corporate sustainability (see also Kong *et al.*, 2002).

So there are conflicting signals from stakeholders on how companies should deal with corporate sustainability issues, which implies that companies will have to rely on their own resources to decide what to do. A clear business case for corporate sustainability would be an important aid to this process.

Value drivers and sustainability

Value drivers – the link between sustainability issues and economic performance

Rappaport (1986) developed the concept of value drivers in his ground-breaking book *Creating Shareholder Value*. Previous attempts to deal with this subject had focused only on short-term stock prices (especially during the dot.com bubble), so Rappaport developed a focused strategy based on a cash-flow orientation and using the cost of capital as a benchmark for added economic value. In his view the accounting approach confused management decisions and created a bias towards non value-adding activities. He took account both of stakeholders, arguing that what the stakeholder mainly wants from the company is cash, and of the broader business environment (ibid., pp. 12, p. 107 f.) Although some of his assumptions and conclusions were very US-specific, and for some critics the purpose of the firm was too economically defined, his clarification of the relationship between managerial actions and economic outcome is helpful, especially for a 'fuzzy' issue such as corporate sustainability.

The extent of shareholder value depends on cash flow from operations, discount rate and debt structure. A number of value drivers determine the cash flow from operations: the first is the length of time over which the value adding activity or investment can be maintained or 'value growth duration' as Rappaport refers to this. This implies a long-term focus, and thus one that is relevant for sustainability. The other value drivers are sales growth, operating profit margin, income tax rate and working and fixed capital. The discount rate, with which the cash flow is equalized to a common time frame, equals the risk-weighted cost of capital as a value driver. A lower discount rate therefore has a positive effect on the net present value.

It is evident that these value drivers are influenced by many factors. The operating profit margin, for example, is influenced by costs, productivity, resource efficiency and so on. Therefore the notion of value drivers is extended to all factors that significantly contribute to economic value added.

Sustainability issues can influence all value drivers in a positive or negative way. If they enable dematerialization and more service instead of fixed capital, the impact is positive because the amount of capital employed can be reduced. If governments establish higher pollution standards that can only be met by improved technology, the consequent cost increase will negatively affect the operating profit margin.

Of special relevance is the cost of capital (although this was not often mentioned by the managers in our research). Corporate sustainability has a risk management dimension that is often dominant (for example in financial services). As the cost of capital is risk weighted, a lower risk will mean lower capital costs and therefore a lower discount rate for the cash flow. This will in turn lengthen the time period under consideration, because future profit streams have a lower discount rate that contributes more to net present value than does a higher discount rate. The overall impact, however, will be small, but could at least mitigate the often-neglected value growth duration to some extent.

Figure 3.9 presents the relationship between value drivers leading to shareholder value, and sustainability concepts, or actions.

As explained in the previous chapter, the business case for corporate sustainability is defined by actions or projects that solve sustainability issues (by internalizing externalities) and economic value at the same time (the 'smart zone' in Figure 2.1). This depends on companies' ability to improve business processes or technology, or influence their customers. If a government wants action to be taken to resolve a sustainability issue that will not add economic value to companies it has to resort to legislation to make them comply.

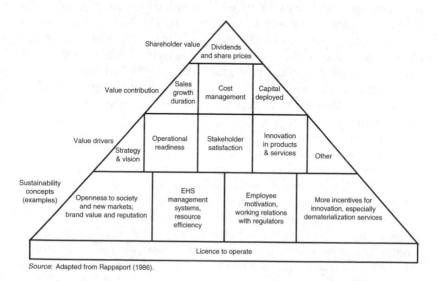

Source: Adapted from Rappaport (1986).

Figure 3.9   Relation between value drivers and sustainability concepts

Value drivers in the business case for corporate sustainability

In order to systemize value drivers in our research concept, we differentiated between their strategic and operational dimensions. Strategic sustainability issues affect all value drivers, mostly in terms of income generation, because they normally require innovation (in Schumpeter's sense, not just in respect of product improvement) in core technologies or business processes, or even a completely new business model. A move from the combustion engine to fuel cells in cars is an example of the type of technological innovation we have in mind. A move from selling cars to becoming a 'mobility provider' would be the equivalent in a business model. The main value drivers here would be increases in both revenue and value growth duration because, as will be discussed later, such innovation tends to occur only if the previous business system or technology is no longer a viable economic activity for the company.

Operational sustainability issues feature a myriad of incremental improvements in occupational health and safety, resource efficiency and small modifications in behaviour or processes. They are basically cost driven; either they decrease costs, for example through lower energy consumption' or they avoid costs, such as by preventing higher capital costs due to perceived higher risk.

In our research we found many other value drivers that managers deem important but cannot easily be subsumed into one of the categories mentioned above. They include soft issues such as brand value and reputation, licence to operate and others. In some cases a decline in brand value is measurable (as described in an IMD case study: 'Under the Spotlight: It's always Coca-Cola, December 2001), but in most cases it is not. Several of the companies in our study had attempted to quantify these intangibles, but had not gone far beyond single project-based estimates. Does this matter? We tend to think not. A company is not driven only by numbers. Politics and power play a significant part in every large company, and many decisions cannot be based on numbers alone. The more strategic a decision the more unreliable its quantitative basis is, due to the fact that many quantification attempts involve uncertain estimates of future trends. To assess their relevance requires knowledge of the context and managerial judgement.

The relevance of a value driver is therefore not a matter of quantification, but whether it supports the core business strategy. After all most share prices do not depend on physical assets, but on such intangibles as knowledge, brand value, competences, strategy and so on. For this value, to quote Rappaport (1986, p. 60), 'there is no unique formula. Its

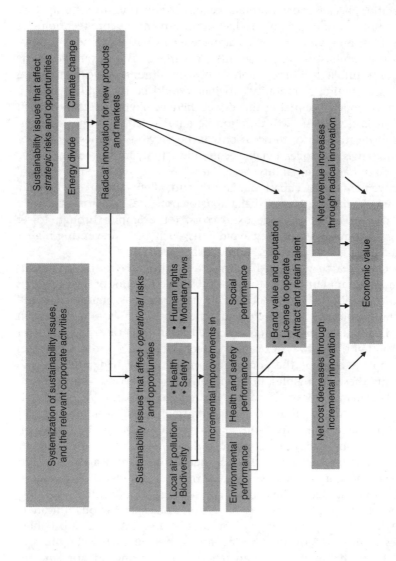

Figure 3.10 Value drivers in the energy industry

value depends on a careful assessment of the competitive position of the business at the end of the forecast period.' This thinking seems to be entering the mainstream; for example in its 2002 annual report Goldman Sachs says that the three key assets in its success are people, capital and reputation.

However our study shows that not all managers see the quantification issue in such a way. There is a certain tendency among laggards and average performers to want to see 'hard numbers', whereas industry leaders care less about quantification of the business case. Given the success of their sustainability initiatives so for, the realization that the monetary costs of sustainability are marginal and the fact that a corporate culture of doing the right thing is often already in place, sustainability officers in proactive companies seem to be under less pressure to provide monetary quantification than their colleagues in less progressive companies, who are obviously still struggling to convince top management and their peers. A typical example of the systematization of sustainability issues, value drivers and the relevant corporate activities is shown in Figure 3.10.

Empirical evidence

As can be seen in Figure 3.11, managers have clearly gone beyond a mere cost perspective; licence to operate, reputation and brand value, and the capacity to attract talented employees and increase employee satisfaction are considered very significant value drivers. They even outweigh the 'low-hanging fruit' (or easily reached cost efficiencies), as

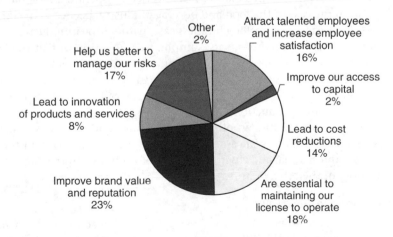

Figure 3.11 Sustainability officers survey: the importance of value drivers

represented in Figure 3.11 by risk management and cost reductions. Finally, our study has shown that improved access to capital is only a marginal value driver. In the following subsections we shall draw cross-industry conclusions on the importance of individual value drivers and their economic potential.

Net cost decreases

Companies traditionally strive for cost reductions through more (eco-) efficient and safer processes. Our interviews indicate that there is still potential for achieving these 'easy wins' (particularly among the laggards in industries), which can mainly be achieved through greater operational excellence rather than by introducing *ad hoc* environmental health and safety programmes.

Data obtained from our questionnaires suggest that the chemical and technology industries put the greatest emphasis on cost reduction, while the pharmaceutical industry puts the least emphasis on this factor, presumably because costs are mainly associated with R&D and less with sustainability issues in that industry. All the industries surveyed, and particularly the utility and oil and gas industries, show considerable interest in risk management.

Licence to operate

Our study has revealed that licence to operate is particularly salient in the oil and gas, aviation, pharmaceutical and food and beverage industries. The aviation industry uses sophisticated models to quantify noise reduction around airports in order to maintain its licence to operate, particularly at night. In the case of the food and beverage industry, licence to operate constitutes the most compelling business case; without the introduction of sustainable fishing methods, for example, the depletion of fish stocks will render some businesses' licence to operate null and void.

Licence to operate is most significant in the oil and gas and utility industries (presumably due to the importance of obtaining licences for exploration and production, and improving fenceline community (in the zone surrounding an oil/gas explortation) and nuclear security respectively), and least significant in the finance and technology industries since their direct social and environmental footprints are minor compared with those of the other sectors.

Reputation and brand value

Reputation and brand value are closely linked to each other and to licence to operate and employee satisfaction. According to some of the sustainability officers in our study, their importance as value drivers is substantial because of global scrutiny of the corporate sector, particularly in the case of the utility and food and beverage industries. In contrast reputation and brand are less significant value drivers in the oil and gas industry. The responses of general managers on the importance of brand and reputation produced a similar picture: brand and reputation appear to be more important in front-line industries such as the food and beverage, financial and automotive industries, and less important in the chemical and utility industries.

With regard to the effect that stakeholders can have on reputation and brand value:

- Media campaigns play a greater role in the chemical industry and financial services.
- NGO campaigns are considered more important in the food and beverage, oil and gas and chemical industries.
- Conflicts with authorities affect brand and reputation more strongly in the pharmaceutical, chemical and aviation industries.
- Consumer boycotts and shareholder opposition generally play a minor role.

In general, the damage caused by incidents affecting reputation appears of less importance (some bias is likely here). It is considered most significant by general managers in the pharmaceutical and aviation industries (presumably in the context of product recalls and safety issues), and least significant in the technology and food and beverage industries.

From evidence obtained in the interviews it can be concluded that industries that have specialized products and brands and are in direct contact with the consumer, such as the food and beverage, financial services and automotive industries, are most concerned with brand value and reputation.

Employee satisfaction

As can be seen in Figure 3.10, the attraction and retention of talented employees is seen as a significant factor in corporate sustainability. It appears to be most important in R&D-intensive industries (particularly the pharmaceutical industry), and least important in more capital-intensive industries such as utilities, oil and gas and technology.

Our interviews largely showed that employees have a desire to be good citizens, and that good corporate citizenship can give companies a competitive advantage over laggards in the industry due to increased employee productivity and the companies' attractiveness to recruits.

Net revenue increases

Our empirical evidence shows that net revenue increases do not constitute a significant value driver since as a rule they only materialize in the medium to long term, and provided barriers such as lack of consumer demand or technological uncertainty can be overcome.

The sustainability officers in our study considered innovation of products and services to be a less important driver for sustainability action within corporations.[4] While this was considered to be fairly important in the financial sector (14 per cent), it was perceived as less important in the pharmaceutical (5 per cent) and utility (3 per cent) industries.

Business opportunities beyond the existing products and services were considered a significant factor in promoting sustainable business practices, and were deemed slightly more important than process and product innovation. The latter were least significant in the pharmaceutical and food and beverage industries and most important in the oil and gas industry, whereas business opportunities were perceived as most significant in the financial sector and least significant in the pharmaceutical industry.

Conclusion

Table 3.2 lists corporate measures that appear to have the greatest economic potential, based on our survey results and additional research.

Based on the preceding discussions, the industries in question can be summarized as follows:

- The principal issues in the oil and gas and chemical industries' are both production-(short term) and product-related (long term). Both industries have cost-intensive assets and tend to focus on cost and risk reduction, plus their licence to operate. The long lifespan of product-related livestock means promotes a trend towards incremental rather than radical innovation of products and services.
- The food and beverage and pharmaceutical industries are more front-line and therefore more vulnerable to damage to reputation and brand value. Upstream activities are to some extent influenced by gatekeepers such as food retailers or doctors/pharmacies. Sustainable product innovations are largely neglected by these industries.

The most pressing issues are sustainable sourcing in the food industry and access to drugs in the pharmaceutical industry.
- The automotive and technology industries differ in terms of their customers (industrial versus private) and the perceptions of stakeholders, but the main issue for both of them is the environmental health and safety performance of their products. The future of the automotive industry also depends on the resolution of such issues as traffic congestion, which will probably necessitate a new business model. The primary value drivers are reputation and brand value.

Table 3.2   Short- and long-term measures with economic potential, by industry

Industry	Immediate measures	Long-term measures
Automotive	Improve product-related environmental health and safety performance (also in relation to climate change)	New transportation concepts and engine technology to retain licence to operate
Aviation	Noise reduction to retain licence for night flights	
Chemical	Improve operational performance in terms of environmental health and safety	New service-oriented business models
Food and beverages	Improve food safety. Attend to new business models to 'serve the poor', resource depletion, manage social issues in developing countries	
Financial	Minimize downside risks	
Oil and gas	Manage social and environmental issues in developing countries to minimize disruption of operations	New climate-friendly products and business models
Pharmaceutical	Improve environmental health and safety performance	Retain licence to operate by providing better access to drugs
Technology	Improve environmental health and safety performance in terms of products and remanufacturing	New business models (service-based)
Electricity	Improve operational excellence	New climate-friendly operations and business model (for example contracting)

- The aviation and financial industries are both service industries but have individual characteristics. Whereas the latter is essentially concerned with reputation and minimizing credit and underwriting risks, airlines are primarily concerned with passenger health and safety) and noise reduction.

Corporate sustainability management: how companies currently manage sustainability issues

Vision and goals

The reader will not be surprised that in this section we once again underline the diversity of ways in which the subject of corporate sustainability management is approached not only across industries but also within industries. The main influence seems to be the previous experience of the company with the matter. Whereas in the much-maligned chemical and energy industries nearly every corporate vision and mission statement contains references to sustainable development, the same cannot be said of the pharmaceutical industry. Moreover industries that are close to the customer appear to be more responsive than companies in the technology industry, which mainly supply other industries. Within companies, junior managers seem to be less aware of sustainability issues than are senior managers (because of their different levels of involvement), and headquarters are more aware than operational units (presumably for the same reason). Departments also differ from each other in degree of awareness, and again there are interindustry differences. Whereas in the automotive industry the strategy and R&D departments are often the drivers of sustainability issues and sales departments pay less attention to the matter, this is not the case in the food industry. Overall, however, few companies make an effort to change the corporate culture and increase their employees' knowledge of sustainable development (apart from companies such as Shell and Unilever).

Clearly defined goals that can be monitored drive business. To do this appears to be much easier in the environmental area than in the social area. Despite disagreements with NGOs, companies find it easier to establish what the 'right' environmental standards are and then define how ambitiously they can be improved and within what time frame. All companies that adopt a standardized environmental management system (ISO 14000, EMAS) are required to set targets for environmental performance. Many of the companies in our study have introduced ISO 14000, mainly in the mid to late 1990s, and as a consequence have continuously improved their environmental performance.

Attending to social issues is much more difficult and not just because of the national and cultural differences discussed earlier in this chapter. Beyond recognizing employees as important stakeholders, this area is subject to lack of definition and an absence of clear indicators. Nonetheless some industry leaders have sometimes set ambitious goals. These will still exist. One company, for example, has set goals for the number of women in management positions. Others, for improving the compatibility of work and family life.

However most goals are to do with gradual improvement, not radical change. While the former has resulted in significant achievements there is still a large discrepancy between public expectations (and sometimes corporate rhetoric) and corporate reality.

Strategy

There is often a debate within companies on whether there is any need for a corporate sustainability strategy. Meanwhile companies that focus on the cost and efficiency side of corporate sustainability tend to consider that an issue-by-issue approach is sufficient. Others see the need for a – functional – sustainability strategy on the same level as their marketing or human resource-strategy. Such a strategy would describe actions in primarily environmental but also social issues with which the company is confronted. The result of developing a sustainability strategy is greater visibility of sustainability issues at management level and a greater transparency for outside stakeholders (the Global Reporting Initiative, the most widely accepted standard for sustainability reporting, explicitly requires a formulated strategy from companies). However few if any companies can claim to have fully integrated their sustainability strategy into their overall business strategy, or rewarded their top management for meeting sustainability goals. This became evident during the interview part of our study and our review of company documents, hence our scepticism about some of the survey results.

However leading companies are starting to integrate their business and sustainability strategies. At Shell and BP for example, all investment projects have to take into account a type of 'eco-tax' that reflects the potential limits on CO_2 emissions. At DuPont the strategic plan includes targets for improving corporate sustainability by addressing new issues, employing new technology and so on.

Sometimes a pioneering effort becomes mainstream, as happened relatively quickly with the 'Equator Principles'. In this case ten leading banks (ABN AMRO, Barclays, Citigroup, Credit Lyonnais, Credit Suisse, HVB, Rabobank, Royal Bank of Scotland, WestLB and Westpac) adopted a voluntary set of guidelines on bringing environmental and social issues

into the financing of projects in developing countries, thus closely
following the example set by the World Bank and the IFC (the private
arm of the IMF), which were pioneers in formulating sustainability
policies and criteria for the approval of project loans.

However it should be recognized that it is often difficult to integrate
issue-focused strategies into overall strategies, and indeed the activities
of business units into the corporate strategy. There is no 'winning
formula' for this, and there is often a trade-off. In aviation, for example,
noise near airports would be reduced if planes took off more steeply,
but this would increase fuel consumption.

The content and characteristics of sustainability issues can differ greatly
and can therefore affect different value drivers, as discussed earlier, Table 3.3
summarizes the types of strategy adopted by the industries in our study.

Table 3.3   Sustainability strategies, by industry

Automotive	*Aviation*
• Strategies are issue-based and are not usually imbedded in a company-wide approach	• Defined strategies exist for single issues such as noise reduction, fuel consumption and CO_2 – emissions • The noise level of planes have a strategic impact on the fleet acquisition as the allocation of slots and enlargement of hubs can be closely associated with this.
Chemical	*Oil and gas*
• Environmental risks can be important when attempting to divest businesses with low profit margins • Strategies are product-specific and responsibilities are divisional • Sustainability criteria are included in the development of products and processes • There are high environmental health and safety standards throughout the industry	• Focus on going beyond regulatory compliance and ensuring community involvement in developing countries • Development of hydrocarbon power • Research into cleaner fuels and new energy sources • Improving/maintaining environmental health and safety standards
Electricity	*Finance*
• Strategies to reduce CO_2 emissions, for example by increasing the efficiency of conventional plants, fuel-switching or developing renewable energy sources.	• Strategies depend heavily on the size of the bank/insurance company and the markets in which it operates

- Demand-side management and energy efficiency (however, measures are limited as overcapacities exist)
- Sustainability guidelines for operations in developing countries

Food and Beverages
- In Europe companies have changed their suppliers and banned GMOs in response to consumer pressure
- Health risks and obesity are being addressed
- Some companies are entering emerging markets and are interested in serving low-income markets
- High eco-efficiency standards throughout the industry

Technology
- Strategies are mostly based on technical innovations and focus on process innovation to improve environmental health and safety performance, and product innovation to increase eco-efficiency of products and stay ahead of the market
- Environmental and social risks are increasingly taken into account when operationalizing corporate strategies

- Main focus on reputation and sustainability risk management in the case of products and services
- Guidelines and transparency measures in emerging-market projects have been adopted by some institutions

Pharmaceutical
- Few companies try to establish a comprehensive corporate sustainability strategy
- Most strategies focus on single issues such as external partners, HIV/AIDS research and so on
- Very limited development of cheaper medicines for low-income groups
- High environmental health and safety standards throughout the industry

Organizational structure and departmental responsibility for sustainability issues

In most industries the concept of sustainable development first took root in the environmental health and safety (EHS) department, with the human resource department (HR) sometimes becoming involved in the early stages. The situation now is much more diverse, both across and within industries. In some industries the EHS department is still taking the lead in addressing sustainable development issues. In the chemical and oil and gas industries, instead of there being a single EHS department there is an environmental department and a health and safety department. The food industry often distinguishes between environmental issues and food safety. Only a handful of companies in the industries researched have a specific sustainability unit. In most industries responsibility is split between departments. Table 3.4 summarizes the current situation.

Table 3.4   Responsibility for sustainability issues, by industry

	Automotive	*Aviation*	*Chemical*	*Oil and gas*
Historical evolution	First taken up by EHS departments	Environmental management at the operational level	Mainly taken up by EHS departments	Mainly taken up by EHS departments
Situation today	Different companies have adopted different combinations	Comparable approach among companies	Different companies have adopted different combinations	Two main approaches
Unit responsible	R&D or operations in conjunction with the sustainability unit	Mostly EHS, only a few sustainability units	Often a sustainability officer or committee, plus various departmental responsibilities	Either sustainability unit or external affairs department, or split between EHS and HR
Hierarchical responsibility	Sustainability unit reports to board	Responsibility held by board member (public affairs or quality/EHS)	Integrated into all departments, overall responsibility at board level	Strong involvement of board
	Financial services	*Food and beverages*	*Pharmaceutical*	*Technology*
Historical evolution	Evolved within environmental management	Evolved within environmental management	EHS departments early promoters and leaders	Mainly taken up by EHS and quality departments
Situation today	Diverse: different approaches due to differing progress	Diverse options chosen but often taken up by supply chain departments	Diverse approaches chosen	Different combinations in different companies

Unit responsible	Sustainability units within communication, risk management or strategy department	Often a strategic coordination committee and issue groups	Mostly EHS, public affairs, sustainability unit and/or committee	Mostly sustainability affairs unit at corporate level, with EHS experts in operational units
Hierarchical responsibility	Mostly board level	Board level with strong CEO involvement	Board member (either COO or public affairs)	Mostly board level

This diversity among and within industries has led us to conclude that overall responsibility is less dependent on the industry a company is in than on the following:

- The company's sustainability strategy (structure follows strategy).
- The organizational set-up of the company.
- The evolution of sustainability within the company.

Interestingly, across industries most of the staff or units responsible for sustainability report directly to a board member and a surprising number of board members are directly involved in companies' progress towards sustainability.

All the sustainability officers we interviewed agreed that the involvement of all departments is crucial to progress in sustainable development, but it appears that in practice the degree of this varies substantially. Table 3.5 summarizes the current involvement of various departments.

As can be seen, departments that oppose progress towards sustainability and those units which promote the concept of sustainable development are quite similar across industries. Very often it is the marketing and sales department and finance department that strongly oppose the concept, for the following reasons:

- They have a strong quantitative focus and are indicator driven.
- Their incentive systems are based on sales figures and they fear losing customers with little interest in sustainability.
- So far the concept of sustainability has been difficult to quantify, measure and integrate into existing control methods/tools

Table 3.5 Involvement of organizational departments in sustainability issues, by industry

Department	Industry			
	Automotive	Aviation	Chemical	Oil and gas
Human resources	Interactions with sustainability unit on labour-related issues	Traditionally strongly involved	Key to setting up guiding principles for corporate values and so on	Naturally concerned with social issues
EHS	Traditionally heads the move towards sustainability	Drives progress towards sustainability	Sustainability issues organizationally integrated in all companies	Traditionally heads the move towards sustainability
Finance/control/ Investor relations	Short-term profit orientation, provide information to capital markets	No involvement so far	Short-term thinking acts as barrier, nevertheless goals set, controlled and revised	Usually resistant, although control staff take soft factors into account
Operations	Works on a daily base on issues such as eco-efficiency	Historically, this is where EHS first evolved	Involved in setting EHS standards for production	Concerned with local issues and stakeholders, less aware of long-term strategic challenges
Marketing and sales	Mostly sees sustainable development as a revenue-reducing practice	No involvement so far	Trying to offer additional services in the case of winning situations	No involvement so far
Corporate strategy	No direct link to corporate strategy	No involvement so far	Involved in risk management and issue management systems	No involvement so far

| | Industry | | | |
Department	Automotive	Aviation	Chemical	Oil and gas
R&D	Working to improve environmental and safety performance	No involvement so far	Working to improve sustainable development performance through innovations	Relatively proactive attitude, since they are responsible for anticipating future developments
Communication/ public affairs	Argues in favour of a value driver perspective	Strong promoter of sustainable development	Regular dialogue between key people	Neutral to proactive attitude, increasingly interested in profiling renewables
	Financial services	*Food and beverages*	*Pharmaceutical*	*Technology*
Human resources	Promotes the drive towards sustainability	Interacts with sustainability unit on labour-related issues	Need for strong collaboration, mostly promotes the concept of sustainable development	Naturally concerned with social issues, sometimes responsible for corporate citizenship
EHS	Environmental management units often take the lead	Involved with operations in the production process	Key promoter and leader of sustainability measures	Strong advocate of sustainability and enforcement of environmental management system (ISO 14001)
Finance/ control/IR	Limited involvement so far (however strong involvement in risk management)	Opposed to the concept of sustainable development	Erect obstacles, mostly opposed to the concept of sustainable development	Most resistant to sustainability, although control staff have started to integrate softer issues
Operations	Involvement via sustainability teams/ representatives	Opposed to the concept of sustainable development but at the same time regarded as the biggest promoter	Long history of positive engagement, considers that sustainable development can reduce costs	More concerned with local issues, but integrates sustainability through eco-efficiency of products and services

Table 3.5 (Continued)

Department	Industry			
	Financial services	*Food and beverages*	*Pharmaceutical*	*Technology*
Marketing and sales	Limited involvement so far	Opposed to the concept of sustainable development	Opposed to the concept due to focus on revenue maximization	Opposed to the concept but uses eco-efficiency as a sales argument
Corporate strategy	Involved in sustainable development in some companies	Part of the strategic coordinating committee	Only minor involvement, neutral about the concept of sustainable development	Focuses more on the sustainability issues of customers than on its own
R&D	Generally of limited importance in the sector	Involved on the product-innovation side	No involvement	Key promoter of sustainable development through innovation and life-cycle management
Communication/public affairs	Strongly promotes the drive towards sustainability, sustainability units are often part of the department	Strong promoter of sustainable development	Close relations with sustainability unit 'Mouthpiece' of the sustainability unit	Strong promoter of sustainable development, especially in companies that deal with hazardous materials

Table 3.6 shows the results of our survey of general managers on the topic of departmental opposition to and support of sustainable development (top three in each category, percentages in brackets).

Across industries the R&D department is generally seen as the strongest promoter of sustainability while the finance/control departments are seen in all but the financial services sector as the strongest opponents. Interestingly, in some industries the manufacturing department is seen as a strong opponent. This differs from company to company and from issue to issue and is always related to product complexity. We discovered that a department might promote a specific issue in relation to sustainable development but oppose a specific sustainability-related measure for another issue.

Table 3.6 Strongest departmental opponents and promoters of sustainable development

Industry	Biggest potential promoters	Strongest opponents
Automotive	R&D (32.2) Manufacturing (27.3) HR/corporate staff (27.3)	Finance/control (43.5) HR/corporate staff (15.9) R&D (14.49)
Aviation	R&D (35.3) HR/corporate staff (29.4) Manufacturing (15.9)	Finance/control (50.0) Manufacturing (22.2) Marketing and sales (12.9)
Chemical	R&D (31.0) Manufacturing (27.6) Corporate staff (20.7)	Finance/control (37.2) Marketing and sales (25.6) Manufacturing (23.3)
Energy	R&D (31.8) Manufacturing (30.2) Marketing and sales (17.1)	Finance/control (45.3) Manufacturing (27.3) Marketing and sales (12.9)
Financial services	R&D (28.2) HR/corporate staff (27.6) Manufacturing (23.1)	Marketing and sales (38.6) Finance/control (33.3) HR/corporate staff (17.5)
Food and beverages	Manufacturing (31.3) R&D (26.6) Marketing and sales (22.6)	Finance/control (32.7) Marketing and sales (25.7) Manufacturing (18.8)
Pharmaceutical	Manufacturing (27.8) R&D (25.7) HR/corporate staff (19.5)	Finance/control (38.6) Marketing and sales (31.6) Manufacturing (12.3)
Technology	R&D (29.6) HR/corporate staff (26.9) Manufacturing (22.8)	Finance/control (39.3) Manufacturing (20.0) Marketing and sales (15.7)

In general, across the industries researched company mind-set definitely influences the approach a company takes to sustainability, and every function is guided by a function-specific mind-set, ranging from the technical orientation of many R&D functions to the quantitative focus of the finance and control departments. But as already stated, many managers across the board are reluctant to become too involved in corporate sustainability matters.

Processes

The processes, systems and tools that relate to corporate sustainability management can be categorized according to the stages of building the business case for sustainability: identification of issues, building the business case, implementing the business case, and monitoring and controlling. Companies must go through all these steps in order to comprehensively integrate corporate sustainability management.

A cross-industry comparison reveals that the progress an industry has made in this process determines its success in the implementation of the related tools. Obviously the degree of achievement differs among the companies in an industry. Therefore the results from the industry comparison relate to the industry average. Table 3.7 lists the most frequently used tools across all industries.

Interestingly, none of the companies in our study had developed or implemented an integrated corporate sustainability management system. Nonetheless the need for such a system was stressed by a number of more advanced companies, though not in all industries; for example in the financial services industry it was not regarded as a goal.

Issue identification and strategy building

The identification stage includes both issue tracking and issue evaluation. The tools used in this process can also be collectively referred to as an Early Awareness System (EAS). The results are used as inputs in to the subsequent process of strategy building. Both identification and strategy building are issue-specific, meaning that the related activities deal predominantly with issues rather than overall corporate considerations. Together, issue identification and strategy building can be defined as issue management. This is often more reactive than proactive, is not always linked to the overall strategy and is rarely informed by sustainability issues that have already been dealt with. For example, although the pharmaceutical industry successfully managed issues such as animal testing and the use of genetically modified organisms (GMOs), it did not apply what it had learnt to new issues.

Table 3.7 Tools most frequently used by companies to promote sustainability*

Tools to identify the BCS	Tools to build the BCS
• Stakeholder/industry dialogue	• Coordination committee (discusses and pushes strategic decisions at the corporate level) (29%, 55%)
• Media screening	• Business teams, task forces to resolve conflicts and push CSM (31%, 45%)
• Surveys / Public opinion polls	• Strategic planning and accounting procedures that take account of environmental and/or social issues (26%, 32%)
• Benchmarking • Risk management tools	

Tools to implement the BCS	Tools to monitor and control implementation
• Corporate values, policies and standards that take account of environmental issues (75%, 85%)	• Measurement tools to increase transparency (for example to measure material usage and waste flows) (54%, 61%)
• Reward and punishment systems (for example salary partly based on social and/or environmental performance) (14%, 21%)	• Tools to measure resource allocation (for example environmental expenses) (29%, 20%)
• Management development (for example environmental training courses, workshops on sustainable development for senior executives) (31%, 49%)	• Environmental (EHS) and/or social auditing
• Sustainability/environmental innovation awards	• Eco-efficiency analysis
• Product stewardship	• Environmental accounting
• Communication tools to increase awareness and understanding	• Due diligence environmental assessment
• Internal information systems/ services (for example intranet, corporate TV, corporate magazines)	
• Sustainability indices and ratings	
• Sustainability reporting initiatives	

* Tools with percentages were identified in both the survey and the interviews, while tools without percentages were identified in interviews only. The first percentage refers to general managers and the second to sustainability officers.

A comparison reveals that there are slight variations in the progress made by the various industries in terms of issue identification. The outstanding players are the energy and chemical industries and some automotive companies. Due to the diversity of their clients and hence the number of issues they have to deal with, some companies in the financial sector, and reinsurers in particular, have developed sophisticated issue management systems.

It is generally agreed that preventing a crisis is better than managing it once it has emerged. However in practice few companies monitor their business environment for signs of a crisis. While there are some exceptions to the rule, such as Swiss Re and other insurers, more often than not companies rely on their intuition or rudimentary monitoring (for example through chat rooms on the Internet) that is often focused on detecting criticisms of products and services. When enquiring about the existence of EAS in the companies we studied it was, common for mainly lower level managers to point to a set of files containing press clippings and declare that they themselves were the early awareness system, although it appears that top management never listened to them.

The main concern is that an early awareness system might lead to another layer of bureaucracy or consume too many resources. However our research reveals that this need not to be the case. Indeed all that is required is a large database – not a great obstacle in today's world – and a number of employees to feed in their observations in a systematic way. Creating such a system requires considerable thought, but the real challenge for managers is to develop the capacity for open-mindedness and keen-eyed observation, and not to be blindfolded by prejudice, dedication to the *status quo* or taking what they see and hear as confirmation of their beliefs.

Most stakeholder confrontations do not come out of the blue and signs of trouble can often be detected at an early stage. However it is essential to know what is being looked for and what is relevant (this can be established by a set of defining criteria), and to investigate whether seemingly unrelated information forms a logical pattern. It is not possible to track the tens of thousands of issues that are on the boil at any one time around the world. Characteristics that make an issue potentially important can be described, based on empirical evidence. The following checklist is also helpful (Steger, 2002):

- Are the arguments against the issue plausible?
- Does the issue evoke emotion in the public?
- Is the issue media-friendly?

- Are there connections to other issues involving the company or other companies?
- How strong is the key activist group?
- How isolated is the company?
- How far have the dynamics of the crisis already evolved?
- How easy is the solution?

While some of the managers in our study, particularly those with sustainability responsibilities, had a fairly good understanding of current issues, others claimed that nothing new was on the horizon. In the aviation industry managers were mainly concerned with how their main issue – the scientific controversy over the climate change effects of NO_x and aircraft water vapour in the stratosphere – would influence the thinking of key stakeholders.

Implementation, monitoring and controlling

Implementation, monitoring and controlling processes are not issue-specific but a general management matter. The implementation process involves decision making, budgeting, incentive systems, guidelines, standard operating procedures, learning activities, feedback/adjustment processes and so on.

Our study has shown that the overall focus of the implementation process is on environmental management rather than on social aspects. This is largely due to difficulties experienced by companies in clearly defining social aspects and related criteria. It appears that companies are only gradually implementing sustainability-related tools in tough areas such as budgeting, decision making and remuneration, and all but a few advanced companies are concentrating on softer measures such as guidelines, non-financial incentive systems and so on.

In conclusion, our study has shown that differencial progress among industries is more marked in the implementation stage than in the identification and strategy-building stages, and that the energy and chemical industries have advanced the furthest in implementing sustainability-related measures.

Notes

1. As well as referring to distinct sustainability issues, the sustainability managers in our study referred to general aspects of sustainability management as issues in themselves. In this category, only responses with no link to social or environmental issues were counted, for example elements of sustainability management such as stakeholder engagement, goal setting and senior

management awareness, the subject itself, such as sustainability and Corporate Social Responsibility (CSR), and environmental legislation such as eco-taxes.

In the previously discussed categories of environmental issues and social issues about 35 responses were also to do with aspects of management, for example waste management, climate change strategy and human resource policies. If these answers were added here, this would imply that sustainability management, with one third of all issues listed by the respondents, was the main issue category.

2. For sustainability officers in the pharmaceutical industry, public pressure groups and private–public partnerships share first place as the most proactive players.
3. In this case respondents from the technology and pharmaceutical sectors agreed with their counterparts in other industries.
4. The significance of a strategic approach is presumably even less, since respondents are likely to associate the item 'leads to innovation of products and services' with incremental rather than radical innovation.

References

Kinard, Jerry, Smith, Michael and Kinard, Brian (2003) 'Business Executives' Attitudes toward Social Responsibility: Past and present', *American Business Review*, June, pp. 87–91.

Kong, Nancy, Salzmann, Oliver, Steger, Ulrich and Ionescu-Somers, Aileen (2002) 'Moving Business/Industry towards Sustainable Consumption: The role of NGOs', *European Management Journal*, vol. 20, no. 2.

Rappaport, Alfred (1986) *Creating Shareholder Value: The new standard for business performance* (New York: The Free Press).

Steger, Ulrich (2002) *Corporate Diplomacy* (London: Wiley).

4

Assessment of the Business Case

Evidence of the business case – and the caveats

All our findings indicate that there is indeed a business case for corporate sustainability, but to varying degrees. One objective of our research was to examine managers' perception of the business case. While most sustainability managers acknowledge its existence it is never as clearly defined as in the 'smart zone' (see Figure 2.1 in Chapter 2) and is more difficult to measure than we had expected. There are many indications that the business case has not yet been fully exploited by most companies. There are many ideas floating around that have the potential to improve sustainability performance and boost profits.

Our findings clearly demonstrate that the business case is industry-specific, probably company-specific, and perhaps even plant-specific, given the diverse sustainability issues with which companies are confronted and the various value drivers affected through a variety of stakeholder "transmission belts". The business case tends to be strongest when companies are in a position to avoid the commodity trap, dematerialize (through services) or redesign key processes (logistics). In focused areas such as these, corporate sustainability can be of strategic importance even if the company is not heading for a major breakthrough in terms of technology or markets served. For example sustainability actions that result in marginal improvements of techno-logy, business models or core processes can increase in operational efficiency. This is what most companies rely on, and here economic as well as quantitative cost–benefit considerations dominate day-to-day business.

But the business case also depends to a very great extent on factors that are difficult to quantify such as reputation, the value of which is probably only known once it is lost, or the company's licence to operate. Although these are difficult to measure, companies regard them as important because they can influence their business environment in so many ways, sometimes through regulators or local communities and even through NGO activism. A strong brand that requires protection (for example in the food and beverage industry), and the need for a good reputation (in financial services) are powerful motivators. Given the risk management dimensions of corporate sustainability, the impact of reputation loss on the cost of capital also appears to present a thus far neglected but emerging potential for formulating a business case.

In any event all business cases require the support of a core business strategy and establishing a clear link between strategy and sustainability is more important than the quantification of relevant value drivers. Finally, the duration of value growth is an important factor that did not show up clearly on our radar screen at the outset of our research and is rarely considered by managers.

Our first hypothesis about the existence of a sector-specific business case is thus tentatively confirmed. However we are less sure about the second, that is, the influence of the national culture and business environment on corporate sustainability. There are indications that the business environment in Northern Europe has a greater influence on sustainability than is the case in, say, Southern Europe. But this influence is by no means as strong as that of the business sector itself. Companies in developing countries, have lower compliance requirements than those in developed countries and are therefore more able to exploit what we call 'low-hanging fruit'. Obstacles and barriers differ from country to country and the worst impediments to progress in sustainability are rarely clear-cut. For example is the German propensity for strict regulation of just about everything more counterproductive for sustainability than the ever-mounting pressure for quick results in the USA?

While we found evidence of all the promotional and impedimental factors contained in our original hypothesis,[1] we learnt that the impact of such factors depends on the context and degree of influence of each factor. As promotional and impedimental factors mostly occur concurrently, it is the overall balance that counts. For example knowledge gaps may be overcome by top management commitment, and investor reluctance may be balanced by promising business opportunities.

Summary of the business case in the eight industries studied

Automotive industry

Current exploitation: A cost perspective dominates, with eco-efficiency, cost reduction, stakeholder acceptance, improved reputation, risk reduction and employee recruitment and retention as the predominant factors. The industry is mainly reactive when it comes to sustainability issues and progress achieved could best be described as low to moderate.

Future potential: Less complex issues such as recycling and safety have not yet been fully exploited. The value perspective of more long-term intangible value drivers such as revenue increase, licence to operate and reputation enhancement is not yet exploited either. There is considerable potential to develop new markets, customer acquisition and retention as well as joint efforts of companies.

Limits: Acknowledgement of the concept of sustainable development by customers and financial markets is not yet strong due to mindset barriers. Thus demand for more sustainability action is limited. Societal change is required on energy (including emissions) and mobility issues in order for the industry to change.

Aviation industry

Current exploitation: Again in the aviation industry, there have been high efficiency gains for fuel, emissions, and weight. The main driver has been eco-efficiency and cost consciousness. Noise is a major 'licence to operate' issue currently being addressed. Safety is a key social issue, but is already closely integrated into the business and is no longer considered a sustainability issue *per se*. The industry has many market inherent problems that are not driven by social and environmental burdens.

Future potential: Noise, fuel efficiency and safety will need to be further addressed from a business perspective (taking into account operating restrictions, fees, operating hours and programmes for residents). There is considerable potential overall for improved sustainability management as environmental and social impacts grow. Keeping ahead of compliance is key to industry leaders so that others do not set the rules of the game.

Limits: The industry is in crisis and airlines are currently not earning their costs of capital; this is the major influencing factor on progress with sustainability strategies within companies. However, it is also true that the inherent structural economic problems will not be resolved by reduction of social/environmental improvements. Nevertheless, economic pressure will delay pressure on the industry to introduce further concrete measures in these areas given the high costs of reducing some impacts (noise, for example). The market structure for the aviation industry is highly international and current strong demand for cheap air traffic indicates that it is unlikely that consumers will pay for more sustainable airlines. The industry is also subject to many bilateral agreements that make introducing change very difficult.

Chemical industry

Current exploitation: The chemical industry has a very strong health and safety record. The industry concentrates on end-of-pipe solutions and combining cost reductions and efficiency increases with improvement in environmental performance. The industry tends to minimize risks of paying fees for non-compliance or litigation for non-regulated damages. For this reason many actions taken could be described as reactive.

Potential: There is potential to take on a more proactive 'shape the trend' direction: companies can use their knowhow to set new industry standards in an efficient way. Further exploitation of sustainability also promotes attraction and education of responsible employees, creation of strong brands and a link to the consumer and in assuring future input, production sites, employees and future markets (licence to operate). There is also a lot more potential to communicate successes.

Limits: There are limitations to productivity increases and creation of new markets for the industry and in customers, investors, regulators, alliance partners valuing social and environmental efforts now or in the future.

Energy industry (oil and gas)

Current exploitation: Few companies have assessed the business case for sustainability in a comprehensive way – approaches so far have been fragmented and *ad hoc*. Exploitation of the business case is currently based mainly on operational (not strategic) risk management, and on incremental innovation of current processes and activities. Disruptive innovations are mainly only at pilot project level. However, NGO campaigns have had significant effects.

Future potential: Licence to operate and grow, reputation, and employee satisfaction present the greatest potential for future exploitation. In addition to this, as the price for CO_2 emissions increases, change will be driven by economic factors at least to some extent.

Limits: Overall, there is a weak case for new business models and a limited potential for extension of pilot projects into the mainstream due to huge required upfront investment to change business models, and the long life span of energy related assets. In addition, the uncertainty of the business climate and the current mindset within organizations also constitute major barriers. In the end of the day, exploitation of fossil fuels is simply the current most profitable solution to rising energy demand.

Financial services industry

Current exploitation: Sustainability is not a main strategic asset to companies in this area; thus its direct impact on the industry is small. However, for a number of reasons outlined more fully in Chapter 8, indirect impact of the activities of the industry is substantial. Currently, the industry is reactive to the demands of public society groups, but corporate social responsibility is still a niche market, although growing. Eco-efficiency potential in this industry is limited but nevertheless not fully exploited.

Future potential: The greatest areas for potential are risk and reputation management with the opportunities they give to influence customers indirectly or directly. Social responsibility investment funds will continue to grow within a niche market. There is also further eco-efficiency potential, but this will not make a big impact on the business case.

Limits: Currently, corporate social responsibility presents limited investment potential. There is a clear 'willingness to pay' issue as investors look short term for biggest payback. Mindset or risk awareness, short-term horizons and confidentiality obligations are major barriers.

Food and beverage industry

Current exploitation: 'No resource = no business' (the threat to raw material inputs) is the strongest business case within all of the industries researched for this study. The industry has been forced through NGO and media pressure to recognize the business case for dealing with a number of issues as a high priority (GMOs, health and safety, traceability). Leaders recognize sustainability as a key strategic asset. There is a high degree of activity in eco-efficiency due to the 'front line' nature of food and beverage business. The most important initiatives can be found in pilot project experimentation in the supply chain and joint industry initiatives in this regard.

Future potential: There is considerable potential for further exploiting licence to operate/reputation value drivers. In an industry that is not necessarily as attractive as others for young people, recruiting and keeping talent is also a driver for further exploitation. The industry is building up a good case for mainstreaming sustainable agriculture supply chain initiatives. However, radically new business models are necessary for reaching the poor in developed countries and this is at a very early stage of experimentation. There is potential for engaging brand managers more fully in sustainability initiatives, but this needs to be handled carefully. Joint industry efforts have potential for more extensive exploitation.

Limits: There is clearly a lack of customer and shareholder pressure. Consumers demonstrate limited willingness to pay for sustainable products, but as long as the consumer does not know what she is buying (through labelling), this situation is difficult to assess correctly. Government subsidies of agriculture/fishing interfere with the establishment of a business case, as do trade barriers.

Pharmaceutical industry

Current exploitation: Eco-efficiency, cost and risk reduction have been first in line for exploitation by this industry, due to the shorter time horizon involved and the immediate 'pay-off'. There are few sustainability leaders in the industry and many laggards. There is also a distinctly high degree of vagueness and uncertainty about sustainability and sustainability concepts, with any economic opportunities being largely undervalued as a result.

Future potential: There is huge potential for exploitation of sustainability in the industry. The as yet virtually unexploited value-driven focus (licence to operate, improved brand value and reputation and attracting talent) have most potential. Revenue increase, risk reduction, innovation of products, improved reputation, improvement of access to capital also have considerable potential. In the pharmaceutical industry, the change process started later than in other industries, and companies are only now engaging in the process. Thus the industry needs to accelerate to catch up with others – increased external public and NGO pressure will precipitate this. Peer group pressure will also increasingly be a factor.

Limits: Engaging top management in sustainability action is a major challenge for the immediate future. As with other industries, mindset is still a major barrier – some companies just simply do not see the value perspective that sustainability could bring to strategic thinking within their organization. External pressure (government, NGOs, and general public) will create increased competition on sustainability issues within the industry. Unless consumers and financial markets demand it, the momentum will not grow rapidly.

Technology industry

Current exploitation: Eco-efficiency of own operations and products has so far enabled reduced costs, improved efficiencies and minimized risk of non-compliance. The current focus is on trying to make sustainability more meaningful for business units. This is a challenge due to diversity of business and high degree of decentralization. There have been limited disruptive innovations of products and business models using pilot projects.

Future potential: Technology transfer to developing countries offers greatest potential. Also, de-materialization of products and processes presents opportunities (improved durability, recyclables, reduced weight and size). New service-oriented business models also offer potential to establish pilot projects.

Limits: This sector is under less pressure because stakeholders generally perceive it as 'behaving well' – therefore lack of stakeholder pressure is a major constraint to further exploitation of the business case. Also, dematerialization is a little-known concept in the industry. In a conservative industry, new business models meet mindset barriers and lack of expertise. The wide range of business activities and high degree of decentralization within the industry make the status of the business case for sustainability difficult to assess.

As already noted, cautious moves rather than bold transformations characterize sustainability strategies. The introduction of breakthrough technologies often extends over decades, fragmented into many pilot projects and hedged in joint ventures and alliances, often supported by government subsidies. The following section explains why this is so.

Why are companies risk averse?

According to advocates of corporate sustainability (for example Elkington, 2001; Liedke, 2003), companies will miss the boat if they do not immediately transform themselves to suit the 'new age'. But few if any companies are doing this. Are they actually missing the boat or is this a case of advocates pressing for what they want to see? Lack of pressure is not an argument in itself, because major breakthroughs almost never result from a perceived need; after all there was no perceived need for electricity, the motor car or the Walkman before these were brought to the market by innovators. Many had to fight against massive resistance until their success forced others to imitate them. Those who then failed to keep up often fell by the wayside because the new solutions (as Schumpeter called them), be they new technologies, services, processes or business systems, did not leave them space for survival.

A certain basic logic could apply here; it is very difficult to construct a 'breakthrough' business case in the current circumstances, but if a company does manage to do so it will achieve a sustainable competitive advantage as well as a competence that will be difficult to emulate – that some things cannot be done only holds true until someone actually does them. There are several reasons why companies are behaving so cautiously:

- Technology: unlike the time when the steam engine or electricity were invented, or when the chemical industry first came into being, companies today are locked into·a technology trajectory. The existing technologies are highly effective, have been developed over a long period and are still being improved (take the combustion engine and polymer-based products as examples). New, unproven technologies find it difficult to compete and are therefore rarely exploited economically – only 10 per cent of all patented products are commercially produced. Radically new technologies only have a chance in specific conditions, usually when there is a mismatch between evolving needs and the dominant paradigm, and even then niche markets have to be used as a springboard.
- The business system: with today's division of labour, large companies are tied into a business system that includes the supply chain, various sales channels and a broad range of service and support facilities. Even dominant players have to move with the system and are locked into it. (This may appear to contradict the assertion that intense global rivalry is causing constant change, but in our view this change amounts to 'more of the same' rather than the transformation that some writers imagine). Moreover part of the business system may be based on bureaucratic regulations that are attuned to an old way of operating and prevent the emergence of innovative systems.
- Consumer inertia: unsustainable consumption patterns in the case of food, car travel and energy and product use in the household are deeply ingrained and culturally supported. They are unlikely to change dramatically, except under huge pressure and with the promise of

economic benefits, neither of which are currently present. In fact, on balance it is more likely that consumers are driving companies in a less sustainable direction.

- The attitude of managers: managers tend not to see themselves as the *avant-garde* of society, and it is rarely in their nature to pick up ideas from society and politics and transform them into business opportunities. However there is some interindustry variation in this. For example fast-moving consumer goods industries are more inclined to capitalize on and even accelerate social trends, but the same cannot be said of technology-driven industries. In any case, managers tend to focus only on trends that favour their business.
- Conflicting trends: at the moment there is no clear trend towards sustainable development. Some favour it, and would like to see less energy and resource consumption, but many seen not to case, as illustrated by hedonistic behaviour and the demand for convenience products. For every trend there seems to be a countertrend, and with no clear political leadership why should companies with no democratic mandate take the initiative? The often-contradictory signals that important stakeholders are sending just add to the confusion.

Many of these arguments hold true not only for corporate sustainability but also, and despite all the rhetoric about 'revolutions', for most other strategic changes in companies. A recent example was the dot.com hype. It is not that new information technology will have no economic impact, but it will take years if not decades to work itself through the economy. Furthermore the most dramatic changes often occur in the most unexpected circumstances.

It therefore makes sense for companies not to risk their future on very uncertain and slow developments. The mortality rate of new innovations is extremely high (Monsanto and its experience with GMOs is but one example), which is why it is wise for companies to be risk averse, move gradually, hedge their bets, invest in technical pilot projects and test new business models in niche markets under favourable conditions. That corporate sustainability is not just viewed as the next big thing is actually good news as this means that it is here to stay. Its importance may vary according to future developments, for example if the effects of climate change worsen the pressure on companies to change their practices will quickly increase. Because of the many issues involved, corporate sustainability will remain even when the next big thing has been forgotten and will contribute to the way in which corporations change and develop.

What's new?

In our view the most important product of our research is an empirical diagnostic tool that can help sustainability officers (or whatever title is given to the position) to identify a company-specific business case. Given the wide variety of sustainability issues, value drivers and corporate contexts it is necessary to build the business case around a specific company situation. The industry reports in part II of this book provide a preliminary framework for tailoring the business case to corporate specifics.

We are confident that the diagnostic tool will work, and will help companies to identify potential areas for action or new issues. Even with 'soft' value drivers, the economic logic of what to do in corporate sustainability can thus be packaged more compellingly for presentation to decision-makers – all the more so since money is often not really the issue. Such a diagnostic tool will allow officers to test new ideas more systematically in a professional framework, as well as increasing the transparency of how companies are dealing with sustainability issues.

If there was any surprise in our research it was how little even proactive companies had thought about the economic benefits of what they were doing in the way of sustainability. Indeed our researchers observed that during the interviews many of the interviewees seemed to be properly thinking about the economic logic of corporate sustainability for the first time.

A second surprise was how many of the perceived value drivers were 'soft'. As we have seen, 'licence to operate', 'brand value and reputation' and 'attracting and retaining talented employees' came top of the list, with the more obvious 'cost reduction' being awarded lesser importance. One reason for this may be that the strategic, revenue-generating dimension of the business case is underutilized and that soft value drivers generally cover the fragmented, incremental steps that could finally lead to a breakthrough. This is not implausible since a good reputation and strong brands allow for a degree of risk taking – if something goes amiss (as it does with most innovations), then the outcry from customers or the public is not likely to be as great.

Finally, we were amazed at how little company-wide communication and consensus there was even on important sustainability issues and how few shifts there have been in traditional lines of responsibility. Too much is left to experts, even though corporate sustainability touches every operation.

Some nagging questions

Customers and capital markets are clearly the main deterrents of greater corporate sustainability action. This has two implications. First, can it truly be claimed that sustainability provides a first-mover advantage? The general indication is that laggards are more likely to be punished than the pioneers are to be rewarded, especially given the selective, but normally low, pressure applied to sustainability issues. For example numerous environmental products have failed to become popular with consumers, and too great a deviation from the norm can result in considerable loss of market share. The automotive industry provides a good example of this: fuel-efficient cars are notoriously hard to sell, although US 'gas guzzlers' are equally unpopular in Europe. The second implication is one of industry interdependence: the industries we looked at are sometimes each other's customers and have a tendency to complain about each other.

How can this vicious circle be broken? Should the chemical industry order only the most fuel-efficient vehicles for its car fleets in order to boost the demand for environmentally friendlier cars? Consumers will behave in a more environmentally friendly way as long as they do not individually have to pay a premium for collective goods such as clean air. But if there is a 'smart zone' there is no such trade-off; fuel-efficient cars also pay off economically – the higher up-front cost is soon outweighed by lower operating cost. There is probably an infinite number of similar examples.

Complexity is the focus of the next nagging question. Today's global companies are extraordinarily complex; their management network covers product lines, regions/countries, functions, projects and customers, all of which have to be aligned. Complexity can be reduced by only two means: decentralization and reduction of inputs. Nearly all the global companies have extensively decentralized, with many responsibilities being passed down the line, and they have reduced their inputs by focusing on shareholder value. However they are still exceedingly complex and only a few very well managed companies can deal with this without experiencing major setbacks. By its very nature, corporate sustainability serves to increase complexity. Therefore is the fact that there are so few leaders in sustainability due not to reluctance or complacency but to a widespread lack of competence to manage increased complexity? If this is the case, can anything be done to remedy the situation? Only time will tell.

The last nagging question concerns relevance. The extent of politically driven rhetoric on sustainable development suggests that the latter should be the most important issue on the corporate agenda, but the reality is different. After all it is not part of the core business of companies, and shareholders and customers count much more than non-business stakeholders. According to one leading NGO representative, 'There is a limit of about 5 per cent of overall company turnover that can be allocated to (and influenced by) corporate sustainability. Corporations tend to be most preoccupied with the daily grind of business and maximizing shareholder value'.

It can only be hoped that empirical evidence will help to take the hype out of well-meaning political propaganda and sharpen the focus on what is actually feasible in the real world.

Note

1. The original project proposal and hypotheses can be found at http://www.imd.ch/research/projects/bcs.

References

Elkington, John (2001) *The Chrysalis Economy: How citizen CEOs and corporations can fuse values and value creation* (Oxford: Capstone).
Liedke, Christa (2003) *Wir Reformer gestalten Unternehmen neu* (Stuttgart: Hirzel Verlag).

Part II
Industry Reports

5

The Automotive Industry

Marc Brunner

The focus in this chapter is on the leading global car manufacturers. In terms of product segment the light-vehicle sector, providing individual transport, is the focal point of the research reported here.[1] However the results also apply to freight transport as most of the sustainability issues are comparable and the car manufacturers in this study also produce trucks. The participating companies were DaimlerChrysler (as the reference company), Volkswagen, Ford, Opel (GM Europe), Toyota and Nissan. This diverse sample ensured that all the important car manufacturing regions in the world – Europe, the USA and Asia – were covered. The findings are based on empirical data from the following sources:

- Close to 60 in-depth, personal interviews lasting an average of two hours each with sustainability officers and executive managers from leading automotive companies, senior executives from suppliers or related industries (such as the railway sector), and stakeholders from various interest groups, such as financial investors, governments, regulatory bodies, non-governmental organizations (NGOs) and experts.
- More than 60 surveys completed by automotive managers.

The automotive industry: economic, social and environmental overview

Economic and competitive overview

The automotive industry can be regarded as a fairly important player in terms of its economic impact on the national economies in which it operates. The GDP contribution of the transport sector has ranged from 4 per cent to 8 per cent in OECD countries in recent years. When related industries are included, 2–4 per cent of the total labour force of the OECD countries work for the industry (USA, 14 million employees; Europe, 12 million; Japan, 7 million). Worldwide, about 700 million cars are currently registered and in 2002 more than 35 million new cars were produced. The industry's sales in 2001 amounted to more than $1000 billion. With an R&D expenditure of $18 billion in the USA and $12 billion in Europe in 2000, the industry is one of the biggest innovators in terms of investment. A brief summary of recent trends is presented in Table 5.1.

The competitive strategies of the big six manufacturers are similar and can be summarized as follows:

- Concentration on the core competencies of car manufacturing.
- Extension of product range to cover all market niches. The current focus of new product development is on luxury and sports utility vehicles.
- Differentiation strategies through branding activities.
- Alliances and cooperation with competitors in R&D and sourcing of components and systems.
- Integration of new service concepts for customers (mainly in the fields of financial services and insurance, plus telematics).

Social and environmental relevance and impact

The negative externalities caused by the production and disposal of cars include emissions and other types of pollution, consumption of non-renewable resources and the need for landfill sites. Car-use externalities include injury and death from traffic accidents, congestion and emissions. Finally the related infrastructure (for example roads) severs ecosystems, disrupts communities and causes visual annoyance. The vast majority of the positive effects of the car industry and the use of its products – such as mobility as a facilitator of economic activity, and the car industry as both an employer and, with related industries, a contributor to GDP – are internalized by market mechanisms. Although by definition they cannot be regarded as externalities, they play a key role in both developed and emerging countries.

The generally high environmental impact of the automotive industry is comparable to that of the aviation, energy and chemical industries. Together these industries make up the 'usual suspects' group of environmental polluters. Within this group the automotive and aviation industries lag behind in terms of achievement from a stakeholder

Table 5.1 Recent developments and trends in the automotive industry

Consolidation	• The six largest manufacturers account for approximately 80 per cent of global sales • Over the past 40 years the number of independent companies has declined from 52 to 12 • Nearly all the remaining independent companies are allied to one of the big six • Consolidation has resulted in a strong mutual dependence among companies • Industry specialists consider that the automobile industry is in the so-called end game of consolidation
Market demand	• The demand for new cars has fallen in recent years, mainly because of market saturation in developed countries • Growth opportunities remain only in emerging markets and smaller niche segments
Overcapacity	• There was a capacity utilization rate of about 87 per cent in 2001 (European manufacturers) • It is difficult to reduce production capacity because the financial and political exit barriers are high
Price deflation	• As a result of interrelated competition and in order to address overcapacity, manufacturers have introduced a series of price reductions, mainly in the US market
Financial performance	• There has been a low return on capital investment (about 5 per cent) over the past 10 years • Stock market performance has been relatively week in recent years • Balance sheet issues pose a potential threat to financial performance (namely pension funds in US companies and the dollar exposure of European companies) • Overall the industry is a relatively unattractive investment proposition, with potential problems in attracting new equity capital

perspective (including the general public, NGOs, regulators and scientific bodies). Conversely the social impact of the automotive industry can be regarded as significantly lower than that of the pharmaceutical and food industries. Here the level of achievement, especially by European manufacturers, is already substantial as a result of regulations (for instance extensive labour rights, company-financed healthcare and pension systems, and high corporate taxes).

Related issues and their economic relevance

History and overview of sustainable development in the automotive industry

Sustainable development in the automotive industry has its origins in the field of environmental, health and safety (EHS) in manufacturers' production facilities. In the early 1990s automotive companies started to improve environmental aspects of their products. The focus was on emission limiters such as catalytic converters, fuel efficiency, recycling and alternative propulsion systems. Parallel to these developments manufacturers began to incorporate better safety features into their products, including Antilock Brake Systems (ABS), airbags and electronic drive stability systems. The key drivers of these activities were stakeholder and regulatory pressure, technological innovation and customer demand.

In recent years there have been a number of developments that are likely to be sustained. First, there has been a shift in focus from production to product-related issues. This is the result of the relatively high level of achievement in the production field as well as growing public awareness of and concern about the externalities of car usage. Second, in parallel with the globalization of the industry (in terms of markets and production), attention to environmental and social issues has shifted from the national to the global level, with awareness and acceptance of increased corporate social responsibility leading to global initiatives such as the UN Global Compact.[2] Third, companies have increased their cooperation in these fields through industry and even cross-industry initiatives to address complex issues such as sustainable means of mobility. Stakeholder pressure and technological progress remain key drivers in this regard, but they are increasingly supported by the industry's awareness and understanding of and commitment to the concept of sustainable development.

Finally, the single most important influence on sustainable development in the automotive industry is increased complexity. The number of players (for instance stakeholders and markets) and interactions between them are increasing dramatically, with mutual dependence in respect of sustainability issues, such as mobility concepts, energy and emissions.

Sustainable mobility and transport[3]

Overview and economic relevance

The free movement of people and goods is a prerequisite for economic activity in all regions. It is regarded as a driver of the globalization of markets and of economic growth in emerging countries. For instance the transport sector's contribution to GDP ranges from 4–8 per cent in the OECD countries. Different modes of transport are ranked according to their importance on a global basis, as follows: car travel, air travel, bus travel and train travel. This discussion will concentrate on the environmental and social implications of car travel, but its interaction and links with other modes of transport will also be considered. Table 5.2 summarizes the negative externalities of car travel.

The main business objective of the automotive industry is to sell cars to individual consumers,[4] but the demand for new cars is stagnating or even falling in developed countries. One reason for this is that the lifetime of vehicles has increased because of improved quality and maintenance; other factors are listed in Table 5.3.

Solutions to these threats to sales will require a change of approach by car manufacturers and the creation of new sources of revenue. Table 5.4 provides a brief overview of alternative concepts and their implications.

The threats to the automotive industry are strongly related to the environmental issues of emissions and energy supply, as well as safety. The uncertainties inherent in the determinants of sustainable transport and their implications for the automotive business model as well as their relation with other issues, make the challenge of sustainable transport potentially the most significant issue for this industry. In addition

Table 5.2 Negative externalities of car travel

	Social concerns	*Environmental concerns*
Inner city travel	• Road safety • Economic viability of public transport • Creation of transport-disadvantaged social groups • Community disruption • Traffic congestion • Depletion of community space	• Consumption of a non-renewable resources • CO_2 emissions • Other noxious emissions • Vehicular noise • Local air pollution, especially in developing countries
Intercity travel	• Road safety • Congestion • Financing of motorway infrastructure, especially in developing countries	• CO_2 emissions • Disruption of natural habitats through road building

Table 5.3 Factors in the demand for new cars

Determinants of demand	Underlying factors
Costs of car travel to user	• Opportunity costs, such as time wasted in traffic jams • Direct taxation on car ownership • Indirect taxation on fuel • Cost of fuel
Environmental and safety regulations and taxation	• Potential for increased internalization of externalities through regulations, leading to large investments in technological innovation • Direct taxes levied on car manufacturers
Quality and cost of alternative modes of transport	• Potential shift of demand towards public transport
Consumer preferences	• Potential change in consumer preferences because of concern about the environmental damage caused by car travel
Demand in developing countries	• Trade barriers originating from environmental or social concerns

Table 5.4 Overview of alternative mobility concepts

Alternative concept	Requirements	Financial potential for automotive industry
Car sharing	• Operating system	• Sale of mobility units* instead of new cars
Integration of modes of transport: • Cars used to drive to public transport connections • Railway or bus connections for distance travel	• Advanced information systems • Improved public transport (management capacity, railway infrastructure)	• Delivery of IT infrastructure • Acquisition and operation of public transport systems • Increased bus sales • Diversification into train production
New vehicles for urban travel: • Smaller, lighter and cheaper cars	• Technological innovations	• New market segment

* for example, number of passengers or kilometres travelled.

the possible alternatives will require fundamental changes in current mobility schemes (ways in which people travel). These changes will only be possible if there is cooperation among the affected industries, members of society and regulators, so progress is likely to be complicated and time-consuming.

Industry perspective

The automotive industry as a whole does not address the issue of transport in a comprehensive manner and its activities are limited to small-scale research or prototype projects such as Mobinet[5] and INVENT.[6] However car manufacturers are part of a global project to promote cross-industry discussions and conceptual work. So far this initiative has not progressed beyond preliminary proposals and possible blueprints for sustainable transport, but it has given rise to more global awareness and thinking.

Automotive managers do not view the challenges of sustainable transport as a threat to their existing business model and claim that there is no adequate substitute for the individual mobility provided by cars. Due to the shortcomings of alternative systems (for example the railways suffer from inferior infrastructure, poor connections, inflexibility and distance from station to home), the quality and comfort of alternative modes of transport is not comparable to that provided by cars. While automotive managers do see some potential in better managed and operated public transport systems, they continue to lobby hard for their industry. Attempts to change the transport system fundamentally through regulatory initiatives are always countered with the argument that the automotive industry is essential to the national economy and employment. The alternative mobility concepts presented in Table 5.4 have so far posed little threat to the industry, but the risks associated with them are regarded as high. They would require the industry to come up with new products and services and improve their marketing (the credibility of the industry could be damaged by contradictory messages), and they could find it difficult to sell the idea of a new business model to the capital markets.

Emerging markets offer the possibility of extending the life cycle of existing products that do not meet customer expectations and regulatory standards in developed markets. The automotive industry is approaching emerging markets with the same products (or concept of mobility) it has used in its established markets, and it argues that cars and trucks are the fastest, cheapest and most effective mode of transport for developing countries.

Stakeholder Perspective

NGOs are lobbying for a reduction in car travel and increased use of public transport. Their proposals focus more on measures to make car travel less attractive (for example higher taxes) than on improving the quality of other modes of transport. The complexity of the issue makes it difficult for NGOs to persuade public and political opinion to support fundamental change, as do their emotional and ideological rather than fact-based and economic arguments.

Consumers can be considered a key factor in the private–public transport divide as the final decision about whether to use a car or choose another means of transport rests with them. While many acknowledge the negative impact of car usage on the environment and society and say they would welcome a reduction in car usage, they continue to use their cars for reasons of convenience, comfort, flexibility and intangible benefits such as status. Consumer behaviour will only change when the cost–benefit relation of other modes of transport outweighs that of the car.

Summary

Establishing sustainable transport will be difficult and time-consuming. It will require cooperation among many players, ranging from regulators and government-owned enterprises to private companies and consumers, all of which have different goals and intentions. There seems to be no immediate threat to the automotive industry's current business model, but changes to the underlying determinants could necessitate fundamental changes to its practices. It should take bold steps today to ensure future gains.

Energy

Overview and economic relevance

The transport sector accounts for approximately one third of the world's energy consumption. Of this, cars consume over 30 per cent, more than any other mode of transport. On balance the total amount of energy consumed by cars has grown relatively moderately (a 0.4 per cent annual change over the past ten years) as the growth in car use has been offset by savings from increased fuel efficiency. About 99 per cent of the energy consumed by the transport sector comes from fossil fuels (petroleum and natural gas). Just 0.5 per cent is generated from renewable sources.

The future supply of oil will depend on a large number of factors, including the discovery of new oil fields (requiring improved search methods of surveying) and more efficient extraction technology. In order to calculate when the known oil resources will be exhausted, scientists compare the forecasts for supply and consumption (for instance as a function of world economic and population development). Such forecasts are subject to substantial uncertainty and experts' opinions on how long supplies will last range from 40 years to over 100 years.

Over the past century the price of crude oil has ranged from $10 per barrel (based on the 2001 dollar value) to more than $75 during the oil crisis in the late 1970s. The uncertainty of supply – potentially exacerbated by unstable political situations in oil-producing countries – means that fuel prices can fluctuate unpredictably and widely. Moreover the sector's dependence on oil has important environmental, social and economic implications.[7] Assessment of the economic relevance of energy in the automotive industry should include both existing and alternative sources of energy. One of the most important factors in determining the future sale of new cars is cost efficiency to customers, which can be expressed as follows:

Reduction in cost of fuel – increase of costs for more fuel-efficient technology + incentives > 0

Total cost of fuel = fuel consumption × price of fuel

The total cost of fuel is determined by the total amount of fuel consumed multiplied by the unit price of fuel. The fuel consumption itself depends on the potential technical reduction in fuel consumption delivered by innovation minus offsetting factors such as power increase, weight gains and energy-consuming features. The price of fuel is determined by the pretax price of fuel plus the tax on fuel. The share of petrol and oil in the total cost of running a car is high: ranging from 10 per cent to 20 per cent per kilometre, depending on national fuel taxes. Fuel-efficiency-related product costs depend on the cost of innovations to improve engine technology, itself a prerequisite for further increases in fuel efficiency. These costs could possibly offset the savings to the customers' operating cost. Incentives to innovate include indirect tax advantages to non-car users and subsidies to the car manufacturers to reduce fleet consumption through innovative technologies. Besides cost efficiency, less tangible factors such as comfort and status influence buying behaviour, but these are hard to quantify and will therefore not be discussed in detail here.

When it comes to assessing alternative sources of energy and their potential use in cars it is essential to ask the right questions. Public debates are often characterized by intense discussions about important but secondary technical details rather than fundamental questions. The

Table 5.5   Fundamental questions about alternative energy sources

Source of energy	• How much alternative energy can be supplied at what point in time?
	• What is the likely unit price for this energy?
Infrastructure	• What technological infrastructure will be necessary for the distribution and storage of alternative energy?
	• What will this infrastructure cost?
	• Who will bear the cost of the infrastructure?
	• When could it be ready for operation?
Propulsion systems	• Which technical solution is feasible?
	• How much will R&D for serial production of this technology cost?
	• What will be the unit cost to the consumer?
	• How much energy will be necessary to operate the vehicle? How much will it cost the consumer per kilometre?
	• What other environmental implications can be expected (such as emission levels)?
Transition	• Will it be possible to make a transition to alternative sources of energy in terms of financing, timing, regulations and cooperation between different industries, nations and other stakeholders?

latter need to be answered separately for each source of energy and should cover the energy source itself, the required infrastructure and suitable propulsion systems (Table 5.5). The discussion should include a perspective on total system efficiency, ranging from energy production through to distribution and consumption.

The answers to these questions would enable an overall feasibility and cost-efficiency assessment of the applicability of a particular alternative energy source. Given a positive assessment, there remains the decisive factor of consumer acceptance. As with the choice of transport issue, in the end it will be the consumer who will have to choose and pay for the alternatively powered vehicle, and cost efficiency will be only one of several factors in the decision, the others including ease of use, comfort, power and status.

Industry perspective

At the moment companies are defending the internal combustion engine on technological and regulatory grounds while at the same time conducting research into alternative energy technologies. The principal reasoning for defending petrol-powered vehicles is to extend the utilization of existing technology for as long as possible in order to maximize returns. It is assumed that the supply of oil will be constant and petrol will remain cost-effective for at least three decades. In order to secure a constant energy cost level for car users, car manufacturers lobby strongly against fuel taxation. Overall, their progress in increasing fuel efficiency is driven by energy-price pressure and regulatory pressure on fleet fuel consumption, but and also, more recently, by marketing strategies offering powerful vehicles with sophisticated features.

Activities in the field of renewable energy are limited to technical research and feasibility studies such as the Clean Energy Partnership[8] and TUT.[9] Only in the area of gas-powered and hybrid vehicles can real market activity be observed. In the USA – the most advanced country in terms of alternative vehicles – such vehicles account for only a small market share, with a total ownership of about 280 000 vehicles. In general the automotive industry refrains from investing in alternative energy technology because it considers that the associated risks (both technical and financial) are too great and the time frame for the implementation of a worldwide system too uncertain.

Stakeholder perspective

Overall, public pressure on this issue is moderate because of the diversity of industries involved in car production and the limited possibility of linking the problem largely or entirely to one entity. One frequently raised criticism is that the industry is not committing itself to alternative propulsion systems and is merely using alternative prototypes and field study projects as public relations instruments.

Summary

The energy issue is comparable to the travel and transport issue in terms of complexity. There are many interrelated factors, and a fundamental change from a strictly oil-based economy to an economy based on new sources of energy would require the cooperation of all stakeholders, as well as considerable public and expert debate. In the meantime the automotive industry should continue its research into alternative propulsion systems so as to be ready when change does occur.

Emissions

Overview and economic relevance

The transport sector accounts for 28 per cent of total CO_2 emissions worldwide, and is one of the biggest producers of the greenhouse gases that are causing climate change. Other air pollutants include carbon monoxide (CO, 55 per cent of which is produced by cars), nitrogen oxides (NO_x, 35 per cent) and volatile organic compounds (VOCs, 30 per cent).

The emissions issue is directly related to the energy issue in the automotive industry as all the emissions mentioned above are a consequence of burning fossil fuels. As with the energy issue, the scope of emissions is spread among different industries on the supply and demand sides (for instance the energy sector is both a supplier and a consumer, and the aviation sector and its customers are consumers). The economic significance to the industry can be summarized by a number of key factors in the industry's potential to sell new products and retain its licence to operate (Table 5.6).

As with conventional sources of energy, any assessment of alternative energy sources and their potential to reduce emissions should pay attention to the emissions from production as well as usage. Current research shows there is still scope for improvement in fossil fuel use, and diesel and natural gas appear to be promising alternatives. However the real solution to the greenhouse gas problem would be a cost-efficient supply of renewable energy.

Table 5.6   Economic factors behind the handling of emission issues

Economic factors	Key drivers
Licence to operate	• Regulatory pressure due to ratification of the Kyoto Protocol on the reduction of CO_2 emissions • Public pressure, mainly from NGOs, to reduce greenhouse gas and other emissions • Credibility and image effects due to commitments by the industry (the ACEA/JAMA* commitment to a 25 per cent reduction in total CO_2 emissions between 1995 and 2008–9)
New car sales	• Conflict between emission reduction and the sale of more powerful, multifeatured vehicles • Positive potential through enforced emission standards (via taxation) on older vehicles
Investment in R&D	• The reduction of emissions needs investment in innovative technology, but it is doubtful whether the costs could be passed on to customers through increased prices

* ACEA: European Automobile Manufacturers Association; JAMA: Japan Automobile Manufacturers Association.

Industry perspective

Driven by the threat to its licence to operate, the automotive industry is addressing this issue seriously, as illustrated by its voluntary commitment to reduce fleet CO_2 production by 25 per cent to 140 g CO_2/km between 1995 and 2008. Measures to realize this target include the improvement of engine and exhaust-system technology and increased production of more fuel-efficient diesel vehicles. However these efforts could be offset at the global level by increased vehicle ownership in developing countries.

Stakeholder Perspective

Public pressure in this area is mainly focused on the climate change issue, with added weight being given by climatic catastrophes in recent years, including floods in some countries and severe drought in others. In addition some NGOs have raised the issue of negative health effects on urban populations from vehicle emissions. They claim that the emission of diesel particulates is causing lung cancer, with about 50 000 people per year in Europe falling victim. They blame certain manufacturers for not installing exhaust filters in their vehicles, despite the fact that the technology has been available for quite some time.

Summary

The emissions problem can only be solved by a reduction in fossil fuel consumption. Climate change is an issue of growing public concern, and this could drive the search for alternative sources of energy and cleaner technologies.

Conclusion

In all of the sustainability issues discussed above, the automotive industry is a vital player, whether as a transport provider, a consumer of fossil fuels or a producer of emissions. These key sustainability issues are characterized by a high degree of complexity. The underlying factors are numerous and interrelated, and changes will have implications for current systems architecture in the developed world.

However the automotive industry's approach to sustainability is reactive rather than proactive. It is stakeholders who raise relevant issues and put direct or indirect pressure on companies, which react by making internal economic assessments and eventually taking appropriate action. When there is no external pressure, companies merely comply with regulations. Where no regulations exist, companies act purely according to their economic interests. Action beyond compliance is only taken when public pressure exceeds regulations or when regulations are on the horizon.

Companies' approach can only be understood from an internal perspective. As an economic entity a company needs to evaluate each activity or issue in terms of the impact on its bottom line. In this context a cost versus value-driver evaluation could provide useful insights. At the moment the industry's focus is mainly on the cost side, but in the future a shift of focus to a value-driver perspective could help companies to develop a more proactive approach to sustainability. They could raise issues on their own, initiate dialogues with their stakeholders and go beyond regulatory compliance without compromising their economic performance. From a general sustainability perspective this would result in better performance in all areas. Figure 5.1 summarizes these ideas.

Corporate sustainability management

Introduction

As sustainability issues become more complex and public pressure mounts, some companies are in the process of setting up comprehensive corporate sustainability management (CSM) programmes, and others are redesigning or adapting their approach towards CSM. In our survey 66 per cent of general managers claimed that their companies had launched at least two internal sustainability initiatives (for example to promote better environmental performance), of which 32 per cent were regarded as successful or even very successful.

The degree of accomplishment varies widely among industries for different areas of CSM. In the areas of awareness, 'vision', culture and organization, the automotive industry is positioned in the middle of the field. As a result of past incidents, on average automotive companies have achieved a leading position in communication and stakeholder interaction and are fairly advanced in issue management, but in the area of strategy design for sustainability the industry is among the least advanced industries. These findings relate to the industry average and are limited to the companies in our research. Obviously there are significant differences between individual companies' achievements.

Awareness, vision and culture

Awareness and understanding of the concept of sustainable development among employees are crucial prerequisites for CSM, with awareness marking the starting point. Compared with other industries

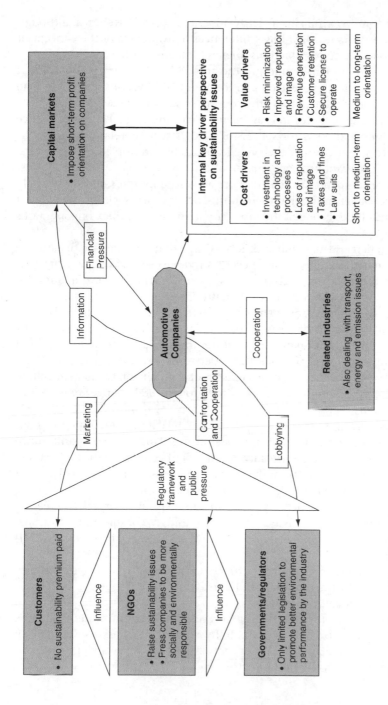

Figure 5.1 Stakeholder relationships and current behaviour of automotive companies

the automotive industry is fairly advanced in the latter area, although our interviews revealed huge differences in awareness of the concept of sustainability across functions, hierarchies and companies.

The predominant opinion in the automotive industry is that there is no need for further development of companies' visions and goals. Due to the broad nature of these the concept of sustainable development fits – and is already reflected in – 'all-inclusive' visions. In general the relevance of visions and goals for successful CSM is seen as relatively minor as managers consider that their role in deciding and implementing general business operations is only marginal.

Those companies which are more advanced in terms of CSM strongly believe that ensuring that their culture reflects their social and ecological responsibilities is one of the most important and complex ongoing tasks of CSM.

In general sustainability officers think that the idea of sustainable development should be part of every corporate culture as it gives direction to the organization's activities, just as customers, cost and quality do. It is believed that culture is the main driver of CSM. As one executive put it, 'In our company managers in all functions and on all levels make tens of thousands of decisions every day that have an impact on our sustainability performance. How, if not through a sustainability-oriented culture, could we influence these decisions?' However the interviews revealed that neither the characteristics of a sustainability-oriented culture nor the means and time frame needed for cultural change were clear to the managers concerned.

There are differences between corporate cultures on different continents, based on different historical norms. European companies have a history of strong (officially enforced) social orientation, Japanese companies are traditionally focused on environmental issues, and US companies have a history of individuality and voluntary donations. Difficulties occur when trying to merge disparate cultures to create a common one, which is becoming increasingly common due to transatlantic mergers and acquisitions and post-merger integration (PMI) activities.

Our interviews showed that there is unanimity among sustainability officers about the importance of persuading top managers and CEOs to make sustainability a priority, as it is they who are in the position to drive awareness through the organization, make organizational changes and design a corporate sustainability strategy. Although sustainability officers are familiar with the concept of CSM and agree about its importance, not all actively promote it.

Sustainability strategy design

Our research revealed that there are two types of sustainability strategy with different approaches and levels of achievement: there is an overall corporate approach to and strategy for sustainability, and there is formulation of strategies at the issue level. Both are obviously interrelated, but differ in content, time horizon and impact.

Only a few of the companies surveyed have designed a corporate sustainability strategy or are convinced of the need for one. For them, such a strategy is a prerequisite for a structured approach to CSM. The interviews revealed that what are called sustainability strategies are often a combination of plans to address certain strategic sustainability issues and lack a comprehensive perspective. Analysis of the way they handle issues shows that some companies have chosen a strategy of compliance but do no more than they have to, indicating a cost-reduction rather than a value-adding perspective.

Corporate strategies define a company's business model, and, in the automotive industry, the model is related to its most important sustainability issues. Therefore, the corporate strategy of car manufacturers provides direction for strategic management of their sustainability issues. The lack of comprehensive sustainability strategies shows that the influence of the concept of sustainability on corporate strategies is rather limited. According to one senior manager, 'The discussion about sustainable mobility is necessary and relevant to our industry's future, but there is no way that this issue will change our business model, which is [aimed at] selling cars.'

Organization

Organizational structure

The matter of sustainability and corporate sustainability management in the automotive industry has mainly been taken up by the environmental health and safety (EHS) departments of companies, but with growing public pressure on product-related issues, R&D, public affairs and communications officers have also been forced to confront the concept of sustainable development. Hence the standard-bearers of CSM now come from various organizational backgrounds. At the board level, those in charge of R&D and operations take most responsibility. The sustainability officer mainly acts as a company–stakeholder go-between and as an internal coordinator of sustainability-related activities.

Many of our interviewees were able to identify the main internal barriers to CSM. Closed mindedness by managers (14 per cent), managers' lack of knowledge and expertise (15 per cent), organizational culture (17 per cent) and the lack of appropriate tools and processes (11 per cent) were the most frequently mentioned barriers. Departmental opponents to the concept of sustainable development include finance, marketing and sales, and strategy. These departments typically interact with the sustainability unit only on an irregular basis.

Organizational processes, systems and tools

Executive managers who participated in the discussions admitted that few of the organizational processes implemented by their companies reflect overall sustainability criteria. So far, no specific sustainability processes or even a comprehensive system for CSM have been set up, unlike the Eco-Management and Audit Scheme (EMAS) for environmental management, which exists in most companies.

Only in areas that have been related to sustainability for a long time have issue-specific criteria been introduced into existing processes. These areas include production-related issues of EHS, and product-related issues of fuel efficiency, emissions, safety and recycling. For the latter the integrated R&D criteria are based on regulations or self-commitment. Processes and systems that include 'hard' factors or quantitative indicators such as budgeting, incentive structures and standard operating procedures do not yet reflect sustainability criteria. Nevertheless many companies explicitly or implicitly use tools that relate to or promote the concept of sustainable development. The majority of these tools are used only for environmental purposes, but they have the potential to be used for social purposes as well.

Communication and stakeholder interactions

Internal communication: selling the business case

The goal of internal CSM communications is to sell the concept by raising awareness and understanding. Different methods are used for different hierarchical groups. In order to gain the support of top management sustainability officers use economic reasoning and focus on the long-term influence of sustainability issues on the automotive business model. Communication is interactive and takes the form of speeches, presentations, cost–benefit analysis and scenario planning. Communication with all other employees is aimed at raising awareness by providing information and best practice examples through sustainability/environmental reports, training, sustainability awards and newsletters.

Stakeholder interactions

Dialogue with stakeholders is regarded as a top priority for CSM. In the automotive industry, 56 per cent of the general managers surveyed ranked 'Listening more to stakeholders ideas and feedback' and 'Greater transparency' as the most effective ways of improving relations with stakeholders, 35 per cent considered 'Public relations' to be the most effective tool for improving these relations, and 'Donations' were regarded as less or least effective by 55 per cent.

Goals include early awareness of potential sustainability issues and reducing the risk of being publicly accused by NGOs or other stakeholders of misconduct. NGOs are usually open to dialogue to achieve their aim of improving the social and environmental responsibility of the industry. However radical pressure groups tend to base their arguments on rather emotional or ideological stand points and neglect scientific facts.

Financial markets are always open to dialogue on sustainability but tend not to seek out information on the concept, for example at company road shows. They treat sustainable development as a niche investment market, with only a slowly growing potential for mainstream markets. While increasing attention is being paid to specific sustainability-related technologies, such as fuel cells, the weak financial performance of and pessimistic outlook for the sector continue to dominate.

In general the managers surveyed expressed strong support for industry initiatives to promote sustainability. However cross-industry initiatives are only undertaken when the industry's own interests will not be put in danger. In general there is a fear of disclosing knowledge and losing competitive advantage. As a result industry initiatives focus on discussions, conceptual work and field tests of new technologies that require limited investment.

Government and other regulatory authorities are only marginally interested in the concept of sustainable development in the industry. Instead of comprehensively approaching major sustainability issues their focus is mainly on product-related legislation. The industry involves itself in the design of regulations by lobbying strongly at all political levels. The development of car-related regulations is seen as a deal-making process. So while automotive companies try to defend the *status quo* on sustainability issues they also try to defend trade barriers to protect national manufacturers.

In conclusion, the industry interacts extensively with its key stakeholders.

Issue management

Activities in the field of issue management vary widely between automotive companies. Some companies have developed sophisticated issue management processes as a consequence of past incidents. They actively manage emerging sustainability issues and heavily involve their key stakeholders. But the majority of companies still take a reactive and unstructured approach, either by muddling through or resorting to crisis management. Often issues are detected too late as a result of poor awareness within the organization. In the worst cases companies react unprofessionally to external pressure and cause further damage to their corporate image.

Assessment of the business case, its potential and exploitation

Value drivers

The previous sections have shown that companies have two general perspectives on dealing with social and ecological responsibility. First, the cost perspective focuses on potential cost increases in all activities in the field of CSM, such as investment in new technology, managerial costs, taxes and fines, the cost of lawsuits, and so on. Second, the value perspective focuses on the possible value creation offered by CSM. On the most general level, value is created in one or more of the following categories: revenue increase, cost reduction and intangible values (licence to operate). This value perspective clearly defines and supports the business case for sustainability.

Our interviews showed that the vast majority of sustainability officers believe in the business case for sustainability and its underlying value drivers. The surveys also provided the same insights on reputation. Company reputation was deemed either important or very important by 92 per cent of the general managers surveyed. Thirty-one per cent of the companies had experienced significant or severe damage to their brand reputation in the previous three years, mainly as a result of NGO (8 per cent) or media (20 per cent) campaigns. This finding indicates adherence to the cost perspective, but it could be argued that appropriate countermeasures could have prevented the cost of lost reputation. Figure 5.2 summarizes the value drivers for going beyond compliance in terms of corporate social and environmental responsibility in a cause and effect relationship. The majority of sustainability officers and some forward-thinking general managers in automotive companies are convinced that at least some of these value drivers could be exploited by

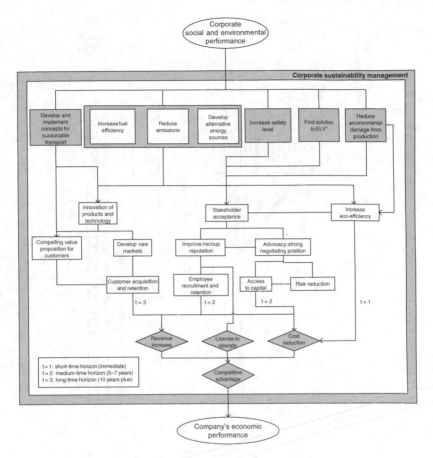

* end of life vehicle

Figure 5.2 Value drivers for CSM in the automotive industry

structured CSM and proactive handling of the industry's major sustainability issues.

Exploitation and future potential of the business case

Analysis of the progress made by automotive companies in respect of the different value drivers reveals that the overall level of achievement is low to moderate. Obviously the degree of achievement differs among companies, and interestingly this does not relate to the regions from which the manufacturers originated.

The greatest progress has been made in the areas of professional management of stakeholder relations and eco-efficiency, mainly due to

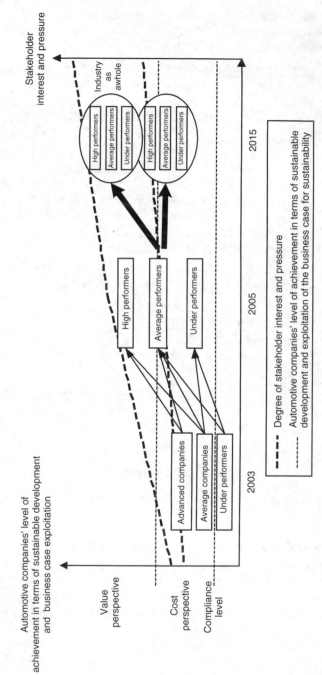

Figure 5.3 Scenarios for the future development of CSM in the automotive industry

production-related performance improvements. Least progress has been made in the financial, product, market and customer areas. The overall conclusion is that to date the automotive industry as a whole has only marginally exploited the business case for sustainability.

Our interviews and surveys revealed the industry's views on the most important factors in promoting CSM. Peer pressure (30 per cent), meaning increased competition based on environmental and social issues within the industry, will tend to push individual companies activities. Pressure from NGOs (50 per cent) on certain issues (for instance diesel emissions) and public pressure for a better environmental performance, by cars will stimulate appropriate measures. Increased commitment by top managers and leaders (71 per cent) will help to promote the concept of CSM, and further verification of the value drivers will help to obtain the necessary support.

The forecast presented in Figure 5.3 is based on conclusions that have been drawn on sustainability issues, the current status of CSM in the industry and the value drivers that define the business case. Further progress with sustainable development will depend on companies and stakeholders jointly addressing the issues discussed in the third section of this chapter. There is also room for companies to make progress in less complex areas such as recycling and safety. Individual and joint progress can only be achieved if companies switch from a cost perspective to a value-driver perspective. One can identify companies that are more advanced, average or underperforming, but most are clustered relatively closely together and maintain a cost perspective. In the medium term greater differentiation among companies is likely, with the more advanced companies' changing to a value-driver perspective. In the long term individual achievements will be strongly bound to the stance taken by the industry as a whole. Either the industry will change its behaviour in respect of the important energy issues (including emissions) and transport, or it will continue to defend the *status quo* on these issues. It is difficult to predict the outcome.

Notes

1. For the full empirical findings see the Automotive Industry Report at http://www.imd.ch/research/projects/bcs.
2. The UN Global Compact is a voluntary corporate citizenship initiative to address human rights, labour and environmental issues in the context of globalization.
3. In this section only the key sustainability issues are presented. See the Automotive Industry Report at http://www.imd.ch/research/projects/bcs for a detailed analysis of safety and end-of-life vehicle issues.

4. Buses account for less than 0.5 per cent of total vehicles sold.
5. Mobinet is a public–private partnership to develop technological solutions for traffic management.
6. INVENT (Intelligenter Verkehr und Nutzergerechte Technik) is a corporate initiative by 23 companies in the automotive, automotive supply and IT industries to develop IT-based solutions for intelligent traffic management.
7. The environmental impact of greenhouse gas emissions (mainly CO_2) from fossil fuel consumption is significant. This topic will be discussed in a separate section.
8. The Clean Energy Partnership (CEP) is an initiative to test the feasibility of hydrogen-powered vehicles, including the necessary infrastructure.
9. TUT ('Tausend Umwelt-Taxis für Berlin', or 1000 Eco-Cabs for Berlin) is a public–private partnership to field test the practicability of gas-powered vehicles.

6
The Aviation Industry

Achim Gebel

Taking airlines as an example, this chapter examines how companies in the aviation industry can improve their social and environmental performance in line with value creation. The industry offers the opportunity for a concentrated study of the challenges of sustainability management in the areas of transportation and logistics. On the one hand the industry is an important economic player in its own right and a catalyst for economic growth and intercultural and interregional exchanges. On the other hand, despite enormous efficiency gains the social and environmental impact of air traffic is growing and the industry faces both global and local problems.

We sampled a number of airlines and evaluated their corporate perspectives. The results presented in this chapter focus on the main sustainability issues and their business relevance, and management of these issues with regard to strategy, organization, implementation and communication (corporate sustainability management, CSM).

The empirical research was based on semistructured interviews with airline managers and stakeholders in the area of sustainability. Our starting point was the European premium carriers. Because of their tradition and size it was probable that their approaches to sustainability would be quite elaborate. To permit broader conclusions we also conducted interviews in different regions (North America and South-East Asia) and with companies with different business models (air express, medium-sized carriers). The other main groups were industry associations, regulators, NGOs and consultants working in this area. More than 50 interviews with an average duration of just over one hour were conducted. The principal participants are listed in Table 6.1.

Table 6.1 Principal participants in the aviation study

Airlines:	Industry associations:
Air Canada	Association of European Airlines (AEA)
Air France	Air Transport Action Group (ATAG)
British Airways	International Air Transport Association
DHL	(IATA)
Iberia	*Regulators*:
Japan Airlines	Umweltbundesamt
Lufthansa (reference company)	EU Commission
KLM (Royal Dutch Airlines)	*NGOs*:
SAS (Scandinavian Airlines)	Greenpeace
Singapore Airlines	Aviation Environment Federation (AEF)
Spanair	European Federation for Transport and
Swiss	Environment (T&E)
United Airlines	*Others*:
	Consultancies, researchers, sustainability
	managers in other areas

Sustainability in aviation

Definition

As in the other chapters of this volume, the term sustainability will be used here in an explicit environmental and social context. We based our research on two of the most common definitions of sustainability: that of the 1987 Brundtland Commission – 'development which meets the needs of the present without compromising the ability of future genera-tions to meet their own needs' – and the well-known 'three pillar model' of economic growth, ecological balance and social progress, as used by the World Business Council for Sustainable Development (WBCSD).

In our research we interpreted these definitions from a company per-spective. A company's goal is value creation and it therefore contributes to the economic pillar. Because the concept of sustainability includes social and environmental aspects, improvements in these areas must be achieved together with value creation (Figure 6.1). The economic impera-tive is reflected in the term 'business case for sustainability'. We shall refer only to improvements that go beyond compliance.

Use of the term

In the course of our research it became evident that the term sustainability is not commonly used in the aviation industry. Only a few companies explicitly include it in the titles of their reports and publications (for

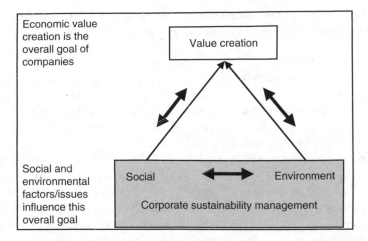

Figure 6.1 Internal perspective on the management of external social and environmental issues

example Air France, British Airways and Lufthansa), and even fewer apply the term to organizational functions (for example British Airways has a Sustainable Business Unit and Lufthansa has a Manager of Sustainability Communication).

Most managers who deal directly with sustainability management – such as environmental, human resources and public affairs managers – are familiar with the term and use it in the context of the Brundtland and WBCSD definitions. In contrast managers in other areas relate the term to long-term economic perspectives, risks and indirect effects, for example a 'sustainable' finance strategy. This could imply fundamental misunderstandings between the two managerial groups.

In the following discussion all management tasks that fall within the scope of sustainability will be referred to as sustainability management and all managers who deal with it will be called sustainability managers, regardless of whether or not the term is explicitly used in the sample companies. This simplification is made to cover with one term the management of and managers who work on environmental or social sustainability issues, or explicitly deal with sustainability as a whole.

Industry and competitive analysis

Before discussing sustainability issues and their management, this section will provide an overview of the structure of the interviewed companies and a brief overview of their economic situation. This is essential to discussing the business aspects of sustainability.

Airline companies

Our core research sample consists of civil airlines that offer scheduled passenger services. We have also included their cargo/freight operations, which are handled at the same airports and cause similar sustainability problems, such as noise and emissions. Moreover this is a business unit of most of the passenger airlines researched.

The interviewed companies are conglomerates of different businesses, the main parts being services, planning and marketing, manufacturing, sales and corporate functions. The sustainability challenges are different for each service. For example maintenance has a direct impact on the environment (toxic substances, sewage), service units have social implications for customers, and network management has a minor direct but considerable indirect impact in terms of fuel consumption and noise. Most of the researched companies have a holding structure that reflects the various business types highlighted above, with a number of different subsidiaries and affiliated brands.

Market environment and inherent structural problems

Air traffic grew strongly at 5–6 per cent per annum between 1980 and 2000 and is projected to grow at the same rate for the next 15–20 years. Nevertheless profitability has remained low. With few exceptions, airlines have not recouped their capital costs. Despite their frontline position they are the weakest part of the value chain (the others being manufacturers, leasers, caterers and airports). Moreover the exponential growth of air traffic (doubling every 12–14 years) regularly leads to capacity shortages, especially at airports and in air traffic control. Box 6.1 considers

---

Box 6.1   Inherent structural problems in the aviation industry and their effects on sustainability

Regulatory confusion

On the one hand aviation markets are liberalized and competition is stimulated by regulators (the USA in the late 1970s, Europe in the early 1990s, Asia in progress); on the other hand airlines are still treated as a public good, receive subsidies or are protected by their government's shareholders. As the example of Swiss Air shows, it is not only developing countries that consider their national airlines as sovereign and an economic asset, for example in terms of job creation, market access and advantage of location. (Related political discussions show that public air traffic is generally seen as a vital part of a sustainable society. The concern is about how further growth measures can be designed in a sustainable way, not whether air traffic is sustainable.)

Market restrictions

There are several constraints on market forces:

- Airports, airport services and air traffic control are natural monopolies.
- Time slot allocation is more a consequence of political agreements than of market forces.
- The plane manufacturers' market is an oligopoly or duopoly.
- Markets are still not completely liberalized – even in the USA there are strong restrictions on foreign airline ownership.

Such restrictions determine/hinder both social and environmental improvements and lead to inefficiency. Optimization of the air traffic control system in Europe could reduce flight times by 5–10 per cent, thus reducing environmental damage.

Unpredictable and extremely elastic demand

Overall demand is very sensitive to outside effects and is therefore difficult to predict, especially in the short and medium terms. Determinants are the security of air travel (The threat of terrorist attacks or accidents), economic downturns or upturns, and factors such as war and epidemics. At the same time demand is very elastic at the lower end of the price curve, resulting in the temptation to sell off empty seats – 80 per cent of the cost structure is fixed by the schedule, and available seat kilometres are a highly perishable good.

Low entry barriers, high exit barriers

Periods of air traffic growth make entry to the airline business attractive because of low entry barriers and assumed economic stability. But in times of economic downturn the exit barriers are

---

Box 6.1   (continued)

high. Overall capacity is difficult to reduce and planes last for more than 30 years, the consequence being overcapacity. Moreover airlines lose their rights to unused time slots.

Increasing returns on size

With the exception of most low-cost carriers, airlines are network operators with an incentive to grow. Furthermore scheduled flights are a necessary product for business travellers, who pay up to five times more than leisure passengers.

The last three factors provide pressure for growth and to some extent artificially generate demand. Opponents of air traffic criticize this and cite sell-off prices when arguing that air traffic is too cheap in relation to the relatively high damage caused to the environment.

---

the main reasons for the inherent structural problems of the aviation industry. These not only explain overcapacity, price wars, runaway costs and poor returns, but also determine the framework for social and environmental improvements.

Recently these long-term trends and problems have been exacerbated by two major developments: an economic downturn in the industry due to the events of September 11, the war in Iraq and SARS; and the overall global economic situation. In the worst crisis in the history of the industry, by spring 2003 airlines had accumulated $30 billion of losses and the situation is worsening. Another factor is the introduction of no-frills carriers. These airlines have enjoyed extremely high growth rates and some are profitable despite the current crisis. For example Ryanair and Southwest have always recouped their capital costs.

Cost cutting and downsizing are the main topics on the management agenda of the major airlines, and this also has an effect on the management of social and environmental issues. A typical question asked by the CEO of a premium carrier is: would Ryanair do this? If not, what is the economic rationale for us doing it? This situation will probably delay the introduction of concrete sustainability measures, but when the market comes back into growth the topic will sooner or later return to the agenda and could fundamentally affect the business model.

Sustainability issues and their economic relevance

This section first provides an overview of the environmental and social issues that were raised in the interviews and then discusses current challenges, the complexity of sustainability issues and the points of view of various stakeholders.

Environmental issues

Most airlines have a clear picture of the environmental issues inherent to their business. There are established checklists, for example in the context of environmental management systems (EMAS, ISO). One of the airlines in the study stated that it had an exhaustive list of more than 200 issues. The environmental impact of the industry is illustrated in Figure 6.2.

Social issues

Most of the interviewees conceded that they lacked a clear picture of the social issues involved in their business but were beginning to address the matter. Whereas environmental issues (noise, emissions, waste and so on) were often raised by the interviewees, even in a general context, social issues were only discussed when the interviewees were prompted

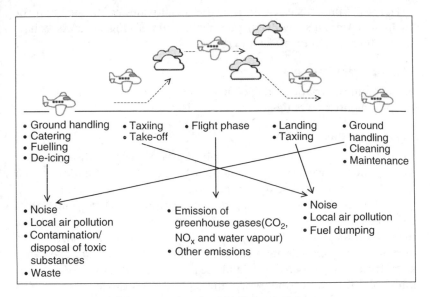

- Ground handling
- Catering
- Fuelling
- De-icing

- Taxiing
- Take-off

- Flight phase

- Landing
- Taxiing

- Ground handling
- Cleaning
- Maintenance

- Noise
- Local air pollution
- Contamination/ disposal of toxic substances
- Waste

- Emission of greenhouse gases(CO_2, NO_x and water vapour)
- Other emissions

- Noise
- Local air pollution
- Fuel dumping

Figure 6.2 Sustainability issues involved in flight operations

and examples were given (deep-vein thrombosis, immigration issues, air safety, leadership behaviour, working conditions, employee skills, corporate cultural issues such as integration after a merger, and societal issues such as war, poverty and noise acceptance).

One reason for this may be the environmental background of many of the interviewees, another the perceived vagueness of social issues. Maslow's famous pyramid of needs exemplifies the range of issues covered: from basic physiological (food, air, water), safety, social and esteem needs to the need for self-realization. But when it comes to specific management tasks, as discussed here, 'everything means nothing', as one interviewee put it. It is important to define which social issues are included and which are not, because this influences the entire discussion of the economic importance of sustainability and its management. For example 'flight safety' can be seen as a major social issue and the entire aviation business depends on its management. However this issue was only mentioned a few times in the interviews and questionnaire answers. One sustainability manager said that when he had been explaining the overall concept of sustainability and its social component, his superior (a board member) had cynically asked him whether he wanted to take over HR responsibilities and what he thought the business advantages of social sustainability would be.

Figure 6.3 presents a selection of the social issues mentioned and the main social groups involved, plus factors underlying business behaviour, which indirectly affect all groups.

Major current issues

Noise from air traffic and global warming were by far the most frequently mentioned issues.

Flightpath and airport noise

Air traffic noise has long been perceived as a problem, although major improvements have been made and noise has been kept at a fairly constant level despite the increase in traffic.

The International Civil Aviation Organization (ICAO) recommends a balanced approach to further improvements, consisting of source control (research indicates the possibility of a 10 decibel reduction within the next 10 years), operational measures to reduce noise (to be aligned with air traffic control procedures), land use planning and restrictions. As airlines are quite vulnerable to operational and even capacity restrictions (for example at Schiphol and Heathrow airports), the challenge for

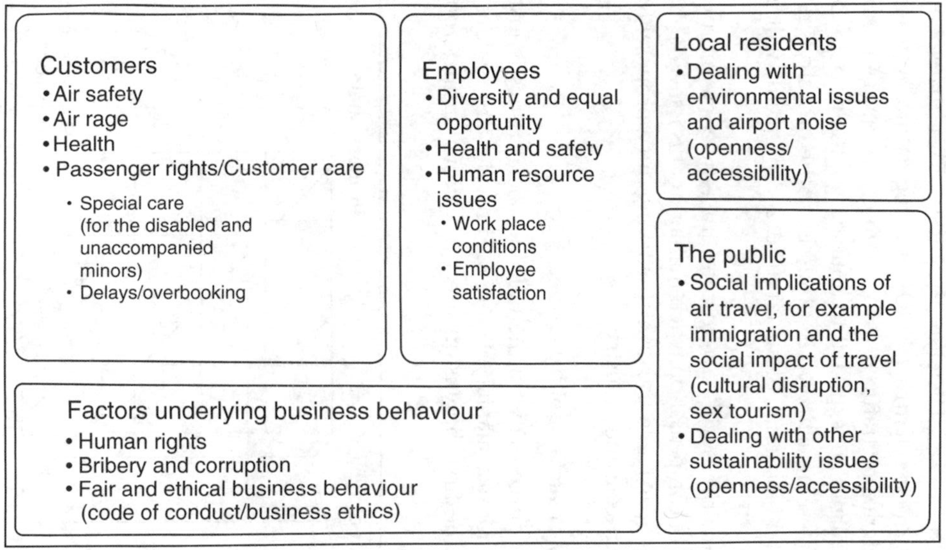

Figure 6.3   The main social groups and social issues in aviation

sustainability managers is to find the right balance, with investment in improvements in other areas.

Greenhouse gases

The problem of greenhouse gases is a relatively new one for the industry. Unlike noise, the negative effects of greenhouse gases are not localized or detected by the senses. Therefore the pressure for abatement comes primarily from expert scientists, NGOs and regulators. Any efficiency gains are outweighed by traffic growth, so much so that greenhouse gas emissions from planes are expected to double over the next 15–20 years. As reductions are being achieved in other areas the industry's relatively low share of total global emissions (around 2–3 per cent) will increase dramatically.

It is likely that airlines will have to combine efficiency improvements with some form of compensation when managing this issue. As a first step the ICAO has been assigned the task of working out a proposal for emissions trading in the airline industry.

The complexity of sustainability issues

Differentiating between environmental and social issues is just a first step in the drive for sustainability. Figure 6.4 provides a three-dimensional illustration. In the first dimension are the various business/operating

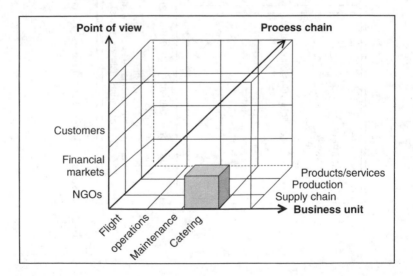

Figure 6.4 The complexity of sustainability issues

units, for example catering, ground handling and flight operations. In the second there are the elements of the process chain (supply chain, production and products/services) and in the third the point of view of stakeholders. A sustainability issue is one that is perceived as an issue, and stakeholders' opinions are quite variable. Despite the differentiation, each part of the cube contains a range of potential issues that could affect a company's entire business. For example in the case of the catering/supply chain/NGO subcube, potential issues could be rules for working conditions on the supply side, genetically modified ingredients and the inclusion of endangered fish species on menus.

Another dimension, which is not included in Figure 6.4, is time. Sustainability issues are not static. Some issues are not fully understood, for example the environmental impact of water vapour from planes is still unclear, while the effect of CO_2 emissions is well known and strengthened regulations are likely. For other well-understood issues, such as waste, strict regulations exist and airlines manage them rationally. Conversely the effect of other activities is no longer perceived as critical, for example fuel dumping.

Issue awareness and evaluation

Only a few airlines have explicit overviews on sustainability issues, but one airline interviewee reported a list of more than 200 environmental issues. Most airlines work with indirect overviews that can be found in their databases, monitoring systems, performance indicators or reports (for example British Airways' report for 2002).

None of the airlines have a formal early awareness system to track changing and emerging issues – or at least the term is not in common use (after being given an explanation of the term, one interviewee working in the environmental department of an airline said that *he* was the company's early awareness system). Most of the interviewees claimed that the relevant issues were well known and that they were adequately informed about changes through knowledge dissemination (congresses, articles, stakeholder dialogues) and information from other employees. However there is still uncertainty about some issues and some aspects of major issues such as emissions and noise. Some airlines, including Air France and Lufthansa, are trying to overcome this by supporting research in the areas in question.

When developing a business strategy, sustainability issues can be assessed according to their importance and economic relevance (see the following section). One airline conducts an annual review of all potential issues based on qualitative and quantitative assessments of the following exhaustive criteria: social/environmental impacts, regulatory scrutiny, stakeholder interests (airport authorities, NGOs, the public), business risks and benefits, and the likelihood and magnitude of the effects on business. This airline highly recommends its system and says that once it has been set up it is not costly to maintain: most issues just require confirmation of last year's analysis or minor changes, and in-depth analysis is only required for a few new changes and issues.

Overall economic impact and value drivers

From a company's perspective there is a need to base the management of sustainability issues on a sound business footing. The effects on business operations and value creation will be discussed in the following subsections in relation to the main value drivers.

License to operate

This major value driver is of greater importance to airlines that have a significant market share and use a major hub with capacity problems (for example British Airways at Heathrow and Lufthansa in Frankfurt) than to minor airlines such as Spanair and Air Berlin. The structure of operating hours and airports served also has a bearing on the significance of this value driver. For express companies such as DHL, night operations are an essential part of the business model. Avoidance of curfews may drive measures such as complete renewal of the fleet. In contrast the threat of operating restrictions is rather minimal for no-frills carriers that use secondary airports such as Pisa in Italy and Hahn in Germany. This value driver may become even more important in the future due to further traffic growth and increased public awareness of noise and emissions.

Eco-efficiency

Potential savings from efficiency gains are the second most important value driver. On its own, fuel consumption (which is closely linked to the major issues of resource depletion and greenhouse emissions) absorbs more than 15 per cent of airline revenues and is likely to become even more expensive due to resource depletion and higher taxes. Compared with other value drivers, eco-efficiency is quite easy to quantify and is therefore more often considered in business decisions. Further efficiency gains can be made in the consumption of electricity, raw materials (recycling) and water.

Regulations

The economic importance of regulations, charges and taxes varies significantly from airline to airline since there are country and airport specificities. In the environmental area, general regulations are of greatest relevance to production-oriented maintenance and service units. There are some aviation-specific regulations, charges, taxes and fees, especially in respect of flight operations. It is likely that regulations will increase in importance, for example in response to the Kyoto Protocol. In the EU the question is not whether there will be regulations but what they should be.

Employee motivation, retention and recruitment

This is an important value driver since airlines have quite high staff turnover rates and a consequent demand for recruits. Moreover airline employees often live close to airports and are seen by other local residents as representatives of their companies and in some way responsible for airline-related issues near airports. Some interviewees said that this is a major reason for communications on sustainability, and even for comprehensive environmental management approaches (see the following section) that allow employees to build their arguments on concrete facts, improvements and personal experiences.

Reputation and positioning

This value driver is especially important for premium carriers in West European and Nordic countries. As one interviewee put it, 'You don't know the value of your reputation until it's damaged', which could happen through a media/NGO campaign on sustainability issues. Reputation is mainly an indirect value driver that promotes other value drivers: employee motivation, retention and recruitment, regulations and licence to operate.

The following example shows how the value drivers are linked and how they affect each other. On the advice of its environmental department one airline decided to invest millions of dollars in quieter and more efficient engines when expanding its long-distance fleet. It valued the efficiency gains made and its new reputation as a leader in environmental performance, which could influence the expansion of its major hub (licence to operate) and a discussion about new noise regulations implying costs that were higher than the additional investment costs for more efficient engines.

In any assessment of the business case for sustainability, negative value drivers must be considered as well. Besides the direct costs of sustainability management, there are indirect costs that are often ignored. These include opportunity costs and risks. For instance opportunity costs can arise when employees are required to engage in social or environmental improvements, which draws their attention away from other business activities (lost business momentum), and there can be risks involved in introducing 'green' technology, operating procedures or strategies. Several airlines are thinking about emission-free flying initiatives ('green miles'). The direct costs of such programmes may be reasonable compared with the positive impact on value drivers such as reputation, regulation or licence to operate. However there are several potential risks that could reverse the effects, for example the initiative might not be accepted by the market, or compensation programmes such as reforestation could fail or turn out to be unsustainable. Moreover instead of reducing the pressure on airlines such programmes could increase public scrutiny of their environmental performance. One interviewee thought it would be better to 'Let sleeping dogs lie'.

All in all the foregoing discussion of value drivers shows that sustainability issues can have a significant impact on value creation and business development at airlines. The main determinants of their economic importance are the company's size (small niche player versus market leader), business model (premium versus no-frills carrier) and the culture of its home market (the USA versus Europe). This is especially true for value drivers such as license to operate, reputation and positioning, and employee motivation and retention. Accordingly sustainability management, as discussed in the following section, varies significantly from airline to airline.

Corporate sustainability management

This section discusses how airlines can react to and manage the challenges of sustainability issues at the corporate level, and the extent to which there is a business rationale (business case) for doing so.

Strategy

A prerequisite for any strategy is the existence of concrete, feasible measures to react to challenges, in our case, for example, investment in noise control or a communication campaign. Furthermore, according to our research hypothesis there has to be a business case for introducing these measures; that is, their economic assessment – including the evaluation of contradictory goals – has to be positive and specific to the context of the company, and the measures must fit into an overall strategy.

Improvement options

The improvement measures revealed by our study can be grouped into internal improvements, external alignments and communication.

Managers reported that a survey of the company for existing initiatives and compliance measures is a necessary step towards gaining an overall picture and detecting redundancies and gaps.

Internal improvements include all measures that have a business case within the company, that is, social or environmental improvements that have a positive pay-off. These include measures for direct improvements (for example fleet renewal, taxiing procedures, diversity programmes) as well as research or sponsorship. Elements of the sustainability management functions described in other subsections can also be seen as potential measures in this category: they may facilitate greater awareness among employees and lead to better management of environmental and social issues.

External alignments consist of measures that only have a business case within a large group of airlines, since some important environmental issues, such as greenhouse gas emissions and noise, can only be solved at that level. Examples are voluntary agreements, lobbying, joint research and joint efforts (for example to influence engine/plane manufacturers). Here industry associations such as IATA, ATAG and the AEA play an important role. When pushing for improvements these organizations often face the challenge of unanimous decision making or the 'prisoner's dilemma'.

Communication is an important measure as sustainability is closely linked to values and perceptions and requires a response to stakeholder demands. It is important for airlines to communicate the impact of their activities, for example in the case of fuel dumping, and to defend their legitimate interests and positions.

Assessment of potential improvements

Among our interviewees there was a broad consensus on both the necessity of a business case and the difficulty of assessing it. Assessment is difficult because most improvements in the area of sustainability require decision making in the face of uncertainty and the indirect, long-term economic effects are hard to evaluate (for example quantifying improved reputation or the fact that new regulation was avoided). However this is not specifically a sustainability management problem. Managers in other areas face the same difficulties, for example network managers in respect of revenue allocation or marketing managers in respect of the effectiveness of a new advertising campaign.

The interviewees did not mention specific sustainability management evaluation methods and referred to 'normal' management practices (for example cost–benefit analysis). To carry out a synthesis by analysing potential value drivers (see the section entitled 'Overall economic impact and value drivers' above) using a combination of quantitative and qualitative criteria may be helpful.

Management of contradictory goals

Possible solutions/measures may have complex and sometimes contradictory effects on different aspects of sustainability, which is another reason why an economic assessment is unavoidable. Obvious examples are the contradictions inherent in the issue of abatement of noise and NO_x and CO_2 emissions. The faster an aircraft takes off and climbs, the less noise is heard by local residents, but the higher the fuel consumption. The higher the temperature at which fuel burns, the greater the fuel efficiency and the lower the CO_2 emissions, but this results in NO_x emissions. Even if improvements are feasible in the long term, in the short term priorities have to be set. As economic entities, companies should manage this conflict by focusing on the options with the best cost–benefit ratio and the greatest acceptance. This could mean taking off during the night at full engine power in order to be as quiet as possible, and ascending more slowly during the day to enable greater fuel efficiency.

Overall strategy

Most airlines have a clear understanding of their strategy in specific areas, functions or business units, but there is just tacit knowledge of the overall approach. Only a few airlines have a clear and explicit overview of all improvement measures and how they fit into an overall strategy to address the challenges of the sustainability issues the company is facing. Figure 6.5 shows a strategy design (business plan) used by one of the airlines in our study. It is used to avoid gaps and overlaps, and to ensure adequate adoption of the strategy across the company. It starts with directive goals (for example licence to grow) that are first broken down into subdirective goals (for example achieve measurable improvements) and then into measurable goals (for example an x per cent CO_2 reduction/revenue passenger kilometre RPK). All existing and planned improvement measures in different functions and business units are listed and allocated to these goals. Measures can consist of projects (for example investment in noise reduction) or changed routines/business processes (for example altering procedures). To avoid adding complexity to the overall concept there can be different strategy plans for the main issues (such as for noise reduction and fuel efficiency).

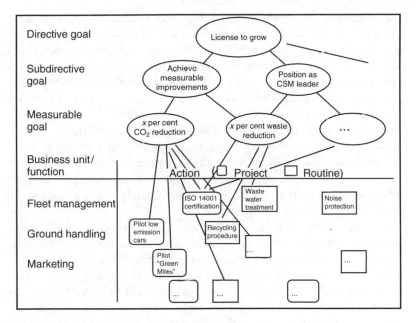

Figure 6.5 Airline business plan for improvements

Organization

Only a few of the airlines in our study have functions or management positions that explicitly bear the term sustainability (as mentioned earlier, British Airways has a Sustainable Business Unit). Some airlines do not explicitly use the term but have a transparent virtual structure to cover sustainability matters with clearly defined responsibilities in all areas (for example Lufthansa).

Sustainability management can be poorly defined due to the diversity of interpretations of what corporate social responsibility (CSR) encompasses. At the end of the interviewing process in one company, it was mentioned that there were 'some others working on Corporate Social Responsibility CSR', meaning, 'HR issues such as worldwide working condition standards or codes of business conduct'.

Managers with a direct responsibility for sustainability issues can normally be found in the following departments: environment, human resources, communication, public relations, quality management and sustainability management. Direct responsibility means that they act internally as promoters of environmental and social improvements, and externally as communicators of their company's performance, achievements and policies. In the main it is environmental managers who are in charge of sustainability management. During the late 1980s and early 1990s most of the airlines in our survey embarked on environmental management at the operational level, for example in maintenance. During the past decade this has been gradually extended to all business units and the corporate centre. Today all the airlines have a corporate environmental department, or at least an officer. Interestingly, most of the airlines were in the process of reducing or had recently reduced their environmental staff by about 25–50 per cent. This could be seen as a sign of a reduction in the business relevance of sustainability. However some airlines stated that the percentages just corresponded to the overall goal for corporate staff reductions.

Most managers involved in corporate sustainability management have a background in engineering, public social sciences or economics. The majority of the interviewed managers started their careers outside the company, in consultancies or research institutions. Just a few had moved internally from other departments or planned to do so in the near future. Obviously companies have often looked for employees with an outside perspective on the company and its business in order to ensure openness, a better understanding of stakeholders or an early awareness of external issues that might constitute business risks or opportunities. Nevertheless such managers have to adapt to the management and company culture. The importance of top management support was emphasized by some of the interviewees, and was seen as a starting point for dealing with social and environmental issues. Thereafter support could be obtained by presenting sound strategies and business cases.

According to our interview results an effective organizational sustainability management structure should include the following:

- There should be a clear and transparent structure covering all dimensions of sustainability.
- A separate sustainability department is not necessary, but one department (for example environment) should be in charge of coordination.
- The structure should be aligned with and reflect the overall corporate organizational structure.
- The main social sustainability issues should be managed by their traditional departments (for example HR for employees and Customer Care for customers).

Implementation and integration

Most of the interviewees reported that standard management practices are applied when integrating and implementing sustainability improvements. Sustainability managers are involved in the decision-making process rather than in integration management. They emphasized that everything planned in the area of sustainability, investment and altered business or operating procedures should be incorporated into the company's general business plan to ensure that implementation conforms to the standard management procedures. According to one airline manager, 'the challenge is to integrate it into the normal business processes. At the operational level, for example, a pilot wants to have clear, precise and integrated guidelines. He is not interested in whether this is an environmental standard or a manufacturer's handling instruction.'

Alongside general approaches such as project management, frameworks for business process redesign and quality management, an effective environmental management system has been cited as essential to managing direct environmental impacts (for example in maintenance) and integrating improvements into business and operating procedures, as its use implies regular updates and continuous improvement measures. However the benefits of an environmental management system have to be carefully assessed as its implementation absorbs resources. Moreover managers and employees are increasingly reluctant to adopt such systems, as they claim to be over-certified already (for example, in the area of catering)

Eco-Management and Audit Schemes (EMASs) are not widespread in the aviation industry. Lufthansa Cityline is the only certified company in the EMAS air transport category. Beyond this there is some certification of flight operations business units, for example maintenance, catering and airports. The strong geographical focus on Austria, Germany, the Netherlands and the Scandinavian countries is notable. ISO 14001 certification is more common. On the basis of our interview data (there are no public statistics available), just a few corporations have certification for their entire business section, but certification of business units or subsidiaries is common, especially in technical and operational areas such as maintenance and catering.

Managers' perceptions and attitudes are also seen as vital to successful implementation. Other than through corporate culture, values and business ethics, these can be influenced by incentives and setting goals and objectives. Balanced scorecards were mentioned by several interviewees, but none of the companies surveyed use them. Other incentives are awards to employees for suggestions. The provision of information is also seen as an important driver of motivation, for example through training (specific or integrated modules), road shows and other forms of communication (see below). One US airline considers that information on managers' personal liabilities is the starting point for the professional setting up of environmental management.

Controlling and monitoring

It is important to monitor changes in social and environmental perform-ance, but an overall assessment of sustainability is almost impossible. More easily observed are the business and management processes that ensure consideration of social and environmental issues (proactive monitoring) and performance and compliance with social and environ-mental impact parameters (reactive monitoring).

Most airlines have internal monitoring and control systems. To monitor the process of implementation, most of the interviewees again pointed to the need for integration of sustainability issues into normal business procedures. For more specific information on social and environmental issues, nearly all the companies surveyed have separate databases for each department, plus key performance indicators (KPIs). Some airlines are attempting to improve their KPIs and the consistency of the latter among the various business units and subsidiaries. Moreover better alignment of indicators throughout the industry would aid performance comparison between airlines and – if accepted and supported by regulators and NGOs – facilitate planning reliability. In this context the importance of external auditing is emphasized.

Communication

Communication is an important part of the work of sustainability managers. According to our survey, even managers whose work is not dedicated to communication issues spend more than 50 per cent of their time on internal and external communication. This is apparently because sustainability is closely linked to values and perceptions and requires a response to stakeholders' demands, for example to inform the public about environmental matters. It is also important in influ-encing and supporting sustainability awareness and improvements, as well as increasing employees' motivation and changing their perceptions. In addition it enables a company to influence the regulatory envir-onment, both directly by influencing the regulators themselves, and indirectly by changing the thinking of other groups, such as the public and NGOs.

One airline reported two interesting experiences. First, the airline had been confronted by an NGO about animal transportation concerns. The airline did not react to this because it had complied with the relevant regulations and even applied higher standards in some areas. But the public's perception was influenced solely by the accusers. Eventually the pressure became so intense that a senior executive was forced to take change of the matter and operating procedures had to be changed to avoid severe damage to the airline's reputation. Second, a few years later and based on its previous experience, the same airline reacted in a completely different way to an accusation that by transporting fruit and vegetables it was adding to the degree of environmental damage. It made itself available for discussions and, adopting a constructive approach with the NGOs in question, proved that the impact was marginal and that some of the changes were wrong. The campaign faded away without creating a negative image.

Another of our interviewees said that company information 'should not be perceived as a whitewashing exercise but rather as providing verifiable and valid information. One example is a widespread public misperception of fuel dumping, which is reported as rare (according to the bigger airlines it only happens up to 15 times a year) and has no measurable environmental impact. The policy of some airlines is never to dump fuel unless there is a threat to passenger safety. Some European airlines have been in the public spotlight for carrying illegal immigrants, even though they were legally obliged to provide the transportation for which they were being criticized.

However there is a significant difference between positive influence and manipulation. All the airline interviewees thought that it is in the legitimate interest of airlines to defend their position. However interviewees at regulatory governmental institutions, NGOs and consultancies felt that the industry must be careful to maintain credibility, avoid denying or purposely omitting scientific facts, and be willing to compromise. If they are not the industry could lose influence and be accused of 'green-washing'.

Reporting/publications

Over the past decade most airlines have started to publish reports dedicated solely to environmental issues, but only a few produce sustainability reports or refer explicitly to sustainability in their environmental reports. However in 2001 IATA and ATAG published a comprehensive survey on airline environmental reporting.

Reports are used externally to maintain reputation and provide information, and internally to boost employees' motivation. Surveys indicate that reports have a high popularity rating among employees. However some of our interviewees questioned the need for an annual publication and wondered whether the time and money could not be more effectively spent on other endeavours, such as articles and reports in external media (public relations), in the published timetable, in the staff magazine or in special publications on specific issues (such as airport noise and immigration).

Internet and intranet

The Internet pages of the researched airlines vary between offering no information on sustainability to well-elaborated details. As some of the interviewees pointed out, the Internet is an easy and inexpensive way to make information on sustainability available to a broader community. In addition to reproducing printed communications, such as current and past reports, plus the text of speeches and policies, home pages may contain facts and figures on aviation and the environment (Lufthansa), links to sponsored research projects or initiatives (Air Canada) or interactive tools such as an environmental impact calculator (SAS).

Companies' intranet pages may contain additional internal information such as top managers' notes and speeches, guidelines and policies, suggestion boxes, information on awards, social projects and web-based training modules.

Stakeholder dialogue

Our interviews revealed the existence of two types of stakeholder dialogue. The first is via mail, e-mail or telephone. Some companies only publish a postal address, even on their Internet page. Others include an e-mail address, while some publish the contact details of managers in all areas, and even photographs of them. The provision of such information demonstrates accessibility, sincerity and openness in Western cultures, but in other cultures it may well be perceived differently, as one Asian manager pointed out. The published e-mail feedback or Internet discussion forums provided by other industries (such as 'Tell Shell') are absent in the aviation industry. The second type is personal, dedicated dialogue. Such dialogue may occur on an *ad hoc* basis and relate to current issues, as in the immigration and cargo example, or they may be regular and long term. An example here is the extensive dialogue that European airlines have with people who live near their major hubs and airports. This is normally handled by managers in the infrastructure departments in cooperation with the airports in question.

Some managers reported difficulties in establishing long-term cooperation with NGOs, sometimes because the latter refuse to cooperate, sometimes because they lack resources. Among the few cooperative NGOs is the WWF. A number of industry associations facilitate this process on behalf of the entire industry, such as the Air Transport Action Group's work with the Union for the Conservation of Nature. Other important means of communication are the provision of representation at forums, congresses and conferences, and participation in industry initiatives such as the World Business Council for Sustainable Development, and in international working groups such as the Committee on Aviation Environmental Protection.

Framework for sustainability management

Figure 6.6 shows a framework for the four elements of corporate sustainability management discussed above: (strategy, organization, implementation/integration and communication). All four elements are interrelated, for example organizational structure influences implementation/integration and *vice versa* (management capacity), and communication and implementation/integration are closely related in respect of employee motivation, information on new business processes and so

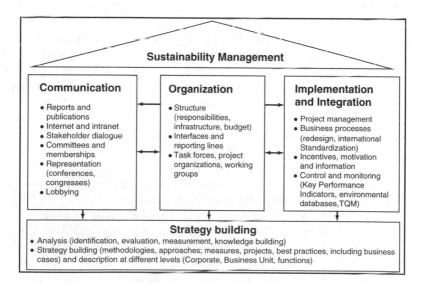

Figure 6.6 Framework for corporate sustainability management

on. Finally, strategy is influenced by the preceding and other factors, for example the qualifications of the people assigned to work on it.

Conclusion

This chapter has shown that sustainability issues have a significant impact on business operations and value creation in the aviation industry. Various examples of how airlines can manage these issues according to an economic rationale have been discussed. In this sense a business case for sustainability management can be said to exist. However its significance varies considerably among airlines. The goal for all airlines should be an adequate sustainability performance that fits their specific circumstances. The main criteria for assessing this are the business rationale (the existence of a business case) and the balance between the sustainability performance and management elements (for example between communication and environmental improvements, see Figure 6.6). The extensiveness and sophistication of measures and management elements are not criteria for assessing performance. For example publishing a sustainability report does not necessarily make sense for a small airline as its resources may be used more efficiently to improve its environmental performance.

Effective sustainability management requires several barriers to be overcome:

- The complexity of sustainability: Ambiguity of the concept, uncertainty about issues, contradictory goals, lack of standards and measurements.
- Market constraints: inherent structural problems, highly international market in which decisions/regulations are based on the lowest common denominator.
- Behavioural and cultural factors: 'hope' and positive image, fatalism ('inherently unsustainable') and positivism/ignorance, differing values.

One of the main barriers is the ambiguity of the concept of sustainability. There is a need for sustainability performance indicators that are accepted by the entire industry and its stakeholders. Such indicators would inevitably represent a compromise (due to differing values), would have to be adapted from time to time (following advances in knowledge) and would not solve the problem of contradictory goals. However they are a prerequisite for transparency, planning reliability and sustainable performance. Market constraints and behavioural and cultural factors can hinder sustainability improvements in all areas and cannot always be influenced by sustainability managers.

An additional challenge is that the problems of noise and emissions can only be overcome by a joint approach by airlines or the industry as a whole, and there are likely to be widely differing opinions on the most suitable measures. Some of the interviewees in our study were in favour of voluntary commitments rather than regulations as this would allow greater flexibility. But it would run the risk of cartelization and lack of public acceptance. Moreover the incentive for individual companies to renege would be high. Regulations, on the other hand, would enable greater planning reliability and ensure equal conditions for all participants.

Airlines should not be hesitant about managing sustainability issues in an open manner. The improvement of social and environmental sustainability may in some cases hinder growth, but not necessarily value creation. And as one manager stated, 'The problem for airlines has never been growth, but profitability and value creation.' The economic problems being experienced by the industry are mainly to do with the market and are not due to social and environmental burdens. Hence addressing these problems should not be accompanied by reduced attention to social and environmental improvements. This is the task not only of airlines but also of international regulators.

7

The Energy Industry

Oliver Salzmann

This chapter is based on empirical evidence gathered from 44 personal interviews (22 in the oil and gas industry, 13 in the utility sector and nine with external stakeholders), and 205 completed mail, fax and on-line questionnaires (30 completed by sustainability officers and 175 by general managers, that is non-experts on sustainability). We gratefully acknowledge the participation of the BG Group, ConocoPhillips, EON, the European Commission, ExxonMobil, Friends of the Earth UK, Fortum Oyj, Gaz de France, Greenpeace Germany, the International Energy Agency, Norsk Hydro, Royal Dutch/Shell, RAG, RWE, Scottish Power, Suez, Total, the United Nations Environment Programme (UNEP), the World Business Council for Sustainable Development (WBCSD) and the World Economic Forum.

General industry analysis

Energy (both primary and secondary, such as electricity) is a strategic and cheap commodity that is essential to most economic activities. Demand, and hence price, is closely linked to economic up turns, downturns and climatic conditions.

Commercial consumption of energy has risen by a factor of five over the past 50 years, mainly fed by fossil fuels (95 per cent of the commercial and 83 per cent of the total supply). Demand will continue to grow due to economic growth, urbanization and the spread of Western lifestyles in developing countries, particularly in Asia. Estimating the remaining reserves of fossil fuels is difficult since new discoveries and price shifts can suddenly make uneconomic reservoirs commercially viable. Even if the ratio of reserves to production happen to rise, supply shortages, particularly in the case of oil, can be expected from 2030.

Resource depletion and short-term supply disruptions due to geopolitical factors are clearly of great significance to the oil and gas industry – indeed one may trigger the other, leading to price increases. They are less important to electric and gas utilities mainly relying on coal, gas and nuclear fuels that are available domestically or are purchased from more politically stable regions. Furthermore coal has by far the largest reserves of all fossil fuels. In contrast to the global activities of the oil and gas industry, electricity supply tends to be more localized.

Competition

As is often the case in markets with high entry barriers, concentration in the oil and gas industry has increased significantly in recent years. Because the cost of extracting and producing oil and gas is so high, joint ventures are common. Nevertheless there is significant competition, particularly in the refining and marketing of oil and gas products. Figure 7.1 summarizes the competitive situation in the industry.

In Europe the degree of competition in the electricity industry has traditionally been relatively low in comparison with the oil and gas industry. The competitive forces are summarized Figure 7.2. However the strong government influence over and monopolistic structure of the electricity sector has come to an end with the liberalization and opening up of Europe's gas and electricity markets. This has brought several significant changes, including increased investment risk because customers can easily change their supplier, a reduction of overcapacity and consolidation through mergers and acquisitions.

Furthermore competition between oil and gas companies and European electricity companies is increasing in a converging market. Whereas the latter are building up their capacity in the upstream gas business, oil and gas companies are entering the power supply market through their gas and power business units.

Environmental regulation

Environmental regulations in the oil and gas sector primarily focus on fuel quality, for example the reduction of lead and sulphur. Some EU member states have already introduced eco-taxes on fuels, and refineries will be subject to the forthcoming EU emission trading system. Companies are also engaged in voluntary initiatives such as internal and external emission trading (the UK) and reduction agreements (France).

The electricity industry is now facing stronger regulatory pressure in respect of atmospheric emissions, particularly CO_2. The most significant

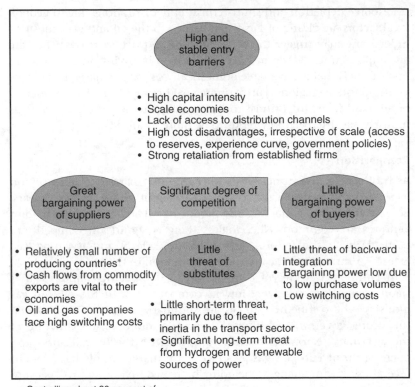

Figure containing the following labelled elements:

High and stable entry barriers
- High capital intensity
- Scale economies
- Lack of access to distribution channels
- High cost disadvantages, irrespective of scale (access to reserves, experience curve, government policies)
- Strong retaliation from established firms

Great bargaining power of suppliers
- Relatively small number of producing countries*
- Cash flows from commodity exports are vital to their economies
- Oil and gas companies face high switching costs

Significant degree of competition

Little bargaining power of buyers
- Little threat of backward integration
- Bargaining power low due to low purchase volumes
- Low switching costs

Little threat of substitutes
- Little short-term threat, primarily due to fleet inertia in the transport sector
- Significant long-term threat from hydrogen and renewable sources of power

* Controlling about 90 per cent of reserves and 69 per cent of production of the world's oil and gas.

Figure 7.1 Competition in the oil and gas industry (based on Porter's five forces model)

initiatives are the EU CO_2 emission trading system, to be launched in 2005, and the voluntary UK trading scheme. Companies are also engaged in voluntary agreements with domestic governments (for example in Germany).

Sustainability issues

The general managers in our study showed considerable familiarity with the concept of sustainable development and expected its importance to increase in the future. They considered environmental issues to be more significant than social issues, mainly because social issues are more difficult to grasp. However the sample was strongly biased towards European companies, which are confronted with higher regulatory

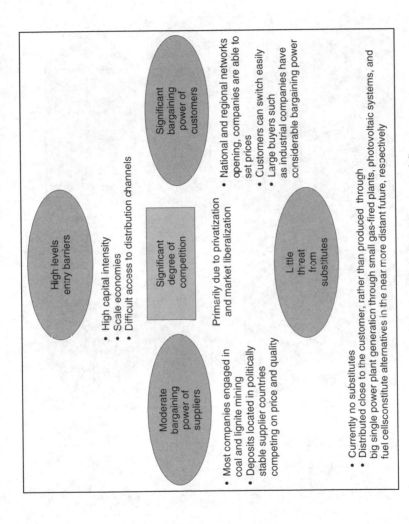

Figure 7.2 Competition in the electricity industry (based on Porter's five forces model)

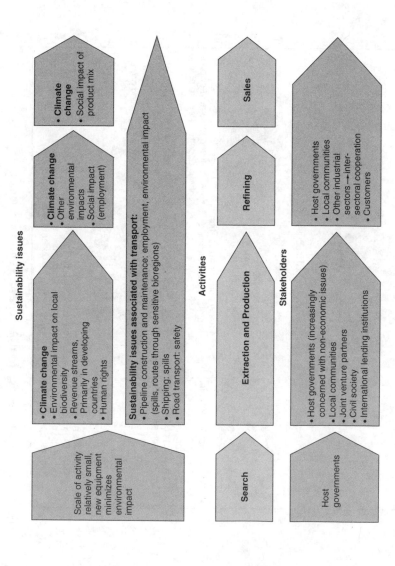

Figure 7.3 Sustainability issues and stakeholders – oil and gas

Sustainability issues

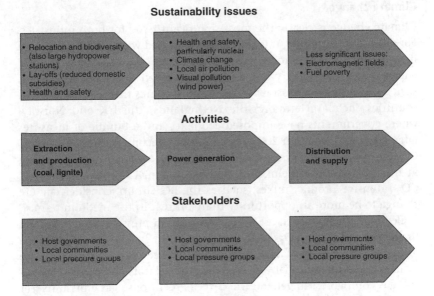

Figure 7.4 Sustainability issues and stakeholders – electricity

standards and less severe social problems than their counterparts in developing countries, particularly in the case of electricity.

Climate change and the North–South energy divide are associated with major externalities in both sectors. As can be seen in Figures 7.3 and 7.4, sustainability issues are strongly associated with particular activities and locations (for example biodiversity). We shall elaborate on their economic relevance in the following subsections.

Health and safety

The running of major installations and hazardous fuels obviously present health and safety (H&S) challenges. H&S issues are considered well-handled and thus performance is often argued to be superior to other industries. Location and fuel/technology are the major influencing factors:

- Developed countries put more regulatory emphasis on safety than do developing countries.
- Nuclear power and gas present special safety challenges.

Health and safety incidents clearly have an impact on costs (for example insurance premiums, clean-up operations), licence to operate, brand value and reputation.

Climate change

Climate change is clearly the most significant issue for both industries. For oil & gas companies, it is primarily associated with product use even if emissions from operations play a significant role in areas with little energy-intensive industry and a high proportion of renewable energy, such as Scandinavia. Most external pressure comes from NGOs, even in countries such as Germany, the Netherlands, the UK and Norway, where governments have imposed eco-taxes and a bundle of measures targeted at end users. In 2005 refineries will become subject to the EU CO_2 emission trading system, and BP and Shell are already participating in the UK's voluntary emission trading system. Companies with less CO_2-intensive product mixes, such as the BG Group, consider climate change to be more an opportunity than a threat in the medium term.

Electricity companies face stronger short-term pressure – being among the largest industrial CO_2 emitters in Europe (in contrast to the millions of car owners and private households that use oil and gas) they are easier targets for national and European legislators than upstream oil and gas companies. In general the cost of greenhouse gas emissions (set by eco-taxes and allowances) is expected to increase over time, including in the USA,[1] where liability risk associated with climate change is particularly high. The Carbon Disclosure Project, run by a group of institutional investors, is currently scrutinizing the CO_2 portfolio of the corporate sector.

Substantial investment in emission reduction is being made in both sectors as part of strategic management. Companies' stance on climate change has a significant impact on brand value, reputation and exposure to litigation. Brand value and reputation appear to be more significant in the liberalized oil and gas industry.

Biodiversity

Biodiversity is strongly affected by emissions from the oil and gas industry into water and the soil (foremost through oil spills) and the industry's extraction and construction activities (platforms, pipelines), particularly in developing countries. While the mining activities associated with the electricity industry are highly regulated in developed countries, large hydropower projects in developing and emerging economies have adverse effects on biodiversity, and on populations when relocation is necessary.

Since damage to biodiversity is often concentrated at the local level (the laying of pipelines, surface mining), local stakeholders and NGOs play a key role in protests, and are sometimes more influential and effective than national and global NGOs.

Significant economic costs are associated with formal and informal licences to operate, brand value, reputation and clean-up operations.

Local air pollution

In the OECD countries local air pollution has fallen since the 1980s and early 1990s. For the oil and gas industry, local air pollution is associated with production and refining, and particularly with product use (in cars and so on). In urban areas of developing countries the immediate environmental effects of atmospheric emissions are more closely scrutinized than those of climate change.

In response to increasing regulatory and public pressure over the past two decades the industry has agreed to phase out lead and reduce the sulphur content of its motor fuels. However the production of cleaner fuels is itself an energy-intensive process and the implications for production and emission costs are significant. The industry is currently developing 'designer fuels' that will reduce emissions still further. It is also cooperating with other industries to research fuel-cell and hydrogen technology. These activities are important not only in terms of portfolio development but also for reputation and brand value.

Local air pollution through the emission of NO_x, SO_2 and so on by the electricity industry has decreased as companies have made significant investments in cleaner technologies in response to external pressures (for example EU directives and domestic emission limits). Therefore the economic significance of externalities will be limited in the future. In several European countries, however, secondary (waste) fuel-fired power plants will continue to face the growing challenge of emission standards.

The energy divide

In developing countries, particularly in rural areas, energy is needed for economic and social reasons.[2] Some oil and gas companies have established local energy infrastructures around their facilities, and some have entered the urban electricity business. The supply of electricity to rural areas is poor because of the high fixed costs of grid extensions to remote communities with sparse populations. Alternatives such as photovoltaic systems are costly and are therefore limited to demonstration projects that can attract funding from third parties. The following factors also prevent engagement in developing countries:

- Customers' lack of purchasing power.
- Lack of local experience in technologies and markets, largely due to specific local conditions. Companies' technical and commercial activities are dominated by the strong pull from wealthy countries and urban areas, particularly in the case of the electricity industry, which is focusing on the European market.
- Mindset (see the later section on corporate thinking and attitudes).

Bridging the North–South energy divide will require the issue of funding to be resolved. Companies could contemplate provision to those at the bottom of the pyramid (four billion people with the limited purchasing power of less than US$1500 per year) and maximize the positive externalities of providing the energy required for the economic development of underdeveloped areas.

Monetary flows in developing countries

Assessing the social impact of local activities and determining an adequate level of engagement in communities constitute major challenges for oil and gas companies. International lending institutions and NGOs are increasingly scrutinizing major investments in developing countries in terms of payments to host governments (corruption), and the allocation of revenue streams between national governments and local communities (that is, assessing how local communities benefit). A relevant issue for any industry operating in developing countries that lack democratic structures is reduced employment when a project switches from construction to maintenance. The economic relevance of the issues described lies in companies' formal and informal licence to operate (for example employment, changes in purchasing power due to price increases associated with migration to sites), reputation risks and access to third-party funding.

Human rights

Energy companies' facilities in poor, less democratic countries such as Myanmar and Libya have been attacked for a number of reasons, including civil war, ideological/political motives, local social and environmental problems and so on. Moreover police or military forces contracted to protect the sites have been accused of violating human rights. Media coverage and lawsuits filed by NGOs have significantly affected the reputation of companies.

Other social issues

Electricity companies face two additional challenges:

- Lay-offs: the deregulation of markets has significantly increased competitive pressures, resulting in companies laying off employees. The gradual phasing out of subsidies on domestic mining activities is associated with shutdowns, which are expected to be managed in a socially acceptable manner.
- Relocation due to surface mining and large hydropower projects: these activities are scrutinized by local pressure groups and NGOs.

Both issues are economically relevant because they can affect companies' reputation and formal/informal licence to operate.

Stakeholders

The following subsections consider individual stakeholders and the part they play in certain sustainability issues.

Governments and regulators

As discussed earlier, regulatory pressure on the oil and gas industry is rather weak but is compensated by increased scrutiny by civil society. However in the case of the electricity industry, and particularly in Europe, regulators are the most important promoters of corporate sustainability through measures such as obligatory reporting (France), emission trading (the EU) and so on.

Consensus is growing on the need to internalize the external costs of fossil fuel use (not extraction and production) and to introduce effective policy instruments (carbon taxes, emission trading and so on). Governments in developed countries are clearly more concerned with social and environmental issues than are their counterparts in developing countries. The latter primarily focus on revenues (with profits being split between companies, the national government and local communities), although their awareness of sustainability issues is increasing.

Civil society

NGOs are monitoring corporate activities in developing countries and criticizing governments' fossil-fuel-based energy policies. They lobby governments to internalize external costs and provide subsidies to offset the competitive disadvantages of renewable sources of energy. NGO's activities appear to have had a significant effect on the perceptions and expectations of younger employees, who constitute an important internal pressure group.

Electricity companies are already strongly regulated and are less powerful than the major oil and gas companies. Moreover their extraction activities, even lignite surface mining, are low profile and provide much needed employment in some countries. Hence the pressure on them by NGOs is less confrontational and focuses on single issues such as nuclear transport, surface mining and the construction of plants. In general local pressure groups tend to play a greater role than global NGOs.

In contrast NGOs are the main pressure groups in the case of the oil and gas industry, and focus on climate change and local environmental/social issues in developing countries. In addition to boycotts and protest campaigns, global NGOs are encouraging shareholder responsibility, which is gaining more and more support from socially responsible investors.

The financial community

Although oil and gas shareholders have increasingly supported social and environmental activism, their overall role in terms of corporate sustainability is very reactive. Our study suggests that the scrutiny exercised by socially responsible investors differs from NGO pressure in both quality and intensity, so that companies are better able to react on a conceptual and strategic basis. Some 79 per cent of the general managers surveyed expected shareholders to take on a more proactive role in the future.

International lending institutions are playing a significant part in setting standards for activities in developing countries (for example revenue management and human rights). Private banks are also increasingly important, as reflected in the Equator Principles adopted by 15 significant players, including ABN Amro, the Credit Suisse Group and so on. Electricity shareholders are aware of the relatively high environmental standards in the OECD countries, and particularly in Europe, so are mainly concerned about provisions for operational accidents and transparency in the post-Enron period. However, as can be seen from the activities of the Carbon Disclosure Project, they are likely to play a more proactive past in the future. European shareholders, and insurance companies in particular, tend to have a more progressive attitude than their Anglo-Saxon counterparts.

Customers

Customers tend to serve as a deterrent to sustainability measures. Although NGOs' boycott campaigns have had a noticeable effect on oil and gas companies, especially in the UK and Germany,[3] the majority of customers are hampering progress by demanding cheap and convenient fuels. Both household and industrial customers are largely ignoring environmental and social issues and the 'green pull' is marginal.

Other stakeholders

Joint ventures, which are common in the oil and gas industry, are seen as promoters of sustainability since corporate sustainability performance converges at the level of the more proactive joint venture partners. However laggards veto progressive action. In the electricity industry, municipalities can drive corporate sustainability by purchasing 'green' electricity, and producing competitive electricity from small and highly efficient gas-fired plants.

Value drivers

According to one sustainability officer, 'The business case for environmental health and safety performance has almost no limits. More radical innovations are the tricky part, pushed only by enthusiasts in R&D and environmental affairs rather than top management.' The sustainability officers we interviewed recognized the significance of the value drivers behind all the issues described. Their counterparts in other business functions focused more on local and short-term issues that affected their companies' exposure to operational risks (low risk, low gain), for example cost savings through eco-efficient and safe processes.

In general the rationale for net cost reductions through more efficient, cleaner and safer processes appears to be well understood, so that quantification and monetization is sometimes argued to be unnecessary; investments are built around environmental, health and safety issues. Oil and gas companies use revenue management in developing countries to maintain their informal licences to operate, based on local communities' acceptance of corporate activities.

Improvements to social and environmental health and safety performance (for example community involvement) are often interrelated and can enhance companies licence to operate, brand value, reputation and employee satisfaction. The interviews we conducted have led us to conclude that the latter have become more and more important. In the oil and gas industry they appear to be key value drivers, particularly since companies are facing considerable scrutiny by civil society. Companies aim to differentiate themselves from their peers more through improved reputation than through environmental health and safety performance – at least in the upper tier of the industry. In contrast electricity companies focus more on environmental, health and safety improvements as key value drivers, even though the importance of their licence to operate, reputation and employee satisfaction can be expected to increase in the liberalized European market. (see Figure 3.10, Chapter 3).

The strategic risks and opportunities associated with climate change and the North–South energy divide, together with the need for radical innovation in technologies and business models, are largely recognized, by sustainability officers and most key decision makers. However this has not yet led to a significant paradigm shift because the current business environment favours an incremental approach, that is, increasing the efficiency of fossil fuel production. The economic argument for radical innovation is weak as companies' licence to operate and reputation have not yet been seriously challenged. Radical innovation is currently limited to internally and/or externally subsidized pilot projects, or in some cases pilot business units, and will require substantial and risky investments to produce significant long-term net revenue increases.

There are also two systemic barriers to a strategic paradigm shift: long-term effects are hard to quantify, and the discounting of both positive and negative future cash flows decreases the relevance of long-term investments.

Oil and gas companies, particularly Shell, have a more comprehensive approach than electricity companies. Leaders in sustainability have given up on complete economic quantification of the business case for sustainability (BCS – see Box 7.1) because of its complexity. However they are currently developing methods of quantifying the economic potential of certain corporate activities, and focusing on value drivers such as formal and informal licences to operate (for example the economic gains of speeding up permitting and minimizing disruption by operations in developing countries through comprehensive stakeholder dialogues, community involvement and sound environmental management) and employee satisfaction (for example the economic gains from sustainability leaders' ability to attract, retain and motivate talented employees).

Box 7.1   Value drivers

At company X the elements of a generic set of value drivers were identified by a senior management committee consisting of members of the corporate sustainability function and the top managers of all business units.

The committee worked on the BCS for several months without ever putting a list of value drivers together. The latter 'only took a couple of minutes'. The list is seen as a set of tools for strategy formulation, investment decision making and day-to-day activities (for example the recycling of coffee cups).

An external consultancy was engaged to quantify the BCS and examine the applicability of emerging techniques and so on, but without much success. The company refocused on its core values and business principles that were 'self-evidently right'. Some strategic decisions were made under considerable uncertainty, however *ex-post* evaluation is proving the usefulness of the value drivers as tools. The next step will be to quantify the economic potential of individual value drivers, including employee satisfaction and licence to operate.

So far value drivers have not been incorporated into strategy-development processes under their own label. They are fed into these processes through risk assessment procedures that focus on projects and issues rather than individual value drivers.

Corporate sustainability management

The electricity industry's approach to corporate sustainability management lags significantly behind that of the oil and gas industry, and its performance is less uniform (for example in terms of environmental reporting and corporate values). The key areas of corporate sustainability management will be discussed in the following subsections.

Corporate vision

The oil and gas companies in our study have similar strategic agendas for growth and competitiveness. The industry's contribution to economic growth and welfare improvements on a global scale is highlighted by pointing to the link between economic development and local environmental improvements.

The companies in question stress that their corporate visions must be realized in a responsible way. In contrast to earlier times, local and regional issues such as human rights and biodiversity are taken into account at the operational level, not least since they are associated with improved reputation, brand value and licence to operate. Corporate visions are based on the following assumptions:

- The industry will have to meet a growing energy demand, particularly in Asia.
- Although the share of renewable sources of energy will grow rapidly, they will not be able to meet the demand in the medium term.
- Substantial investment will be necessary to develop oil and gas resources to fill the energy supply gap.

Changing the current business models to address long-term global issues (climate change, the North–South energy divide) is often discussed but in practice it has been limited to incremental changes to the conventional models (for example cogeneration, reduction of no flaring), plus research, development and pilot projects. BP's 'beyond petroleum' rebranding was a prominent way of signalling a change in stance, but it was widely criticized by NGOs and others as 'greenwashing'.

Electricity companies have a significantly more regional – that is, European – approach to their business. Like oil and gas companies, they strive for profitable growth, geographical diversification (primarily expansion within Europe) and competitiveness, and also to incorporate welfare improvements into their corporate vision. Due to decreasing profit margins as a result of the ongoing EU liberalization process, companies' focus on financial performance is particularly strong – similar to the downstream oil and gas sector. Securing profits through an efficient base load has first priority. For reasons of supply security, diversified fuel mixes constitute an additional part of companies' strategies.

Corporate visions are largely based on meeting customer's demand for an affordable and reliable energy supply. Environmental damage and climate change are addressed mainly on a business-as-usual basis (via incremental innovations). The North–South energy divide is barely considered due to the focus on European and North American markets. However the E7[4] has established a fund for renewable-energy, rural-electrification and greenhouse-gas-reduction projects in developing countries. Strategies and corporate thinking vary according to the fuel mix in question.

Corporate thinking and attitudes

Oil and gas companies tend to have a strong focus on science and technology. This is associated with the reactive and defensive corporate thinking of the past. The current situation in the USA illustrates how public perceptions and lifestyles shape companies' thinking and PR approaches. European companies, which face greater public pressure in terms of climate change and have more open corporate cultures, have adopted a more proactive approach that is reflected in public statements by their chief executives. Exxon Mobil has recently changed its stance on climate change and published its first corporate citizenship report, mainly because of increasing pressure in Europe. Although the transatlantic divide in attitudes and corporate mindsets is still significant, strategies and operations do not significantly differ between US and European companies.

Electricity companies' corporate thinking has largely been determined by the industry's previous status as a state monopoly. To date, brand value and reputation have played minor roles. Furthermore companies have a strong focus on engineering expertise. Managerial thinking that is still primarily conservative and dominated by a strong short-term focus on securing the newly liberalized European energy markets.

The following barriers to changes in thinking appear to be significant:

- Continuous technical challenges, particularly in the upstream oil and gas sector, have perpetuated companies' customary focus on science and technology.
- Lack of pressure from customers and shareholders: oil, gas and electricity are strategic commodities and customers are largely unconcerned about the related environmental and social issues.
- Lack of urgency: issues such as climate change and renewable energy are long-term matters that do not fit into the short-term focus of key decision makers.
- Addressing climate change and the North–South energy divide will require technologies, expertise and business models that are very different from the current ones.

The concept of BCS appears to be well understood by managers, but opinions vary on the need for its quantification – that is, monetization of the results of integrating external effects into strategies and operations. In general companies that think reactively demand a quantified business case, while progressive players rely more strongly on their corporate values and visions. We conclude that corporate thinking remains a major barrier, against which an elusive case, particularly for long-term issues, cannot compete.

Sustainability strategy design

In both industries, corporate sustainability strategies are not labelled as such. Essentially, companies have different means of ensuring that their corporate vision ('What to do') is operationalized in a responsible way ('How to do it'):

- Corporate values: e.g. honesty and respect for people.
- Business principles (integrity, attention to health, safety and the environment), policies and guidelines.
- A 'beyond compliance position': operational managers are required to prove that they have gone beyond compliance by taking sustainability issues into account.
- A strategic focus: making the corporate vision operational in terms of its contribution to sustainable development (e.g. become a leading international renewables operator; research and develop cleaner fuels and new energy technologies).

In their internal and external communications most companies, particularly those in the oil and gas industry, stress the potential economic value of internalizing sustainability issues, for example enhancing their licence to operate or opportunities for growth, being a preferred partner for host governments, improving their reputation and so on. Shell appears to be the only player to present its business case as a set of value drivers.

Whereas some companies have publicly committed themselves to certain sustainability strategies, such as reducing their greenhouse gas emissions and investing in renewable energy, others are keeping a lower profile. In the case of greenhouse gas emissions this may be due to a conflict between production growth and reduction targets. In general, however, the main reason appears to be conservative thinking.

Changes in operations obviously focus more on environmental than on social issues:

- Increasing the efficiency of conventional technologies (fossil fuel extraction, refineries and power plants) to reduce CO_2 emissions.
- Power generation from renewable energy sources is being developed on a small scale. In Europe, access to the electricity grid is an area of major concern both for promoters of renewable energy, who demand fair access and criticize cross-subsidization, and for grid owners, who demand cost sharing and point to technical challenges. Electricity companies that operate in developing countries concentrate on

urban areas and industrial customers but see distributed generation as a future option. Emerging economies such as the Philippines and Indonesia are preferred targets because of their more stable business environment. The E7 have drawn up best practice guidelines for sustainable methods of operation and multistakeholder electrification initiatives.

- Oil and gas companies that have not participated in the privatization of electricity supply in developing countries are focusing on pilot projects such as rural electrification by means of home solar systems (for example there is a joint venture by Eskom and Shell in South Africa) and the introduction of renewable energy technology (primarily solar panels).
- There is some research into cleaner motor fuels and hydrogen power (for example a pilot project is being conducted in Iceland).
- Energy services and contracting appear to be of less importance to electricity companies due to their corporate thinking, overcapacity and little demand from industrial and residential customers since electricity is inexpensive. The potential for generating revenues from optimized energy services rather than maximized electricity sales is substantial, and likely to be exploited more strongly in increasingly liberalized markets.

Organizational structures and departments

Although organizational structures tend to be very company-specific, a number of organizational units that are relevant to the business case and corporate sustainability management can be identified. Electricity companies' corporate sustainability governance structures lag behind those in the oil and gas industry, with far fewer employees being appointed to promote and manage corporate sustainability. This holds true both for corporate centres and for business units. Furthermore electricity companies focus more strongly on the environmental dimension of sustainability.

Figure 7.5 shows Scottish Power's environmental governance structure. As one of the leaders in its industry its organizational set-up is similar to the prevalent structures in oil and gas companies, although the latter have a more comprehensive approach that goes beyond a mere environmental focus.

The corporate sustainability unit

In the oil and gas industry, responsibility for corporate sustainability is usually allocated either to a sustainability/external affairs unit or is spread

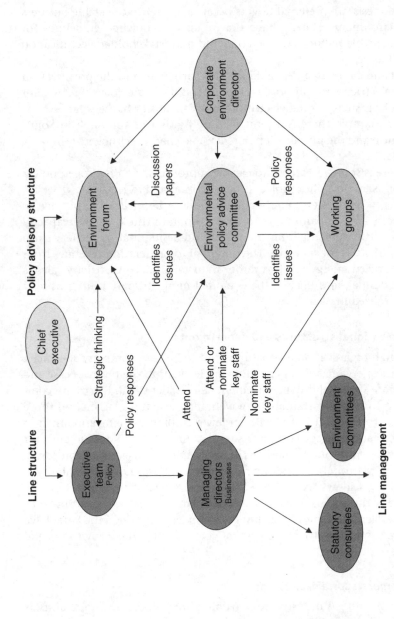

Figure 7.5 Scottish Power's environmental governance structure
Source: Scottish Power Environmental Sustainability Report, 2001/02.

between two departments (for example between environmental health and safety and human resources or external affairs/communication). The unit usually comprises no more than five to ten people, tracks sustainability issues at the corporate level, and collects relevant data from the business units. The BCS is an essential concept in the unit's main task of promoting corporate sustainability management in the business units through its advisory and policy-making role (for example the formulation of strategy, issue tracking and so on) and evaluation role (for example the corporate sustainability officer can reject business plans that do not take environmental and social risks sufficiently into account).

In leading companies the corporate sustainability unit has its counterpart in every department in which sustainability strategies are developed and applied. Our empirical evidence suggests that cooperation between general/functional and sustainability managers can be further improved in order to promote more sustainable business practices. One of the sustainability leaders has recently dissolved its corporate sustainability unit, arguing that there is no longer a need for it as the concept of sustainability has been fully absorbed by all departments.

The importance of non-sustainability departments

Non-sustainability departments feed into issue assessment and strategy development and play a significant role in implementation of corporate sustainability initiatives. They vary significantly in terms of their level of resistance or support, sometimes depending on reporting lines and budgeting procedures, but more often on the nature of the key decision maker.

Data obtained from our interviews and questionnaires suggest that departments that are closer to the issue tend to take on more promotional roles than others, especially R&D and particularly in the electricity industry – this presumably partly reflects the latter's industry-specific focus on technology and engineering. Manufacturing units have a great but as yet unrealized potential for improving corporate sustainability performance.

The following function-specific attitudes have been identified:

- Both R&D and corporate staff have a relatively proactive attitude since they naturally anticipate future developments in the course of technical innovation and long-range planning.
- In general operational managers are concerned with local issues and stakeholders, and are less aware of mid- to long-term strategic challenges. The attitudes of managers and their degree of proactiveness

can differ significantly between up- and downstream divisions, depending on the issues they face. Overall, the management of upstream oil and gas activities tends to be more proactive, since its business is more resource oriented. In contrast downstream operations are more process oriented and face tighter financial controls.

- Finance departments are usually most resistant to sustainability management, although control measures are increasingly taking 'soft factors' into account (for example full cost accounting, investment appraisals). Investor-relations managers tend to be bound to shareholders' wish for financial returns.
- Communication departments tend to have a neutral to proactive attitude. They are increasingly interested in profiling renewable sources of energy, even if their companies' activities in this area are insignificant in economic terms.
- Human resource departments are naturally concerned with social issues (the effects of downsizing, attracting and retaining talented employees).

Processes and tools

The building of a robust business case is a four-step process in which the various organizational units described above participate.

Issue tracking

External effects and sustainability issues are well known to the companies in our study; they commonly use various processes and systems (such as external stakeholder panels, stakeholder dialogues, business intelligence, networking and Internet platforms) to track issues and monitor their business environment so as to avoid unpleasant surprises, depending on whether the issues are global, regional or local and whether they are interrelated, as it is often the case with social and environmental issues.

Global issues such as climate change are identified and monitored at the corporate level. Local or regional issues are monitored through dialogues with community stakeholders. They may be specific to the site under consideration or relevant to a wider range of activities that cause similar externalities. At the corporate level, personal contacts, contact with industry associations and platforms, and stakeholder dialogues are considered most effective. At the project level, environmental and social impact assessments (project and product life cycle analysis) and stakeholder discussions play a key role. The significance of issues tends to depend on factors such as company size (visibility), location of headquarters (the USA versus the Nordic countries), activities (upstream and large-scale projects), product and fuel mix and the 'corporate mantra' (Shell versus Exxon Mobil).

Since scrutiny by civil society is significantly less for the electricity industry than for oil and gas companies, the former's issue tracking processes appear to be less developed.

Issue mapping

When issues have been identified and examined they are mapped to assess their relevance to the entire company and to inform the management of which activities are associated with which issues. The greater the number of activities concerned the greater the importance of issue mapping to assess the significance of the issue on a corporate scale. According to corporate sustainability officers a first quick guess often takes them quite far. Climate change is considered such an obvious issue that mapping is required only to establish priorities for action at the operational level.

Data management tools, such as environmental accounting to measure environmentally relevant material and energy flows and to monitor the social effects of the company's activities and health and safety performance, are necessary for internal and external benchmarking, assessing the significance of the issue (the external effect and potential for the BCS) and prioritizing areas of action. Priority areas of action can be a particular activity and/or a region or country in which engagement with local communities is particularly necessary due to health problems, lack of education and so on.

Local management's awareness and expertise play key roles in mapping. There are more instruments for mapping environmental performance than for monitoring social issues (indicators are unemployment rates, price increases in the area around facilities, and community spent figures as a proxy measure) and the latter are more difficult to grasp. Oil and gas companies are currently looking to standards such as AA1000 and SA8000 for guidance, but the interest shown by electricity companies is limited due to their focus on Europe and emerging economies.

Our study suggests that the laggards in the industry may not be mapping issues comprehensively, either because they lack motivation or because they are struggling to establish the necessary data infrastructure.

Issue prioritization

As mentioned earlier, value drivers are not incorporated into strategy-development processes under their own label, rather they are primarily based on projects and issues whose strategic relevance is assessed through risk assessment procedures.

Companies use internal and external risk reviews to prioritize issues for strategic decision making. These reviews combine bottom-up and top-down approaches. Business units and country managers, who naturally focus on short-term and local issues, submit risk reports to the corporate body, which takes a more holistic and long-term approach and assesses potential cross-impacts.

Risk assessment tools include qualitative and quantitative assessments (risk score, financial figures), incorporate parameters such as probability of occurrence, possible consequences and degree of control, and can be used at different managerial levels (corporate, country or project) as well as provide a risk priority list ('risk register', essentially a tracking tool).

Both sectors appear to focus too narrowly on operational risks. Strategic risks and opportunities tend to be neglected, often because they are difficult to assess (as elaborated above in the section on value drivers). Issue prioritization is based on a pragmatic assessment of the financial risks associated with the issues under consideration and does not involve assessment of the individual business case. A business case may be constructed for a strategy to tackle a priority issue.

Integration into strategic decision making

Issues find their way into strategic decision making via four partly complementary routes:

- A robust (that is, *ex-ante* and universally quantifiable) business case can easily be presented for improvements in environmental health and safety performance since they represent classic win–win solutions. Nevertheless discussions on opportunity costs are common.
- Value drivers such as licence to operate, reputation, employee satisfaction and brand value are more complex and therefore less easy to quantify. However external pressures such as boycott campaigns have been so significant to oil and gas companies that the business case does not require comprehensive *ex-ante* quantification. This is not yet the case in the electricity industry, although a more liberalized and competitive business environment may change the situation in the future.

- Pilot projects, case studies and their *ex-post* quantification can also provide a business case, even if it is less universal and therefore more vulnerable to questioning. Pilot projects are also effective rollout tools because staff learn as they go and familiarize themselves with new ways of conducting the business.
- Corporate visions and values create a common understanding within the company. A quantified business case then becomes less important since improved environmental and social performance is considered self-evidently right. However without quantification projects are less justifiable when financial pressures increase.

The application of measures to integrate prioritized sustainability issues depends on the management level in question and the complexity of the issue. In general decisions are usually taken with a significant degree of uncertainty. At the corporate level, scenario analysis and backcasting, the most complex measures available, are seldom used by individual companies but applied by industry or multiindustry associations. Full cost (that is, carbon cost) approaches are increasingly being used in both sectors when appraising investments.[5]

Recent developments in the oil and gas sector suggest that the leading companies will develop increasingly sophisticated ways of quantifying and then prioritizing the business case for certain activities at both the corporate and the project level. At the project level, cost–benefit analyses address issues that are hard to quantify. Emerging techniques, such as real options, are not used. In general the softer the underlying issues and the higher the degree of strategic uncertainty, the greater the role that business principles and corporate values play in issue integration.

Rollout

Companies use several complementary means to ensure that measures to address sustainability issues are integrated into their operations. Since sustainability management should be an integral part of companies' business, leadership (that is, open commitment by top management) and effective management processes are essential. Leading companies particularly in the oil and gas industry, have established metrics, targets and incentive systems. Corporate policies and guidelines are necessary for creating minimum performance standards, complemented by corporate values and visions to generate a common understanding.

Some measures are particularly suitable for raising awareness and increasing support for the integration of sustainability issues into operations:

- Leveraging pressure from external stakeholders (for example share-holders, rating agencies, NGOs, auditors) demanding greater transparency. Sustainability reporting requires the cooperation of business units and departments.
- Confronting managers with the issues in question, that is, showing them the rough spots.
- Launching pilot projects to facilitate a learning (and possibly a trial and error) process at relatively low risk.
- Providing guidelines and best practice examples to reduce the degree of uncertainty.

Assessment of the business case, its potential and exploitation

Although most of our interviewees were familiar with the concept of the BCS, few companies seem to have formulated a comprehensive case. Companies are at different stages in this regard. In general the oil and gas industry is more advanced than the electricity industry.

The BCS is resulting in incremental changes to processes and activities, and is mainly based on the management of operational risks. More radical innovations are limited to pilot projects and the development of technologies for mostly subsidized and hence profitable renewable sources of energy. Since the latter are more relevant to electricity companies than to oil and gas companies their engagement in renewables is more committed and is business rather than pilot oriented.

While companies' corporate visions and sustainability strategies do take account of climate change, energy poverty in developing countries is seen more as a long-term issue and there have been no changes to business models. Evidence from both sectors suggests that internal factors such as organizational culture and lack of knowledge, are among the main barriers to incremental and radical innovation (Figure 7.6).

Radical innovation faces the following additional barriers:

- Substantial sunk costs and huge initial investments (in extraction sites, pipelines, power plants).
- The long life span of energy-related assets (technological lock-in).
- Major uncertainty about the future business environment (technologies, regulations, climate change and so on).

Whereas the oil and gas industry is mainly driven by the growing demand for energy in emerging economies, electricity companies are concentrating on consolidating the European market. Under the current regulatory framework, making the production, supply and use of fossil fuels more efficient is clearly the most profitable way to meet these challenges.

The business case for a distinct change in business models (for example renewable technologies) is weak in the current business environment, although there are several pressing reasons for moving towards renewable sources of energy (resource depletion, geopolitical instability and climate change). Compared with oil and gas companies, electricity companies are not significantly affected by resource depletion and geopolitics, but they do face regulatory pressure in respect of climate change. We conclude that there is considerable unexploited potential for global incremental innovation based on the BCS. National (upstream) oil companies and smaller integrated oil and gas companies, as well as electricity companies in developing and emerging economies, clearly have room for improvement.

Global scrutiny by regulators, shareholders and civil society on issues such as climate change, biodiversity and adverse social effects in developing countries is likely to increase. The business case in the oil and gas industry can be based on an improved licence to operate/grow, as well as on reputation and employee satisfaction. This appears to be reflected in most of the strategies adopted by the leaders in sustainability, but not enough to constitute a paradigm shift. Increased external pressure and competition

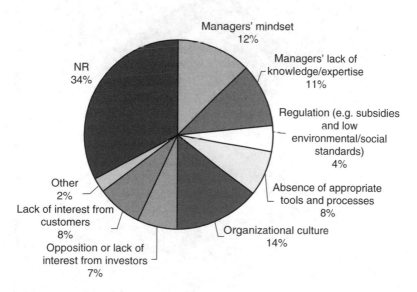

Figure 7.6 Main barriers to corporate sustainability initiatives

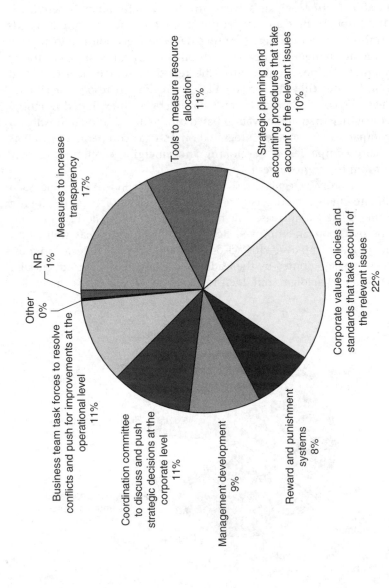

Figure 7.7 Measures and systems related to corporate sustainability – oil and gas

in the electricity industry could also lead to the above mentioned value drivers taking greater precedence over the current narrow focus on cost savings through incremental innovation.

The business case for sustainability is often difficult to quantify, which is why soft factors such as managerial thinking, knowledge and corporate values are important in facilitating sound decision making. While companies need to collect more data in order to identify key challenges and opportunities, they appear to have set the right priorities in terms of processes and systems, as Figure 7.7 shows.

Notes

1. Several US states have filed a lawsuit against the Bush administration for its stance on climate change.
2. People in developing countries spend up to a third of their income on energy, mostly to cook food. The time used to collect, process and use traditional fuels takes away from that available for child care, education and income generation. Alternatives such as liquefied petroleum gas and batteries are very expensive.
3. The Stop Esso compaign in the (UK) and the Brent Spar campaign against Shell (in Germany).
4. The E7 is an initiative launched by nine leading electricity companies from the G7 countries in the wake of the 1992 Rio summit.
5. For an insightful report on full cost accounting in the electricity sector see ICF Inc., 'Full Cost Accounting for Decision Making at Ontario Hydro: A case study', Final Review Draft, 22 March 1996.

8
The Financial Services Industry

Hans-Jörg Hess

This chapter aims to shed more light on the business case for sustainability (BCS) in the financial services sector. It focuses on the business activities of banks and insurance companies with commercial customers, and the findings are based on interviews and a survey of West European and US banks and insurance companies that operate internationally and have a corporate structure. Some smaller financial companies and two banks with a public mandate (IFC and KfW) were included in the sample because of their specific engagement with the subject of our research.

At each company, interviews were carried out with staff in sustainability or environmental units, and when possible with at least one additional line or functional manager. In total 52 managers were interviewed. In addition consultancies with sustainability practices were asked to participate in meetings, as well as NGOs and the UNEP (accounting for 10 interviews). A complete list of the participating organizations is presented in Table 8.1. The survey was distributed to participants in IMD programmes and was also put on-line. Eighty-three managers in the financial services sector returned completed questionnaires.

Industry overview

The financial sector is very heterogeneous. The insurance industry is composed of firms with diverse businesses, such as primary insurance (property and casualty [P&C], life and health insurance) reinsurance, asset management and other special financial services. In the banking industry, business subsectors deal with banking entities related to retail, small and medium-sized enterprises, corporate and investment banking, and asset management. The focus on the banking side is on credit operations with multinational companies (MNCs) and national

Table 8.1 Financial services participants in the study

Banks and insurance companies:
ABN AMRO
Allianz Group
Bank of America
Citigroup
Credit Swiss Group
Dresdner Bank
Fleet Boston Financial
Friends Provident
HVB Group
IFC
ING Group
KfW
Morgan Stanley (UK)
Rabobank
Sarasin Bank
Storebrand
Swiss Re
Züricher Kantonal Bank

Consultancies:
ADL (Cambridge)
Deloitte & Touche (Zurich)
ECOFACT (Zurich)
Ecos (Boston)
PwC (Zurich)

NGOs and others:
Friends of the Earth (USA)
GermanWatch
SAM Group
UNEP Financial Initiative
WWF (UK)

---

companies (NCs), and corporate and investment banking. On the insurance side the focus is on P&C and reinsurance subsectors that have strong business ties with MNCs and NCs.

In recent years the stock markets have suffered their most severe and prolonged decline since the 1930s. Falling equity prices have put many firms under pressure. However the large international banks have come through the economic crisis almost undamaged. In mid 2003, British, French, Swiss and US global financial institutions such as BNP Parisbas, HSBC, Royal Bank of Scotland, UBS and Citigroup reported strong increases in earnings and even record results. Similarly Germany's main private banks, which had to reverse the costs of their past investments in investment banking and still have to cope with a fragmented domestic banking market, are once again reporting profits.

Even with bankruptcies rising sharply in all sectors (the downfall of WorldCom and Enron alone wiped out loans of roughly $34 billion), losses of only a couple of million, rather than billions, are showing up in the credit books of big financial institutions, which have shifted a large share of their lending risk to smaller banks or out of the banking system (for example to insurers offering credit insurance). The practice of passing on loans as quickly as possible leaves more room for large banks to risk trading in securities, derivatives, foreign exchange and investing in private equity (*The Economist*, 16 August 2003).

International P&C insurance and reinsurance business suffered in 2001 after the September 11 terrorist attacks. In 2002, insurance losses due to natural catastrophes and manmade disasters were comparatively low. However storms and floods resulted in large losses in 2002: according to the insurance company Swiss Re, flood-related losses were the highest ever and insurers must expect an increasing number of extreme weather events. Additionally, many asbestos claims are still pending and there are many risks for insurers in America's tort laws. After years of major price reductions in the commercial P&C sector, increased demand for coverage and a shortage of supply raised rates by 15–20 per cent in 2002 (*The Economist*, 8 March 2002). Overall, in mid 2003 the financial statements of large international insurers such as Allianz, AXA and Swiss Re showed profits.

Sustainability and the business case

Our study looks at sustainability in private companies – not what some managers refer to as sustainable profits or finance, but the environmental and social aspects of sustainability, how these influence profits (value creation) and the way in which they are taken into consideration by financial sector companies. A business case for sustainability (BCS) is present when sustainability issues affect value creation – as a threat or an opportunity – and a financial company is in a position to craft strategies to address these issues. If a BCS is apparent, then it is not a luxury to manage environmental and social issues but rather a business rationale.

Our interviews revealed that the meaningfulness of internal environmental and social management should not be underestimated as it is visible to and tangible for the whole organization and helps to raise consciousness about internal and external sustainability issues. Nonetheless the relative direct impact of financial firms is perceived as limited compared with that of their commercial clients. The operations of MNCs and NCs have significant environmental and social effects, and here banks and insurance companies have the most important sustainability leverage. In September 2002, 11 CEOs and chairmen of financial institutions – including ABN AMRO, Allianz, Rabobank, ING Group, Storebrand and Swiss Re – signed the following statement: 'We recognize our role as drivers for change, although the limits of responsibility and influence of the financial services industry need to be further explored. . . . Because we influence the way our clients conduct their business (through policies and processes), the financial sector is a driver for sustainable development rather than the executer of change' (www.wbcsd.org/ Working Group Finance). Therefore our research addresses the indirect influence of banks and insurance companies and their role as 'drivers of sustainability'.

Sustainability issues

Table 8.2 lists the main topics that emerged during our study and were perceived as sustainability issues by financial institutions. It is not an exhaustive list because issues are constantly changing and their importance varies for companies in different lines or areas of business. For example a bank or insurance company that conducts its business mainly in Western Europe may not be affected by issues that are important in emerging markets.

Our interviews and survey revealed that the companies in question deal mostly with environmental and seldom with social issues. This is probably because their commercial customers are subject to numerous environmental laws and regulations. For example banks, extend many loans to companies that are striving to meet the new environmental standards, and insurance companies cover environmental risks such as site-specific clean-up costs or damages to third parties and casualty insurance with pollution coverage, plus insurance to cover the directors or officers of a company if they are sued because of an environmental incident.

Some companies, especially the reinsurers Swiss Re and Munich Re, pay attention to global sustainability topics such as climate change and water shortages in order to identify and prioritize risks and opportunities that could affect their business. For international banks in the trade finance business the burning issues of the moment mainly concern operations in emerging markets, where the pressure from NGOs is most severe and public awareness is high. It appears that internationally

Table 8.2   Main sustainability issues in the business of the financial services sector

---

Environmental pollution:
- Air, water and soil pollution due to building activities and operations (mining operations, oil and gas extraction, agro-business, chemicals and so on)
- Existing residual pollution and contaminated property
- Waste disposal (incineration, landfills and so on)
- Hazardous materials and workplace safety (for example asbestos)
- Nuclear waste and accidents

Environmental damage:
- Water shortages (impact on ecosystems, humans and industries)
- Deforestation and habitat loss (logging and land clearance for agriculture)
- Depletion of fossil fuels (mining operations and oil and gas extraction)
- Destruction of ecosystems (dams, landfills and so on)

Global warming:
- Greenhouse gas emissions
- Extreme weather conditions such as floods and storms

Social issues in industrialized countries:
- Community/society development (ethnic and underprivileged groups)
- Transparency

Social issues in emerging markets:
- Human rights and working conditions (resettlement due to dam construction, child labour and so on)
- Democracy and transparency (despotic regimes, corruption, illegal operations)
- Participation and local development (operations that cause social conflicts, bypass local markets and so on)

---

operating insurers are less exposed to this kind of pressure. In general the sustainability issues to which financial companies are exposed are quite diverse compared with other sectors because of their mixed portfolios of customers.

Companies' awareness and treatment of an issue develop overtime, starting from the point when it is identified and ending when it is resolved or attended to within the remits of mainstream business. Initially an issue is an idea that is developed by scientists and experts and is generally discussed quite rationally outside the company. A company perceives an emerging issue (Figure 8.1) either as a potential problem or as representing an opportunity. However it is often hard to predict at an early stage how an emerging issue will affect the organization and when it will materialize. A burning issue has passed the point of take-off and the organization is affected by and aware of the problem. This might be an 'emotional' phase, going hand-in-hand with media attention, protests outside the company's building or a case pending in court.

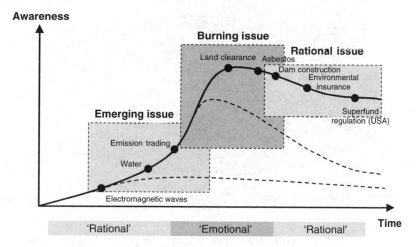

Figure 8.1 Awareness curve for selected issues

A burning issue can either be short-lived and quickly disappear, or it can become a 'rational' issue and a matter for mainstream business policies and processes (as in the case of the US Superfund regulation, which can make banks liable for clean-up costs in the event of hazardous contamination).

The way in which issues affect companies, and evidence of business cases

According to the stakeholder concept, different groups place different demands on companies, but employees, strategic business partners, customers and shareholders all have one thing in common: they interact directly with companies as transactional stakeholders (Figure 8.2). Companies usually have a fairly good understanding of the needs and expectations of these stakeholders' for example employees want additional work to be rewarded by higher salaries, and customers expect better service.

A new development in the context of sustainability is the growing importance of some contextual stakeholder groups that do not have direct business relations with companies. In particular, activist and other groups in civil society are increasingly placing environmental and social demands on companies. According to the Swiss bank UBS:

We realize that simply meeting existing legal requirements is not sufficient. Society's expectations are constantly evolving and often

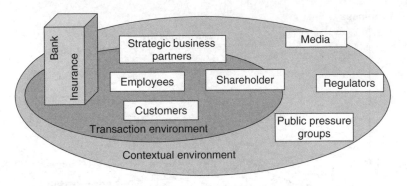

Figure 8.2   Stakeholder groups

precede formal legal and regulatory requirements; we find that we are being held to ever higher standards. Globalisation has added to these demands as multinationals are accused of arbitraging social standards to boost their bottom line.[1]

If a group considers that a company should alter its practices – even though it might not be breaking the law – it may start putting pressure on it.

Until the late 1990s pressure groups focused on the 'dirty' customers of financial institutions, such as oil, gas and chemical companies. Then something happened that banks and insurance companies did not expect: 'The old view was that we are a service industry that was only shifting papers,' a banker remarked. 'We never thought we would be questioned about the activities of our clients.' On 6 April 2003 the *Financial Times* observed that

> Financial institutions have until recently largely escaped the wrath of environmental groups, which have tended to shower their criticism on international institutions, such as the International Monetary Fund and World Bank, or manufacturers accused of operating sweat shops in developing countries. But at this year's World Economic Forum in Davos, over 100 advocacy groups signed the so-called Colleveccio Declaration [www.foe.org/camps/intl/declaration.html], which called on financial institutions to implement more socially and environmentally responsible lending policies.

In the eyes of civil society, public pressure on the financial sector is only just beginning. As an interviewee from an NGO put it: 'It's an innovative thing. So far, banks have not been targeted.' Certainly insurance companies run the risk of being targeted for their underwriting policies, for example in the case of controversial dam or pipeline projects.

Public demands can directly affect banks' business, as occurred in the Dutch palm oil case (see Box 8.1), when a large number of private customers threatened to close their accounts as a result of the campaign by an environmental conservation group. But most of the time sustainability issues are only indirectly relevant for finance companies and their customers: they arise in the contextual environment (researchers, unions, NGOs and so on) and are then taken up by politicians and regulators, who set the rules for the market environment (carbon taxes, security standards and so on).

Our study revealed that sustainability issues can have tangible consequences for financial companies and affect value creation in the following ways:

- By damaging or improving stakeholders' (commercial and private customers, investors, analysts and so on) perception in such a way that the reputation of the business is affected.
- By creating a default on loans or by increasing losses in the case of default (in the case of credit to commercial clients, project finance, and so on).
- By creating liability claims on insurance (property and casualty, Directors and Officers policies and so on).
- By creating new revenues from new products and services (socially responsible investment funds, carbon trading solutions and so on).
- By changing the value of investments in respect of asset management (management of investments/equity capital, assets under management for third party investors and so on).

The cases in Box 8.1 which were encountered during our research, indicate that business cases do exist and that environmental and social issues can affect profits in financial institutions.

The cases described above focused on business with commercial customers. However it is also important to shed light on a direct sustainability issue for financial institutions: financial exclusion in industrialized as well as emerging markets. In Western countries a common objective of high street banks over the past decade has been to cross-sell services such as brokerage accounts and insurance products to wealthier clients, often ignoring low-income groups and rural populations. Likewise in emerging markets, financial institutions have concentrated on wealthy urban clientele. Box 8.2 looks at large untapped markets that could be opened up.

Box 8.1   Business cases for sustainability in financial institutions

Emission-intensive industries: carbon trading schemes and taxes to help combat climate change[2]

The carbon disclosure project – an initiative by 35 institutional investors that involved asking the FT500 global index companies for information relating to greenhouse gas reduction – found that companies and industries vary widely in their degree of risk exposure and the sophistication of their risk management capabilities. Greenhouse gas regulation will be felt most strongly by financial companies' customers in emission-intensive sectors (steel, manufacturing, chemicals, cement production, smelting, transportation, cars, paper and pulp) and the energy industry itself (oil and gas exploration and production, refining, distribution, electricity generation). The initiative also found that loan impairment related to greenhouse gas emissions in emission-intensive sectors could have a significant impact on banks' profits and share prices.

An example of the effects of carbon tax and analysts' apparent reluctance to take climate change into account was provided in 2002 by the Initial Public Offering (IPO) of Xstrata, a London-listed mining company. In a 350-page prospectus, just one line was devoted to climate change. Within weeks the Japanese government began to talk publicly about imposing a carbon tax, and as a substantial portion of Xstrata's revenues come from exporting coal to Japan the market responded by lopping 8 per cent off the company's market capitalization.

Palm oil: resource depletion and social conflicts[3]

Palm oil is the most widely traded edible oil and world production has risen significantly in recent years. In Indonesia and Malaysia production almost doubled between 1990 and 2001. In the years 1995–99 alone, domestic and foreign investments of US$20 billion poured into the sector. Taking advantage of the absence of government control, especially in Indonesia, companies illegally engaged in clearing natural forest land. This resulted in widespread social conflict and huge forest fires that caused extensive air pollution (affecting about 70 million people) and vast economic losses. A successful joint campaign was conducted by Sawit Watch (the

Box 8.1 (continued)

Indonesian oil palm advocacy network), Friends of the Earth (FoE) and Greenpeace Netherlands. In the Netherlands the campaign prompted members of parliament to submit questions to the government on the role of Dutch banks in Indonesia. To emphasize the need for action, in February 2001 FoE distributed 250 000 postcards with which account holders could call on their banks to stop investing in environmentally damaging plantation projects.

After a series of meetings with the campaigners, in early 2002 ABN AMRO, Rabobank, Fortis and ING agreed to cease or restrict their financing of oil palm development in Indonesia on environmental and social grounds (no destruction of rainforests, no burning, acting within legal frameworks and respecting the rights/wishes of local communities). ABN AMRO went even further and opted to apply its new policy to all investments that might affect forests. In other European countries, however, similar campaigns were much less successful and financial institutions could withstand the pressure as their account holders were not sufficiently interested.

Box 8.2 Untapped financial markets[4]

Banks and insurance companies could provide products such as credit and financial services (savings accounts, giro and transfer services, basic insurance) to groups that have hitherto not been served and constitute an untapped source of profits.

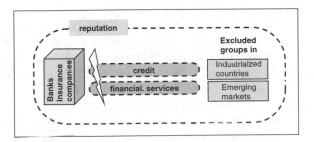

Untapped markets in developed countries

An estimated 35 million people in the USA lack access to banking services and in Britain, the Financial Services Authority has found that over 20 per cent of the adult population do not have current accounts and more than 37 per cent of households do not have savings accounts or investment products. Poor rural people and minorities in inner cities have been excluded because of lack of education or bad credit ratings. However in the USA it has been recognized that Hispanic people constitute a profitable market and financial institutions now offer special accounts and low-cost money transfer services. In 2002 alone, US$24 billion of transfers were sent to Latin America from the USA.

Fair prices for financial services

Large banks typically charge higher fees to customers with small accounts. The Swedish bank Nordea, for example, once charged double for international transfers in areas with a large number of immigrants. Nordea ceased this practice when a newspaper and the Office of the Ombudsman against Ethnic Discrimination brought it to public attention.

Meanwhile people outside the banking system fall prey to predatory lenders and the high charges levied by wire-transfer services. Western Union and Moneygram's fees are disproportionately high in relation to the amounts transmitted, and an extremely disadvantageous exchange rate may be imposed. The result can be a cost of $25–30 for a transfer of $100.

Financial services in emerging markets

Banks are turning to the retail market as their margins on corporate lending are narrowing and fees from investment banking services are falling. Lending to households is a high-growth area in the Czech Republic, Hungary and Poland, and it is thought to be of limited risk as borrowers tend to be middle class. Nonetheless additional tools and effective debt recovery procedures are needed to manage the potential risk of such business. Meanwhile microfinance schemes in emerging markets are hitting the limits of growth and development experts point out the need to mainstream them. Retail finance and credit services to small businesses are expected to offer vast possibilities for small and large banks as margins are significantly higher than in upstream business. The untapped

---

Box 8.2 (continued)

market is huge and information technology can help to reduce costs and construct the necessary financial tools. Three years ago financial institutions insisted that markets such as India were a matter for the public sector; today they are starting to ask 'How can we get involved?'.

Company-specific factors in business cases – value drivers

The preceding section has shown that many different business cases exist and that there is no such thing as a single BCS in the financial sector. A business case is company-specific and depends on:

- The products and services offered and their duration (long-term business engagements are apparently more sensitive to sustainability risks).
- The markets and regions where activities are pursued determine which regulations and societal expectations apply for the financial companies and their customers.
- Market leadership and public image (the larger and better-known companies are generally subjected to higher expectations and greater pressure).

Even though business cases are company-specific and very diverse, all the managers in our study thought that by far the most important value drivers – and therefore the opportunities offered by the strongest business cases – are risk management and reputation. However this finding could be biased as a number of the interviewees worked in functions where sustainability issues were perceived as representing a reputation risk for firms. According to one banker, 'A business case is primarily about influencing down-side risks, as there is no direct feedback mechanism.' In other words, if commercial customers are performing better due to their better management of sustainability issues, financial institutions will still receive the same interest, fees and insurance premiums. They can only indirectly profit from the reduced likelihood that customers will default on loans, create liability claims and damage reputation.

An additional factor from our point of view is that serious management of risk and reputation by financial companies could mean that customers would be obliged to manage their sustainability risks and opportunities

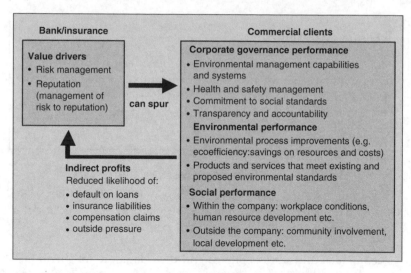

Figure 8.3   Potential effects of risk and reputation management

appropriately (Figure 8.3). The financial sector has always concentrated on being informed and managing risk, but it is not usual for companies to have managers and risk experts who are sensitive to sustainability issues. As one of our interviewees stated, 'Social and environmental risks are often seen separately from financial risks. They are not seen as actually belonging together.'

New products and business opportunities are not major value drivers: carbon trading solutions and broadly defined socially responsible investment funds for example, are seen as future niche markets (see Box 8.3).

Box 8.3   The business case for socially responsible investment[5]

Socially responsible investment (SRI) funds, which usually invest on the basis of broadly defined environmental and social criteria, are still only a niche market, but one with a potentially high growth rate. In Germany for example, ecological funds account for about 1 per cent of managed capital, but institutional investors could become more interested in SRI products as a new law requires certain pension funds to disclose their policy on sustainability issues.

Box 8.3 (continued)

For most banks and insurance companies it is not a challenge to set up an SRI fund, using available expertise is used in combination with the relevant SRI criteria. The real challenge is adequately to monitor sustainability risks in normal funds whose management strongly relies on mathematical models.

From a financial company's perspective, an SRI fund is a business case if investors want to buy the product and are willing to pay extra for transparency and knowledge of where their money is going. A business case can therefore exist even if an SRI fund is underperforming. Research shows that SRI funds normally perform no worse or no better than baseline indices.

Neither are the attraction and retention of human capital perceived as important value drivers.

Why business cases are not exploited

Client companies generally have little incentive to disclose risk-relevant sustainability issues because this might make it harder for them to obtain funding or insurance cover. Therefore assessing a client's corporate governance practices and commitment to managing sustainability issues is important from an investor's or insurer's point of view.

Financial companies do not always know which issues are of importance to their clients. This is understandable because there is a natural limit to their insider knowledge and expertise since they do not play a part in the business operations of their commercial clients. Social and environmental risks are often viewed separately from financial risks in the short term. Also it is rare for staff to have specific experience of the country or industry in question. One of our banking interviewees said that some colleagues accept unrealistic figures from their clients, and fail to scrutinize them sufficiently. In its study of Indonesia's pulp and paper industry the WWF found that due-diligence reports are often based on information provided by the companies concerned, and that independent auditors' reports are not always consulted.[6]

Besides not taking sufficient notice of risks, other potential issues are not properly addressed by analysts or risk officers because of the need for new risk models, which will take time and money to develop. In fact investment bankers may have a strong interest in not looking too closely at the projects they finance: their incentive systems generally have a very short time horizon and they receive a bonus for closing a deal quickly.

The time factor in incentive systems is an especially critical issue in primary and reinsurance businesses, where long-term risks might only materialize some time after the policies are written. Linking a bonus to a specific deal does not encourage underwriters to be cautious. Also, in the case of reputation risks it is hard to balance the interests of the firm and those of the business unit. Business units sell their products and services to meet their targets, and they might not be inclined to put their own interests after those of the firm.

Direct and ongoing contact with clients is essential to influencing and improving a project. As one interviewee put it, 'When you have contact with a client, you have more information and can exert influence. Units that have no direct customer relations often underestimate the importance of sustainability management.' However the risk-spreading strategy of financing projects through a consortium of banks restricts the direct contact that most of the banks have with the client and time is often too short to check the available data properly. Nevertheless the leading bank (or banks) in the consortium does have close contact with the client, and is able to exert some influence. A similar situation exists in the insurance industry, where premiums are written in the reinsurance market or major exposures are shared by consortia. The company in close contact with the customer plays an important part in mitigating risks.

The asset-management arms of banks and insurance companies can also influence firms whose stock they own, for example by means of shareholder resolutions and other forms of intervention. However fund managers, who are working in a highly competitive business, are extremely reluctant to interfere in companies' activities. In his book on global capital and the crisis of legitimacy, John Plender states that asset managers who adopt an interventionist stance with companies may alienate corporate clients whose pension funds they manage, as well as defer potential clients.[7] If fund managers are part of an investment bank, intervention may also alienate companies that use the bank's corporate finance services. In the case of insurance companies, clients may transfer their policies to a more compliant, less interventionist insurer. Plender also points out that the performance of asset managers is assessed by consultants and trustees on the basis of short-term deviations from their competitors. And while their approach to investment is now very theoretical, with growing reliance being placed on mathematical models, their ability to monitor company management is relatively unsophisticated in comparison. And since monitoring is costly, fewer resources are devoted to the task than it deserves from a wider economic and social perspective.[8]

Strategies for addressing sustainability issues

Sustainability issues can affect value creation by financial companies and many different forms of business cases exist. This section looks at measures or strategies that constitute a business rationale for companies because they help to manage relevant issues.

Corporate sustainability management by a staff unit

Of the 18 companies in our study, 12 have corporate staff units to deal specifically with environmental and social issues, four have environmental management units but have not yet officially embraced the concept of sustainability, and two have no special unit, just a single manager working with temporary teams. The 12 corporate sustainability units are primarily charged with internal and external communication of sustainability efforts and the monitoring of issues. The following subsections take a closer look at the tasks of these units and their organizational set-up.

External communication

One of the purposes of external communication is to satisfy the demand for increased transparency. However for obvious business reasons, transparency has its limits. One head of a sustainability unit pointed out that 'In the past, deals were refused for environmental and social reasons. Now we are forced to make it explicit, write it down and measure it against our policies. But a bank cannot be fully transparent for reasons of confidentiality. We have to find a proper balance between business confidentiality and transparency.' Corporate sustainability units inform the public about achievements and, more rarely, failures and difficulties. It is hoped that this approach will increase credibility and public understanding of the fact that transparency and the responsibility of single organizations have their limitats.

Companies propagate their message in several ways: articles in newspapers and corporate publications, speeches by top management, participation in conferences, colloquiums and so on. Many of the units devote a great deal of time to generating environmental, sustainability or Corporate Social Responsibility (CSR) reports. There are different perceptions of the value of reports. Some of our interviewees thought that sustainability reports are ineffective because they do not attract readers; conversely media reports and newspaper articles are perceived as more effective. Information on in-house management is also placed on the Internet and other issues are covered from time to time in a corporate journal. Other interviewees were keen to push sustainability reporting in the direction of value reporting and place it in the company's main annual report so as to demonstrate the link between corporate sustainability efforts and other business issues.

Different perceptions also exist about the timing of reports. Whereas one group of interviewees maintained that a complete environmental report should be published annually, another thought that this is not necessary: in their case in-house management information is available on the Internet and reports are published every two to three years. This is considered sufficient as only small incremental changes take place within the span of a year.

As no common standard exists, the structure and contents of reports vary widely. A consultant in our study noted that 'Up to now, surprisingly, reports are well perceived by normally critical groups, even though they are weak on indicators, tasks and their relation to business.' An environmental manager conveyed his impression that 'In many financial institutions, sustainability is being replaced by a sustainability report.' An NGO representative said that activist groups are becoming increasingly impatient with corporations handing out glossy brochures and giving 'Sunday sermons' about changes, while their day-to-day management moves in another direction. Moreover organizations such as the UNEP FI, which provides a forum for financial companies' activities in the field of sustainability management, is increasingly being seen by activists as a mere talking shop.

Internal communication

Information provided to the general public is also used to create awareness within organizations. In some cases extensive intranet resources are made available, including databases on emerging and known sustainability issues, guidelines and so on. For example the IFC has built up an easily accessible database with a significant number of case examples, ranging from cost savings from improved operational efficiency in a bank to risk reduction through stakeholder involvement in a coal-mining project. This information is intended to sensitize employees to the risks and opportunities involved in sustainability. Corporate sustainability units see the education of upper managers as a key to creating awareness within business units. Swiss Re, Allianz and ABN AMRO, for example, have seminar sessions for upper managers on the topic of sustainability and its impact on business. In presentations and seminars, corporate sustainability staff often use case studies, success stories and risk maps to demonstrate the value of business cases.

Units in most companies are involved in incorporating sustainability criteria into codes of conduct and mission statements. It is expected that this will raise awareness and trigger behavioural changes in the company. However some interviewees pointed out that it is difficult to alter the values and culture of a company. If company leaders do not live up to the new values because they are incompatible with short-term business goals, any changes will have limited effects because employees will take note of what managers do, not what they say.

Issue management

With few exceptions, the companies in our study considered that sector initiatives and networks, such as the UNEP FI and the WBCSD Finance Group, are important forums for gathering information. In half of the companies the sustainability officer, through his formal and informal network, was seen as an early-awareness system (EAS). Some companies have set up procedures and computer-based systems to support EAS capabilities: Allianz, for instance, has created a tool based on functional-ity and efficiency requirements: an interdisciplinary trend assessment team regularly evaluates external reports. Swiss Re has created a database system – a systematic, interactive, risk-perception platform – to support its risk-recognition activities. This database, which consists of loose indicators, inferences and solid facts, is fed by risk-management and underwriting staff and is supported by interdisciplinary workshops. The main problem, as one interviewee stressed, is usually not the availability of signals or information, but their evaluation in the risk management process. Companies with elaborate EASs have found that it is important for an efficient and transparent process to be set up and applied regularly to assess information. Figure 8.4 shows the main elements of the EASs in the researched companies.

If a burning issue erupts – for example if an activist group or the media target a firm – the sustainability units in some companies act in tandem with the 'fire department' (PR/communications) to ensure that the right signals are sent to the outside world. However one of our activist interviewees stated that financial institutions are some-times badly coordinated and various departments communicate with pressure groups independently from each other, thus creating misun-derstanding.

Information	Evaluation	Knowledge sharing
• Sector initiatives • Informal networks • Dialogue with NGOs • Media coverage • External expert reports • Internal sources	• Sustainability officer • Interdisciplinary working groups • Consultation with experts • Risk maps Scenario analysis	• Strategic reports • E-mail lists • Databanks • Workshops • Internal and client seminars

Figure 8.4   Elements of early awareness systems

The organization and integration of units

Sustainability units are attached to different departments (risk management, strategy or corporate communications) in different companies because the latter were initially confronted with issues in different areas (Figure 8.5). Of the 18 units studied, all but two report directly to a board member. Such 'personalized responsibility' at the highest level is seen as essential. The size of units varies: in a few companies there is only one person, but in 10 companies three to five persons are employed. In most cases a committee with high-ranking members from various departments and divisions helps to integrate the unit with the rest of the company. Swiss Re has even set up two committees to ensure effective integration: a strategic steering committee consisting of top-management representatives to influence corporate sustainability management actions from the top down, and an operational committee consisting of divisional representatives to influence bottom-up activities. Also important in this regard are internal and external informal networks.

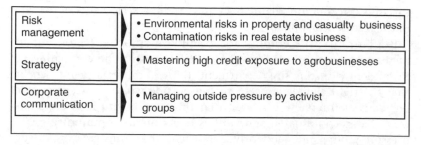

Risk management	• Environmental risks in property and casualty business • Contamination risks in real estate business
Strategy	• Mastering high credit exposure to agrobusinesses
Corporate communication	• Managing outside pressure by activist groups

Figure 8.5   Examples of sustainability issues confronted by different departments

Corporate sustainability units mainly interact with the human resources (HR), communications (PR, investor relations and so on) and risk management departments. Questionnaires from sustainability rating agencies are filled out jointly and seminars, training and communication concepts are developed together, but fields of competence are well defined. HR departments, for example, have established themselves as the internal social conscience. According to one interviewee, 'One gets a bloody nose when trying to poach within HR's territory.' None of the units is organized as a profit centre, but the allocation of a budget, allowing for staffing, project work and travel expenses, is seen as essential.

Comments on the findings

The organizational set-up of units and the issues they deal with are company-specific: large trade-finance banks with a strong private customer base, such as ABN AMRO, are more susceptible to reputation damage by activist groups than reinsurance companies such as Swiss Re. Sustainability units can help financial firms to deal better with outside pressure, but they can also play the role of challenger if core business units are failing to take relevant issues into account. However the existence of a sustainability unit is no guarantee of effective changes being made, so as well as quick-thinking people with good communication skills who can think 'out of the box', sustainability units clearly need members with a thorough understanding of the company's line of business.

Assessing the benefit of sustainability units and their activities is not easy since they do not directly contribute to the company's profits. Departments such as human resources, risk management and communications face similar problems. Sustainability managers can learn much from colleagues in these departments in respect of how to move their business cases forward. Even a simple back-of-the-envelope calculation can be helpful in presenting business rationales and convincing managers; success stories and best-practice can also be useful as cost–benefit arguments are sometimes closely connected. In some cases, however, clear language is lacking when sustainability units communicate with other departments, and the use of jargon and fuzzy definitions can disconcert managers. Failure to demonstrate benefits in strict management terms can have significant negative consequences. Firstly, line managers might formally accept guidelines backed up by the board but privately remain unconvinced and unsupportive. Secondly, if a change in top management takes place or the company finds itself in a crisis, economic justification of the unit's present activities, and even of the unit itself, might be required.

IFC's sustainability framework

The IFC's sustainability framework is applied when financing private companies in regions and sectors underserved by private investment sources and goes beyond the World Bank's minimum standards. These standards are now also applied by some commercial banks to project financing with a capital investment of US$50 million or more: this is because of a recent initiative – the 'Equator Principles' – by ten leading banks, including ABN AMRO, Citigroup, the Credit Suisse Group, the HVB Group and Rabobank. These internationally operating banks have often been attacked for their project finance activities (where the terms of loan repayment are dependent upon the revenues that the project is expected to generate), especially in the mining, oil and gas, and forestry sectors.

The underlying assumption of the IFC framework is that private investment in developing countries may contribute to environmental, social or corporate governance improvements on top of the productive use of capital. The framework is intended to expose of investment officers to risks and opportunities in the area of sustainability. It defines what going beyond minimum, 'no harm' requirements means. As one interviewee pointed out, 'It is not about high sounding goals, it is about making the project better.' Based on the research of an IFC group,[9] the framework divides the sustainability approaches of potential commercial customers into three main areas and a total of eight sustainability factors (Table 8.3). Project teams assess, on a discretionary basis (according to whether it makes sense for the client), whether sustainability factors can strengthen value creation by client companies. Depending on the business case, the payoff to the

Table 8.3   Sustainability factors in the IFC framework

Management commitment and governance
- Environmental management, social development commitment and capacity
- Corporate governance
- Accountability and transparency

The environment
- Eco-efficiency of processes and environmental footprint (impact)
- Environmental performance of product/service

Socioeconomic development
- Local economic growth and partnerships
- Community development
- Improved health, safety and welfare for workers

company in the event of a win–win situation is one or more of the following: cost savings; revenue growth and market access; access to capital; risk reduction; improved human and intellectual capital; and improved brand value and company reputation.

Each of the sustainability factors is differentiated into four performance levels:

- Level 1: factor complies with IFC and national minimum standards.
- Level 2: factor exceeds minimum standards.
- Level 3: high performance due to good practices.
- Level 4: firm is seen as a leader in managing the sustainability factor.

The criteria for each factor and performance level are tightly defined. The IFC is aware that in some frontier markets minimum standards may be all that can realistically be achieved, and to do more may be inappropriate or counterproductive. To encourage investment officers to strengthen projects and improve their developmental impact, a business department's scorecard is linked to the framework and the measured sustainability impact. The percentage of the department's new commitments that meet the framework's criteria for 'high impact' is reported monthly. Reviews of the project and its performance take place once it is completed. Yet there are sceptical voices. When asked what had changed with the new framework one interviewee said, 'You have to write better English now in order to explain that a project has a high developmental impact'. At the time of writing the framework is in its first year of pilot implementation and its impact and utility are still being assessed.

The framework can increase the transparency and monitoring of activities being financed. It can also motivate officers to strengthen a project and its sustainability performance during the investment process, allowing the IFC's extensive environmental and social review process to be better aligned. Indirectly the IFC can also profit from a better performing project as it decreases the risk of default. Privately owned financial companies may consider that the framework is costly in time and resources and that they cannot afford a large environmental and social development department to support their investment staff. But the tool is a first and innovative step, and ten years ago when the first World Bank minimum standards were drafted it was by no means clear that international banks would adopt them in the form of the Equator Principles.

Swiss Re's risk review process for sensitive risks

To encourage staff to highlight potential sustainability risks, Swiss Re has developed a special process that is particularly aimed at cases about which business units have reservations. If staff members are in doubt about the sustainability or ethics of a proposed transaction they are asked to contact their compliance officer or the group compliance officer for guidance. If required the group compliance officer will set up an *ad hoc* task force composed of competent Swiss Re specialists. A formal recommendation is issued by the task force, which may then be passed up the management chain. However the final underwriting decision has to be made by the business unit (Figure 8.6). The procedure is anchored to the group's code of conduct and emphasizes that there are experts elsewhere in the organisation who can be officially consulted and asked for advice. The process enables better monitoring of sustainability-related risks and improves the transparency of decisions on difficult cases.

Conclusion

The aim of the study reported in this chapter was to gather evidence of a business case for sustainability in the financial services sector. The

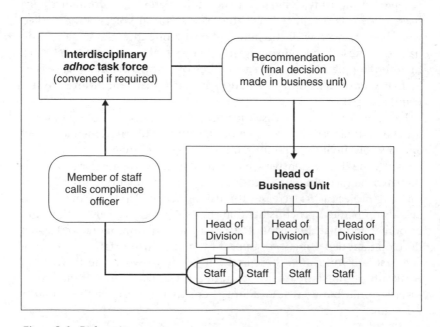

Figure 8.6   Risk review process

results indicate that sustainability management will pay in the long run, even though it does not automatically make good business sense to take environmental and social factors into consideration, especially in the short term. Our research also shows that many different business cases exist. They are company-specific and depend, *inter alia*, on the products and services offered, the markets and regions where activities are pursued and the market leadership and public image of the firm in question. Business cases are often not exploited because customers are not inclined to disclose their risks, the knowledge, tools and guidelines needed to identify sustainability risks are absent, and incentive systems are focused on short-term results and do not motivate staff to tackle sustainability issues.

There are several strategies for exploiting business cases, including the formation of sustainability units, the adoption of RM processes, the application of minimum standards and use of the IFC sustainability framework. Even though effective strategies are company-specific and adapted to their particular needs and line of business, it appears that many firms copy the approaches of their competitors. This is probably because it is easier to get top management acceptance by means of jargon than by suggesting appropriate concrete measures.

It is ultimately in the core business operations that sustainability risks arise, through credit, insurance and other products and services. Useful communication and issue-management strategies exist but they do not necessarily involve changes in these areas. When designing strategies that involve the core business, companies should weigh up the potential costs and benefits and set realistic and realizable goals. They should regularly assess their business operations and processes in order to localize sustainability risks and exploit the opportunities that are inherent to their proper management. Based on company-specific assessments, strategies can be developed for different levels: corporate, business unit, product and employee.

Results are often hard to measure because sustainability activities such as risk and reputation management only contribute indirectly to the company's economic success and there is generally no direct feedback mechanism. Business and risk management models are already complex and need to be adapted to different cultural backgrounds. The additional complexity caused by sustainability measures should be minimal, and they should be easy to integrate into existing processes and procedures.

Besides the economic rationale, there are ethical and political components to sustainability that have not been developed in this chapter.

Financial companies certainly cannot meet all the demands some stakeholders are placing on them, so they need to determine the limits of their responsibility in view of stakeholders' changing expectations of responsible corporate conduct. They have to be aware that they cannot unconditionally dismiss responsibility for the projects they are financing or insuring.

Notes

1. *UBS Handbook 2001/2002* (UBS, 2002), p. 111.
2. Sources: own interviews; Martin Whittaker, 'Carbon Finance and the Global Equity Markets', Matthew Kieman (London) Innovest and Carbon Disclosure Project, February 2003 (www.cdproject.net); Andrew Dlugolecki, 'Climate Change and the Financial Services Industry – Modules 1&2', report prepared for the UNEP FI Climate Change Working Group by Innovest, July 2002 (www.unepfi.net); 'Taking control of climate', *Financial Times*, 25 November 2002.
3. Sources: own interviews; Rob Glastra, 'Oil Palm Plantations and Deforestation in Indonesia. What Role do Europe and Germany Play?', Rob Glastra, Eric Waker and Wolfgang Richert, (Zurich) WWF Germany, WWF Indonesia and WWF Switzerland, WWF Germany in collaboration with WWF Indonesia and WWF Switzerland, November 2002 (http://www.wwf.ch/default.cfm contentstring = 4111); Cheng Hai Teoh, 'The Palm Oil Industry in Malaysia', report prepared for (Zurich) WWF Switzerland, November 2002 (http://www.wwf.ch/default.cfm?contentstring = 4111); Eric Walker, 'Funding Forest Destruction – The Involvement of Dutch Banks in the Financing of Oil Palm Plantations in Indonesia', report by Eric Waker and Jan Willem Van Gelder, (Amsterdam) Greenpeace Netherlands, commissioned by Greenpeace Netherlands, March 2000; 'Campaign Case Study: Dutch Banks and Indonesian Palm oil', *Focus on Finance Newsletter*, March 2001 (www.focusonfinance.org); ABN AMRO, 'ABN AMRO Risk Policies – Forestry and Tree Plantations', October 2001 (http://www.wwf.ch/default.cfm contentstring = 4111).
4. Sources: own interviews; Mark Scher, *Postal Savings and the Provision of Financial Services*, (New York) UN/DESA Discussion Paper (December 2001: UN/DESA,); Financial Services Authority, *In or Out? Financial Exclusion* (London) (July 2000); 'Reaching Out', *The Economist*, 22 February 2003; 'From Communism to consumerism', *The Economist*, 1 March 2003; 'Nordea backar om diskriminerande avgifter', *Dagens Nyheters*, 20 June 2002 (www.dn.se/DNet/jsp/polopoly.jsp?d = 678&a = 29256&maNo = –1); 'Nordea backs down regarding double bank fee (SE)', *Sydsvenska Dagbladet*, 21 June 2002 (www.nordea.com/ENG/media/observer/se_020624.ASP?navi = press&item = empty).
5. Sources: own interviews; 'Nachhaltigkeitsfonds enttäuschen bisher', *Frankfurter Allgemeine Zeitung*, 27 March 2003.
6. Christopher Barr, *Profits on Paper: The Political-Economy of Fiber, Finance and Debt in Indonesia's Pulp and Paper Industries* (WWF Macroeconomics Program Office) (CIFOR and WWF, November 2000).
7. John Plender, *Going off the Rails: Global capital and the crisis of legitimacy* (West Sussex Wiley, 2003).

8. Ibid.
9. SustainAbility and the International Finance Corporation (IFC), *Developing Value: The business case for sustainability in emerging markets*, SustainAbility, International Finance Corporation (IFC) and Ethos Institute, (London) SustainAbility, (2002).

9
The Food and Beverage Industry

Aileen Ionescu-Somers

This chapter examines managers' perceptions of, attitudes towards and approaches to the business case for sustainability in the food and beverage industry,[1] focusing mainly on the economic relevance of sustainability issues, stakeholders, value drivers and internal barriers. Our findings have been obtained from the following sources:

- Forty interviews with a broad range of senior managers at ten leading multinational food and beverage companies (Cadbury Schweppes, Chiquita, Danisco, Danone, Diageo, Kraft, Nestlé, Nutreco, Procter & Gamble and Unilever).
- Ten interviews with stakeholders such as non-governmental organizations (NGOs) and industry associations.
- A questionnaire distributed to 17 sustainability or corporate responsibility officers (mostly senior managers based in Northern Europe).
- A questionnaire distributed to 115 other business managers in the sector (again mostly based in Northern Europe and 50 per cent of whom were either board members or senior managers).

Industry and competitive analysis

Degree of rivalry

There are about 1000 listed food and beverage companies throughout the world. Due to mergers and acquisitions, the industry consists of an increasingly smaller number of global players, but there is still a large proportion of small and medium-sized companies. A few large firms with similar market share dominate the top end of the market, provoking intense rivalry and a significant struggle for market leadership.

The trend towards mergers and acquisitions reflects a drive to take market share away from competitors in slow-growth areas such as developed countries. Larger companies are devoting considerable resources and energy to increasing their market share in developing countries, which constitute their main opportunity for growth. Given the importance of these markets, it is likely that sensitivity to sustainable development criteria in business strategy development will be increasingly important.

The industry is using tactics such as product differentiation, creative use of distribution channels and exploitation of relationships with suppliers to move away from a commodity-type market where no competing firms have a differentiation advantage. This also presents food and beverage companies with the opportunity to put sustainability, with the product differentiation advantages it offers, more firmly on the agenda.

Barriers to entry

Barriers to entry to the food and beverage market are low, as demonstrated by the considerable number of small and medium-sized companies in the market. Government monopolies and proprietary knowledge do not generally restrict market entry, and industry assets can be utilized to produce different products.

Threat of substitutes

The existence of widely available substitutes for food and beverage products is a competitive threat in the industry, and the cost to retailers of switching to a substitute product is low. This typically results in price competition, so it is difficult for companies to raise their prices except when they have a product differentiation advantage. Hence major companies are focusing on product differentiation through perceived brand value or product innovations. Moreover by establishing brand loyalty the leading companies can raise the barriers to entry, thus making it more difficult for retailers to change to new competing products. This again constitutes an opportunity to move sustainability further up the agenda.

Negotiating power

The negotiating power of producers in developing countries is low due to the fragmented sources of supply and an overcapacity in many commodities (such as coffee). This has significant implications for sustainable development in those developing countries which produce the commodities, as producers are at the mercy of fluctuations in the volatile commodity markets. The switching cost of changing from one primary producer to another is low for global companies, thus increasing the vulnerability of producers.

Buyers' power

Large retailers directly purchase a significant proportion of the industry's output and buy in bulk. In developed countries they are quite concentrated, so a large market share is in the hands of a few; moreover there is an identifiable trend towards further consolidation of this sector. Retailers have a large degree of influence on products and their prices. There are always alternative sources of supply and the costs of switching are low, especially in the case of fresh foods. This has led to a trend towards discounting at the retail level. All in all retailers have considerable power over the industry and producers.

Sustainability issues and their economic relevance

We aim to demonstrate that by integrating sustainability issues into their business strategies and focusing on the business opportunities they bring, companies can create economic value through, for example, improved reputation, brand value and risk management.

Given the 'frontline' nature of the industry, employees at all hierarchical levels are exposed to the sustainability issues that affect the sector. In our study 45 per cent of managers from diverse business functions in leading companies declared themselves to be very familiar with the concept of sustainable development, compared with the 27 per cent average across all industries, and 84 per cent felt that the concept of sustainable development would grow in importance in the future. Thus it seems that sustainability is here to stay.

It is a real challenge for companies to establish a coherent sustainability agenda given the diversity of the issues they face. Here we shall focus only on the key global issues in the value chain that, according to managers interviewed, strongly influence the strategic agenda for sustainability in the sector.

Raw material supply

Population growth and resource depletion

The world's present population of 6.0 billion is predicted to grow to 8.3 billion by 2030, an increase of nearly 40 per cent. The world's nutritional requirements are expected to double by 2025, which will place a heavy demand on agricultural productivity. With economic progress there has been a shift towards a more diverse diet and increased consumption of meat, dairy and processed products. However the capacity of the world's food production system to meet these needs is limited. Security of food supply is a major challenge in developing countries, and there is no longer a plentiful supply of land for conversion to agricultural production. Production and productivity improvements are therefore essential.

Since the industry is dependent on a constant supply of high-quality primary agricultural produce the depletion of natural resources (a prime example being fish stocks) is affecting its long-term economic sustainability. This has forced some companies to seek raw materials that have been produced in a more sustainable way so as to ensure their availability in the future.

The environmental effects of agricultural production

Agricultural production can cause extensive environmental damage, including, erosion, soil degradation, loss of biodiversity, destruction of natural habitats, deforestation, groundwater pollution and agrochemical build-up. Companies in the sector are under growing pressure from NGOs, retailers, consumers and regulators to take note of and influence the agricultural methods their growers use. The industry does not currently carry the full environmental and social costs – if these were internalized the final price of food products would rise.

Managers in the industry strongly believe that organic farm produce, the choice of what they see as 'niche' customers, is not a sustainable alternative to conventionally produced food as the reduction in artificial inputs leads to a decrease in production, and therefore the demands of the growing world population cannot be met. NGOs, by contrast, say that due to lack of economic and political pressure, companies are not seeking the necessary alternatives to conventional agriculture to ensure sustainable development.

At the global level, agriculture accounts for 70 per cent of all fresh water used each year, with another 20 per cent being used by industry and 10 per cent for domestic purposes. Since the world's water resources are under increasing pressure from drought, overconsumption and pollution, companies are placing more emphasis on encouraging suppliers to use water as efficiently as possible.

The social impact of agricultural production

Some food and beverage companies have a physical presence in rural areas in various regions and others are dependent on continued supplies from such areas. Economically, therefore is in their long-term interest to aid local economies. For some local populations, these companies are the only major source of employment.

There is growing awareness of and concern about social issues such as child labour, slavery and other human rights abuses, especially in emerging economies. Proving that, for example, no child labour is used in the complex supply chain of the food and beverage industry is a considerable challenge, but companies seem determined to respond to consumers' demand to bring about transparency.

Most global companies procure their raw materials from the global commodities markets. Enormous fluctuations in the prices of primary products and the effects of low prices on production constitute business risks for the sector. Many consumers and activists want local communities to receive a fairer share of the economic benefits of the food they produce and are thus exerting considerable pressure on the industry to change its approach to sourcing.

NGOs insist that the current protectionist agricultural policies of developed countries (for example trade barriers and subsidies) require serious reform as they are detrimental to agricultural progress in developing countries. Many of the managers in our study identified this as the key issue in sustainable development in the industry.

Own operations and downstream

Due to regulatory pressure and image considerations, companies are focusing on output aspects of their operations (emissions into the air, water and soil, energy use, recycling and waste management). Moreover health and food safety considerations (which will discussed further below) have forced companies to pay greater attention to the quality of ingredients, food preparation and factory processing methods. Packaging and recycling are also important issues, given their potential to affect company reputation.

Traceability and food safety

The globalization of world trade has made the industry vulnerable to food scares and public suspicion. Recent examples include dioxin in chicken and beverages, and serious livestock problems such as BSE ('mad cow disease'), scrapie and foot and mouth disease. Since the global spread of telecommunications, companies have been even more exposed to public scrutiny since an event in one part of the world is quickly reported in another. The media tend to focus on companies when any health and safety issues related to their products emerge, even if the companies themselves are not directly responsible. While consumers increasingly expect food safety and traceability, NGOs seem convinced that the increased flow of goods has led to less transparency, not more. In the future consumers are likely to place greater pressure on food and beverage companies to label their products in terms of ingredients, country of origin and even cultivation methods.

Unlike in the USA, European consumers and activists have been effective in forcing companies to exclude genetically modified organisms (GMOs) from their products. NGOs such as Greenpeace have convinced the public that, given the inadequate scientific understanding of the environmental and health effects of GMOs, they should not be cultivated (recent scientific research in the UK has proved the legitimacy of this stand).[2] Other NGOS have pushed for genetically engineered crops to be segregated from conventional ones, and for the presence of genetically engineered ingredients to be stated on food and beverage labels. Meanwhile the EU is implementing tough laws on the labelling of genetically modified foods.

Obesity and diet

The publication in 2000 of a World Health Organization report on preventing and managing obesity was an indication that obesity had become a major global health issue.[3] The marketing of high-fat, low-nutrition products to young people has come under scrutiny and legislators are considering the introduction of a legal requirement for food companies to display more nutritional information on their product packaging. Obesity lawsuits filed in July 2002 against a well-known fast-food company in the USA raised the spectre of similar litigation challenges to those currently faced by the tobacco industry. Indeed some of our interviewees stated that obesity is the largest sustainability issue on their corporate 'radar screens'.

Stakeholders

There are numerous stakeholders with a vested interest in the activities of food and beverage companies, but we shall restrict our focus to stakeholders with a role in either deterring or promoting the corporate sustainability agenda.

Deterrent stakeholder groups

Customers and retailers are the transmitters of consumer pressure and opinion and can strongly influence the business case for sustainability because it is they who provide companies with their revenues. Food and beverage companies' objectives include satisfying changing expectations and meeting the growing demand for healthy, good-quality food by delivering products with a perceivedly higher value than the price consumers pay. This could be a strong force in pushing sustainability further up the industry agenda. As one senior marketing manager in a leading company pointed out, 'What is niche today is mainstream tomorrow'; being ahead of the trend is essential to ensuring the long-term sustainability of the business.

However consumers in developed countries expect greater choice and better quality at a low price and companies have to take account of what people are prepared to pay. Managers claim that if sustainability initiatives lead to a more expensive product, consumers may not be willing to pay the premium, except perhaps that on organic food in niche markets in developed countries. It appears that retailers are not putting food and beverage companies under enough pressure to pursue a sustainability agenda. According to one senior NGO officer, only if consumers know exactly what they are buying (through comprehensive labelling) can they make an informed choice and put the necessary pressure on retailers. Otherwise they will simply opt for products that are perceived as offering the best value for money. Retailers do not tend to be strong promoters of sustainability (with some exceptions in the UK) and sometimes discount their prices to such an extent (retailers in Germany are a prime example) that there is no scope for sustainability improvements in the supply chain. When given a list of suggested barriers to sustainability initiatives the managers in our survey chose customers' lack of interest as one of the most significant. However, as we have seen with the GMO issue in Europe, the potential power of consumers to prompt radical moves by companies is enormous.

Managers expect that the focus on corporate social responsibility will increase in the future, and that much of the momentum for this will come from retailers when they become more aware of the power they have to induce suppliers to change. In the case of capital markets, while progressive companies see sustainability as an opportunity to add value while maintaining value for shareholders (thus not damaging their competitiveness), managers do not generally think that capital markets are likely to become significant drivers of sustainability. The financial managers we interviewed said that the interest of institutional investors in sustainability has grown over the past 10 years, but has now levelled off due to the current economic difficulties. According to our survey only 27 per cent of food and beverage managers expect markets to react much more positively in the future to improved social and environmental performance. Lack of shareholder interest makes it difficult to get sustainability issue on to the agenda, particularly in less progressive companies and despite the trend towards improved standards for ethical and environmental corporate governance. Overall, sustainability officers believe that the opportunities for showing shareholders that profits can be enhanced by efficient sustainability management have not yet been properly exploited, and that they lack the tools to do so.

Promotional stakeholder groups

Governments, regulators, NGOs and employees are important stakeholders that can exert pressure on the industry to take action on sustainability issues. To a much lesser extent, the industry dynamic itself can contribute to promoting sustainability measures in companies. Managers are aware that legal requirements for food safety, particularly in the EU, will intensify and spur sustainability actions, especially in the case of the laggards in the industry. However while regulatory pressure is useful in the earlier stages of promoting a business case for sustainability, it ceases to be the main driver when companies become more progressive and adopt a 'beyond compliance' approach.

Food and beverage multinationals are strong targets for NGOs. Forty per cent of the managers in our study identified NGOs or the media campaigns that supported them as the main contributors to reputation damage in the previous three years. NGOs are particularly effective at creating a sense of urgency about emerging issues, forcing them on to companies' agendas and prompting them to act earlier than they otherwise would. NGOs are well aware that companies will take rapid action when brands upon which their image relies are subjected to critical scrutiny. Some of the leading companies in the sector have moved from a defensive to a proactive stance and now engage in dialogue with NGOs, or even work in partnership with them.

Companies face a number of obstacles when dealing with NGOs. Firstly, because of the diversity of issues included under the label 'sustainability' there are many NGOs to deal with. Secondly, NGOs are perceived by companies as being better equipped to deal with sustainability issues because of their ability to 'speak with one voice' and focus on a single issue, whereas companies find sustainability matters a challenge to manage due to the fragmented and decentralized nature of the industry and the sheer number of issues that come up. Thirdly, companies are mystified by the nature of activism; in cases where a partnership exists with an NGO, managers do not find it easy to accept that the NGO will work with the company on some issues but go against it on others.

Employees can also play an active part in promoting sustainability measures. The degree of their influence in developing countries can depend on how much support the government gives to unions. This stakeholder group is also increasingly important in emerging markets targeted by food companies. Employees can have a major impact on how society perceives a company, since job losses and the way employees are treated are often highly newsworthy. Needless to say, adverse publicity in this regard exposes companies to loss of reputation.

In general the sustainability officers in our study gave a positive assessment of the industry's contribution to sustainability, but NGOs are less convinced. Competing firms are increasingly adopting a united front on issues facing the industry, including GMOs and obesity. In addition quite a few bilateral initiatives exist through industry associations. Leading companies view the adoption of sustainability measures as giving them a 'first mover advantage' that enables them to differentiate themselves from other companies, which in turn gives them a degree of economic advantage.

Companies that wish to engage in sustainable practices tend to look to the industry leaders and learn from them. The most progressive companies compare their sustainability track records with those of peers in other industries, rather than looking specifically at competitors.

Value drivers

A number of 'value drivers' are prompting companies to take sustainability action. For example the cost savings to be had from improved resource efficiency have contributed significantly to the business case for sustainability in this sector. However our surveys and interviews revealed that managers perceived the contribution of sustainability to intangibles such as reputation enhancement, licence to operate and brand value as having the greatest impact on the economic value of their companies.

Reputation enhancement and licence to operate

In the global economy, food and beverage companies face considerable risks to their reputation and hence their profitability. Multinational companies are perceived as having a role in society and a duty to maintain standards that are suited to the fabric of the society in which they operate. The politics of food supply and the importance a company gives to the role of business in society are important determinants of the company's ability to continue its operations (its licence to operate). Some leading companies have a heritage of social responsibility. Going public on a sustainability strategy commits a company to providing credible evidence of sustainable practices and consistency at all locations, and there can be considerable loss of credibility and reputation if the company changes course. If the company's licence to operate is jeopardized in this way there can be an adverse effect on its share price and the success of its business operations.

Brand value and innovation

A food and beverage company's brand is its most important asset, and any tarnishing of its image has a negative effect on whatever premium the brand brings. Therefore product and brand value directly affect the commercial viability of companies in the sector. Not surprisingly then, an overwhelming 84 per cent of the food and beverage managers in our study stated that brand and reputation were very important to their companies.

The association of value with brand is key to brand differentiation (and thus competitive advantage), particularly when a company's name is tied tightly to its brand. In today's competitive environment, product concepts are being expanded beyond technical or physical performance, sometimes using sustainability or corporate responsibility concepts. The relationship between the consumer and the brand is therefore more than a purely functional transaction; consumers want to know the extent to which the values of the brand align with their own. Marketing managers feel that the brand reflects the responsibility of the company and has to be perceived by consumers as trustworthy and healthy. These trends relate to a number of corporate practices that are directly linked to sustainable development. When a product meets sustainability criteria, the media receive the product positively. Given the enormous budgets companies devote to marketing their products, this is clearly a benefit that, although mostly not quantified, indicates that sustainability contributes to brand value.

Attracting and retaining talent

The desire of employees to match their business practices to their personal values is seen by managers as a strong driver for sustainability action. Employees want to be good citizens, to work with a sense of satisfaction and pride, and will generally seek core values that reflect this desire. Attracting and retaining talented employees in a competitive business environment is very much in the economic interest of any company as it adds value to the company. However the interviewees in our study described this as a weak value driver because when jobs become less abundant fewer employees can make choices based on the above criteria.

Value drivers: present and future

Sustainability officers do not consider that value drivers are difficult to identify as those that are most relevant are clearly economically important. Rather the challenge is to define what needs to be done with them from a business perspective and to present them to managers in terms that the latter understand. Some value drivers are not easily measured, so given managers' conviction that in companies 'what gets measured gets done', it is difficult for a sustainability agenda to be pushed throughout the company. Sustainability officers expect the concept of sustainability to be better defined in future, leading to a better understanding of the concept by both society and companies. Managers expect the sector to move gradually away from the focus on environmental impact to a more informed discussion based on research and development, and resource management. Recognition of reputation and licence to operate as value drivers will be enhanced as a result.

Managers believe that when improved tracking and tracing systems are in operation, there will be an increase in branding by food producers, or even dual branding (retailer and producer). If companies reach out to consumers in this way, brand and reputation management will increasingly go hand in hand.

Corporate sustainability management

Corporate vision and organizational culture

The everyday operations of food and beverage companies can provide deep insights into consumer trends; this implies that food and beverage companies can exploit a potential strategic role as corporate citizens that are naturally integrated to society. The corporate visions of companies in the sector can be inspired not only by the objective of meeting consumers' preferences but also by the need for products that improve the quality of life, while at the same time boosting sales and profits, thus creating wealth for employees, communities and investors and fulfilling the company's responsibility as a corporate citizen. Visions that are centred on consumer lifestyle and quality of life can provide a strong case for a sustainability strategy, as long as consumers are pushing in the right direction, which is not always the case. Progressive companies tend to make long-term value creation part of their corporate vision.

The corporate purpose statements, corporate values and corporate principles of the leading companies in the sector align well with sustainability strategy in general, since they are often based on a history of innovative leadership inspired by concern and respect not only for consumers but also for employees and communities.

Organizational culture greatly influences the success of sustainability strategies. One officer described sustainability as an iterative process ('learning by doing'). An open, consensus-based organizational culture lends itself to such a process. All too often sustainable development initiatives are imposed by managers at the top of the corporation rather than emanating from the operating companies, which would spread ownership of the initiatives across the organization.

Our interviewees considered that Northern European cultures lend themselves well to consensus-driven sustainability approaches and managers saw these countries as leading the field in corporate sustainability. However sustainability officers claimed that managers' lack of understanding of sustainability issues and their implications for business is preventing establishment of the continuous feedback mechanisms that are necessary for the early identification of issues. Sales, marketing and manufacturing managers are aware of the many initiatives in their companies but focus primarily on 'their' brand. Unless sustainability is integrated into the business (by establishing targets and incentives), it is unlikely to become a priority. Time and resource considerations can create, if not active opposition, then passivity and inertia in managers faced with what is inevitably perceived as an extra management burden. There is often scepticism about the added value of sustainability action, as well as fear of high costs and little or no return. For business units to push for sustainability action, the links between sustainability activities and their business results must be made visible.

Strategy design

In our survey only 22 per cent of managers stated that their companies are aiming for a high degree of integration of sustainable development into their strategies and operations (sustainability officers were more optimistic as 35 per cent believed that this was the case). Indeed few food and beverage companies in our study have formulated a comprehensive sustainability strategy. Leading companies tend to have a business strategy for certain sustainability issues.

When developing any corporate strategy, companies review their overall growth goals, identify where future markets will be and review global trends. Future markets for food and beverage companies will be in the developing world, where consumers have aspirations for a better quality of life, but currently have much less purchasing power than consumers in developed countries. There are some four billion people at the 'bottom of the pyramid'.[4]

Exploiting this significant business opportunity will require new and creative ways of thinking and acting by companies. Our research has revealed that few innovative efforts are being made to build new business models based on serving the poor. Even the leading food and beverage companies are only just beginning to think of ways of creating, manufacturing, distributing and marketing new products in emerging economies. Meanwhile people in developing countries are already attuned to the concept of sustainable development, and this is all the more reason for putting sustainability objectives on to the corporate agenda.

When looking at how companies have behaved when in crisis we found that sustainability programmes that are integrated into corporate strategic plans run much less risk of being removed from the strategic agenda in difficult economic times, given the credibility risk to the company of withdrawing them. This finding was confirmed by sustainability officers in our study.

Organizational structure and responsibilities

The corporate headquarters of food and beverage multinationals are generally responsible for policy making and strategic overview, but operational responsibilities are usually decentralized. Corporate managers feel that sustainability measures are most successful when implemented by operational units, but given the decentralized structure of most companies in the sector, maintaining an overview of progress in these areas is problematic. The business units of global food and beverage companies are split into geographic markets in order to maintain local focus, and the corporate headquarters provides the 'glue' that holds them together, through strategy, innovation and business development. The latter, if properly utilized, can facilitate the overall monitoring of progress in all areas of sustainability.

One of our interviewees suggested that the key to successful issue identification is constant communication between business and strategy groups. The allocation of responsibility for sustainability issues tends to be company-specific, and may be designated to the public relations department, the innovation department, or a separate unit set up for the purpose.

Most of the leading companies have appointed a central strategic coordinating committee (cross-functional, with appropriate geographical representation) with overall responsibility for the identification of issues. This committee decides whether issues should be addressed at the group or the business unit level.

The committee also nominates cross-functional issue groups to handle the most important issues (for example for human rights and ethical trading). Through the creation of such teams, companies set up a matrix structure that allows, for example, staff working in individual markets to talk to those with global responsibilities, thus ensuring company-wide exchanges on issues and agendas. Information gathered in one market is easily transferred to another, facilitating maximum use of knowledge in the organization; one leading company refers to this process as 'search and spin'.

To optimize a sustainability strategy, having an organizational structure that makes it easy for information to flow across the enterprise and around the world is essential. It makes it possible to put in place an 'early awareness system' (EAS) that allows individuals to identify issues at the market level and pass them on to the corporate appropriate level, and it enables the company to learn directly from stakeholders and consumers. However there is little evidence of a functional EAS in the companies in our study. At the operational level, some companies have concentrated on building a network of sustainability 'champions' at the senior level in business units throughout the organization. This increases the ownership of initiatives by the business units and ensures that matters such as funds and resources for sustainability initiatives are addressed in the context of the business strategy. Given the nature of the sustainability issues that affect the industry, in the most progressive companies the sustainability champions in the supply chain departments are responsible for pushing key issues.

CEOs in the leading companies are the driving force behind their organizations' sustainability strategies. However more than one manager commented that while it would not be possible to pursue a sustainability strategy without top management support, this in itself is not enough for success.

Departments that focus on sales and profit targets tend to view sustainability as a high-risk endeavour. Even in the most progressive companies there are second-tier business managers under the CEO who are oriented first and foremost towards profitable growth, and an 'old guard' of hard-line sceptics at the senior level can be found in virtually every organization. Translating the complex concept of sustainability into the language of such managers is often a huge challenge. Senior managers we interviewed felt that since younger executives have often grown up with the concept of sustainability they are more prepared to integrate it in to their work.

According to our survey, finance and control departments are most opposed to the implementation of sustainability initiatives (22 per cent of responses), followed by marketing and sales (17 per cent) and manufacturing operations (13 per cent). The latter often find it a burden to fit sustainability measures into their target setting, and yet they are regarded by managers as most likely to be able to improve companies' sustainability performance (24 per cent of responses).

Sustainability officers in the food and beverage industry also perceive corporate R&D employees, marketing and sales executives and buyers of raw and semiprocessed materials as potentially key actors, given their influence over product design and sourcing, which are important aspects of any sustainability strategy. Currently, however, they do not have sustainability on their agenda and generally do not recognize the extent to which their work can affect their companies' sustainability model. In fact our survey revealed that lack of knowledge is a significant barrier to the promotion of sustainability, and this was fully backed up by our interviewees. For example sustainability officers asserted that marketing and sales executives do not yet see ways of incorporating sustainability issues in to brand communication, and that they have fixed approaches to their work that make it difficult to adopt a progressive and innovative sustainability agenda. These interviewees felt that increased understanding of the importance of reputation as a corporate value driver might help to overcome this barrier. However developing such an understanding would be time-consuming, and marketing managers tend to change jobs every two to three years, and have tight deadlines and objectives, all of which are significant barriers to changes of attitude.

Moreover sales and marketing executives are generally not included in the cross-functional strategic coordination groups that oversee sustainability strategies, apparently because the industry does not associate specific brands with specific issues, and therefore marketing executives, with their direct association and preoccupation with brand, are dropped from the equation. This is clearly a problem that needs to be addressed if the business case for sustainability is to be promoted downstream.

According to sustainability officers, any sustainability strategy that is not accompanied by a comprehensive communications strategy (perhaps coordinated by the communications or external relations director) will almost certainly fail. Educating line managers about the attitudes the company expects could ensure that supervisors will not erect barriers to change. Most managers support the view that leading by example is one of the most important forms of managerial support in any company.

According to our survey there is considerable scope for sustainability officers to work more closely with various management functions, and to use this contact to promote the business case for sustainability. Only 26 per cent of the managers in our study had contact with the sustainability unit on a day-to-day basis, and 56 per cent engaged in *ad hoc* collaboration. However only 8 per cent of sustainability officers were convinced that greater collaboration would contribute very positively to sustainable business practices in the company, while 24 per cent felt that it would contribute positively.

Processes and systems

Issue tracking

Some of the companies researched have established issue management systems as a direct consequence of defensive confrontations with stakeholders, rather than as a proactive measure. The more affected a company has been by a major issue in the past, the more seriously it treats potential risks and the higher in the company hierarchy it places responsibility for sustainability issues. For effective issue tracking, better-practice companies tend to put mechanisms in place to ensure that information on strategic issues identified in the markets is transmitted around the network. By this means the company can accumulate knowledge sufficient to develop a strategic action agenda based on value creation. As one strategy executive put it:

> We looked at the corporate affairs strategy, starting with identifying issues common to all markets and then focusing on bigger issues that prevent managers from reaching financial targets. We asked each strategic area head, what would ease the licence to operate? Last year every market manager looked at public policy, stakeholder dialogue and how it is addressing corporate citizenship. The benefits were greater awareness of the positive things being done within the company and of diverse approaches. In this way we find strategic alternatives to reach our goals.

Issue mapping

Assessing the relevance and strategic fit of issues to value drivers increases companies' awareness of which business activities relate to which issues. Rather than trying to quantify their sustainability efforts in detail, companies tend to prioritize resources and efforts and work within a matrix framework, particularly with regard to social issues. By benchmarking internally and with other industries or companies, the relative significance of an issue can be assessed. In general, if a risk is likely to be high for the business it will also come high on the company's agenda for action. Data management tools are used to inform the mapping process (continuous measurement of material and energy usage, waste flows and emissions, and other more *ad hoc* environmental impact assessment tools).

Companies are increasingly using standards such as AA1000 and SA8000 to help them to monitor social issues that are elusive and difficult to grasp. However sustainability managers feel that better tools are required for measuring intangible factors such as the impact of relationships with NGOs and so on.

Issue prioritization

Internal and external risk assessment processes are used to prioritize issues. When business units report issues to the corporate level, the issues are assessed against a larger, more long-term picture. Risk assessment tools include qualitative and quantitative analyses and forecasts of probabilities and consequences. The results are incorporated into a 'risk register', which later operates as a tracking tool.

Most of the managers we interviewed felt that greater transparency and a deeper understanding of the way in which issues are tracked, mapped and prioritized by the company and others in the industry would facilitate the earlier and more effective integration of issues into strategic decision making, as well as giving competitive advantage.

Integrating issues into strategic decision making

To convince company managers of the business case for sustainability, most sustainability officers rely on presentations and reports outlining concepts and plans. Progressive companies focus on the value drivers behind sustainability initiatives rather than demanding a complete business case with statistics to back up the proposals, so their sustainability officers tend to avoid referring to costs and concentrate on product differentiation, competitiveness and investment to cut costs in the medium term. Leading companies tend to focus on sustainability issues in areas that are most relevant to their business and where they can have most influence and impact.

Most CEOs in the leading food and beverage companies see a strong business case for sustainability based on reputation and licence to operate but, unlike sustainability officers, are not interested in quantification. Putting a value on reputation loss, for example, is not something that the industry has tried to do. Some managers feel that more work should be done in this area, based on the rationale that if it is possible to value a brand, then it should be possible to value reputation. However as one business development executive stated, 'It is hard to prove that sustainability adds value but it is clear that not paying attention to it destroys value, and rather rapidly. It is not always possible to translate the impact of non-action into money terms. It has more to do with vision – and the fact that if you do not do it, business value is at risk.'

In progressive companies the following tactical methods are used:

- Scenario building, where strategic decision makers consider the consequences of inaction, for example by calculating the impact of NGO activism on share prices.
- Building on previous success stories and implementing pilot projects. Pilot projects involving cash crops in the supply chain have proved an effective way of demonstrating the business case for sustainable sourcing and showing that sustainability can be beneficially integrated into the business at no cost.

If a single issue is very significant, then a focused strategy and an action plan are developed. Position papers are produced on the most important issues.

Integrating issues into operations

Once a business case for sustainability has been established by a multinational company, application of the resulting strategy does not vary from country to country as dual strategies are perceived as risky. However there are significant national differences between companies, for example companies from developing countries will interpret issues differently from their counterparts in developed countries.

Policies and management systems provide an operational framework for promoting sustainability within the company. Central to this are statements of principles and values. According to our findings, managers consider that documents laying out corporate values, policies and standards are vital internal tools. This shows the importance the industry accords to having the right corporate mindset and values, which is essential if sustainability initiatives are to be successful.

Most of the sustainability officers we interviewed felt that the initial message on the business case for sustainability must come from top management, but that employees must first have a basic understanding of the concepts. Developing this understanding involves reinforcing values in managers' minds at every corporate level. One strategy officer remarked, 'A corporate message on sustainability has general themes, but the message has to be...relevant to each region or country; otherwise it is not going to be effective. Operational units have an important role in developing and transmitting this message.'

Pilot projects (mentioned earlier) also have a major advantage in rolling-out a sustainability strategy as they ensure that the processes of building and implementing the business case for sustainability are integrated. By implementing pilot projects, key staff in the company actively engage with sustainability issues in their areas of business.[5] The sustainability officer also learns to 'speak the language' of the business when participating in the process. Previous success stories significantly enhance the business case for sustainability at the operational level.

Managers feel that targets for sustainable practices can help business units to ensure that sustainability action plans become an integral part of the business model. Sustainability managers highlight the importance of focusing on concrete activities with measurable results. Some companies include sustainable development in their goal-setting and management appraisal process or as part of managers' balanced scorecards. Incentive and reward systems are thus linked to performance in sustainability, just as in other business areas, and cooperation and cross-functional initiatives within and among operational teams are encouraged. However few of the companies in our study have moved towards such an integrated approach despite awareness of its usefulness. This is due, according to some managers, to the decentralized nature of management in the sector. However progressive companies have placed target setting firmly on the agenda of future management reviews.

Assessment of the business case, its potential and exploitation

'No resource = no business'

The simple equation 'no resource = no business' is the strongest economic argument for the promotion of sustainable practices in the food and beverage industry, and is clearly the most solid business case for all the industries analyzed in the research project upon which this volume is based. The depletion of fish, stocks, for example, is a business risk within a tight five-year time perspective. This is well within the time horizon of most business managers. The business case for sustainable fisheries can be used as a model that helps food companies to analyze similar risks with even bigger bottom-line effects such as agriculture. However, for agriculture, the time horizon for business risk expands again, and managers less easily perceive benefits unless sustainability officers define them more succinctly.

In the view of one enlightened marketing manager with experience of sustainability initiatives, food and beverage companies will only be able to connect with consumers (who are growing ever more concerned about how their food is produced) if they pursue sound practices that take account of the way in which crops are grown, for example with a view to preserving biodiversity and protecting water supplies. The challenge lies in balancing sustainability measures with continued economic growth.

Although research tends to show that the link between consumers' broad concern for environmental and social issues and their buying habits is still rather weak, there are managers in the industry who feel that the concept of sustainability, if carefully crafted, will ultimately be a major selling point. Brand values and consumer trust are concepts that can be used in marketing and selling high-quality, added value products. Companies are in an experimental phase with pilot projects in the supply chain and do not wish to risk credibility by using their successes to market brands just yet. However these innovative efforts and others like them can eventually be used to make a link between products and consumers' concern about the future of the planet. The opportunity that sustainability gives to innovate can thus contribute to building critical mass and consumer support for these concepts in the markets as a result, radical innovation based on sustainability concepts should go beyond experimental projects.

It has been shown by progressive companies that sustainability can be achieved in some areas without damaging profitability, and sometimes can even save costs, thus proving the business case for sustainability. However all external costs are not included by companies in the cost of raw materials, and managers say that substantial external political and economic pressure will have to be put on the industry if it is to move towards sustainability more rapidly. NGOs say that a major step in sustainable development will only be possible if leaders in the industry join trade initiatives to support changes to the economic and political framework in which the industry operates. Under the present economic scenario the business case for sustainability clearly has its limits.

Notes

1. See http://imd.ch/research/projects/bcs for the full report and the diagnostic toolset developed as a result of the research.
2. 'Proven: the environmental dangers that may halt GM revolution', *Independent*, 17 October, 2003.
3. 'Obesity: Preventing and Managing the Global Epidemic', *World Health Organization Technical Report Series 894* (Geneva: WHO 2000).
4. Stuart L. Hart, and C. K. Prahalad, 'The Fortune at the Bottom of the Pyramid', *Strategy and Business*, 1st Quarter, 2002.
5. See http://www.imd.ch/research/projects/bcs for pilot projects on sustainable agriculture.

10
The Pharmaceutical Industry

Oliver Eckelmann

The focus of the study on which this chapter is based was the leading research-based global pharmaceutical companies,[1] therefore generic manufacturers, parallel importing companies, biotechnology-oriented companies and pharmaceutical service providers were excluded, apart from one leading biotechnology company, which was included in the sample for the purpose of cross-checking.

More than 70 in-depth personal interviews lasting an average of two hours were conducted at the 15 participating companies. The interviewees were sustainability officers and executive managers including some CEOs, (later referred to as general managers) from all relevant functions, divisions and geographical areas. The participating companies were Abbott Laboratories, AstraZeneca, Aventis, Bayer, Boehringer Ingelheim, Bristol-Myers Squibb, Genentech, GlaxoSmithKline, Hoffmann-La Roche, Johnson & Johnson, Merck, Novartis, Pfizer, Pharmacia and Schering.

Interviews were also conducted with representatives of more than 15 institutions and interest groups – such as financial investors, governments, regulatory bodies, NGOs and experts – to ascertain the stakeholders' perspective and identify possible conflicts of interest. Unless otherwise stated, the following discussion is a synthesis of the interview findings and various facts and figures.

The pharmaceutical industry: economic, social and environmental overview

Industry overview

In 2002 the global pharmaceutical industry (producing prescription and over the counter drugs) was estimated to comprise over 2000 pharmaceutical and biotech companies with a reported consolidated revenue of more than $400 billion. The USA was by far the largest market (52 per cent of sales), followed by Europe (25 per cent) and Japan (15 per cent). The pharmaceutical industry consists of two tiers: the top 30 companies account for more than two thirds of sales, or an average of $8 billion, while the rest achieve an average sales figure of $120 million. The market share of the top 10 companies is about 50 per cent.

By any measure the pharmaceutical industry is highly successful. In 2000 the largest companies typically achieved operating margins of 20–30 per cent, and even during the downturn in 2001 the top 10 increased their profits by an average of 18 per cent.

All of the 10 biggest companies invest more than $2 billion in R&D each year, on around 12–19 per cent of gross revenues in 2001. The average total cost to market per approved new drug increased from $467 million in 1991 to $802 million in 2002 (with a time to market of about 14–15 years), but the majority of products launched over the past 20 years have not reached the required annual sales figure of $100 million. This makes the pharmaceutical industry a highly risky business. In 2001 seven of the top 10 companies spent more than 30 per cent of their gross revenues on marketing and sales. Over the past two decades the industry has been affected by significant changes:

- The ageing population and growing health consciousness have boosted demand.
- Mergers and acquisitions (M&As) have rearranged the structure of the industry – pharmaceutical stocks have become more volatile.
- Rising prices and profits have prompted greater regulatory scrutiny.
- The rise of HMOs has driven an aggregation of demand, resulting in pricing pressure by buyers.
- The cost of developing new drugs has increased but R&D productivity has fallen.
- The patents on many highly profitable drugs have expired, resulting in a loss of market share of up to 90 per cent.
- Generic drug marketers have taken an even larger share of the market (approximately 50 per cent of units sold in 2002 in the USA).

Competitive analysis

Relatively high barriers to entry, low to moderate supplier power and relatively inelastic demand combine to give major research-based pharmaceutical companies considerable market power and make the

Table 10.1 Competitive situation in the pharmaceutical industry

• Steep R&D experience curve effects; large economies of scale barriers in R&D and marketing and sales	High and stable barriers to entry reduce the threat of new entrants
• Large number of suppliers; raw materials mostly commodities	Low to moderate but slightly increasing supplier bargaining power
• Significant buyer power influences decisions to prescribe less expensive drugs – increasing price sensitivity; (Health Maintenance Organizations and large distributors) are replacing the role of individual customers	Medium to high and steadily increasing buyer bargaining power
• Generic drugs catching up with branded drugs; technological developments making imitation easier	Low to moderate but steadily increasing threat of substitutes
• Time of product monopoly after market entry fell from six to ten years in the late 1970s to around one year today, and sometimes even less than three months; global competition concentrated among 15–20 large companies; second merger and acquisition wave possible	Moderate but continuously increasing competition within the industry and more intense rivalry

pharmaceutical sector attractive compared with other industries. Table 10.1 summarizes the current situation.

Social and environmental relevance and impact

The business case for corporate sustainability is defined as the 'space' in which companies can reduce negative effects or increase positive external ones without economic loss. Table 10.2 shows the main externalities in the pharmaceutical industry.

As will be discussed below, most of the current sustainability issues cannot be explained and justified by the concept of negative externalities.

Sustainability issues and their economic relevance

In recent decades the focus of sustainability has partly shifted from environmental health and safety to social responsibility. This is a consequence of pharmaceutical companies' successful reduction of pollution and the separation of the chemical industry (bulk chemicals) from the pharmaceutical industry (fine chemicals). Our study has shown that pharmaceutical companies are now well on track when it comes to

Table 10.2   Production and consumption externalities in the pharmaceutical industry

---

Negative externalities caused by production:
- Environmental footprint:* pollution
- Use of non-renewable resources

Positive externalities caused by production:
- Industrial innovation: the returns to society from R&D are more than twice the returns to corporations
- R&D knowledge gained after patent expiry
- R&D knowledge gained in least developed countries, where the industry does not enforce patents

Negative externalities caused by consumption:
- Antibiotics released into the environment

Positive externalities caused by consumption:
- Use of vaccines: people who are not vaccinated benefit from others who are vaccinated (leads to vaccines being undervalued, which is a problem)

---

*An environmental footprint is the amount of land required to support one person's consumption and waste products.

tackling environmental issues. From the 1970s companies' behaviour was purely reactive. It was only when external pressure had reached a critical level that they changed their practices and brought criticism more or less under control. Today companies are confronted with more social issues than environmental ones.

The four most critical sustainability issues (R&D issues, access to healthcare, patent protection and health economics – see Figure 10.1) need immediate attention, have very high stakeholder relevance, are subject to considerable external pressure, present a valid threat to companies' business models and have a strong bearing on profitability. Two of these issues – access to healthcare and health economics – are discussed in detail below.[2]

Access to healthcare

Which drugs to offer at what prices to whom

In 2002, 92 per cent of global drug sales were accounted for by North America, Europe and Japan, with roughly 85 per cent of the world's population receiving the remainder. These figures illustrate the huge imbalance in access to drugs between the developed and developing worlds. The World Health Organization (WHO) estimates that currently one third of the global population lacks access to even the most essential drugs.

Figure 10.1 Position of the four main sustainability issues on the organizational chain

Access to medicines and vaccines depends on four crucial factors: affordable prices, rational selection and use, sustainable financing, and reliable supply systems. Although these are all equally important, in health and trade discussions the focus is usually on drug prices.

Economic relevance

The economic relevance of providing access to healthcare in the developing world is twofold and increasing, as outlined below.

Risk exposure   The external pressure on pharmaceutical companies is increasing. The media and NGOs have successfully publicized the poor access that people in the developing world have to drugs, thus increasing the pressure on companies to address the matter. Despite lowering their prices as a consequence, companies have suffered, a loss of reputation that will require further changes in behaviour to minimize their risk exposure.

Revenue relevance   Almost 99 per cent of the increase in the world's population occurs in the developing countries. The more developed countries account for a mere 1.4 per cent of the increase, and the populations of Europe and Japan – two of the major pharmaceutical markets – are undergoing a constant decrease. If the leading pharmaceutical companies wish to sustain their double-digit revenues and profit growth in the coming decades they will have to start serving growing markets such as China, India and Latin America, which make up the lower tiers of the population pyramid.

Industry and stakeholder perspective

The industry mainly sells its innovative drugs to the markets with the highest allowable prices. The USA – the only significant market in which manufacturers can set the price of drugs without government-imposed restrictions – has by far the highest drug prices, for example on average prices in European countries are 40 per cent below those in the USA. In the less developed world, prices are only a small percentage of those in the developed world, for example in India they are around one twelfth of US prices and the least developed markets have even lower prices. But even at these prices only a small percentage of the population can afford the latest drugs.

Some companies have reacted to external pressure by reducing their prices, but have still suffered an image loss. Not a single marketing manager in our study indicated that social responsibility criteria were included in the price determination process. Some companies offer one-off, not-for-profit prices for specific areas of treatment (mostly antiretrovirals and antimalarials) to a wide range of customers in the least developed countries. Nearly all global companies are donating medicines to developing countries, either directly or indirectly via the WHO or public–private partnerships (PPPs).

The main stakeholder participants in the global health discussion on access to drugs are NGOs and, as moderators, intergovernmental organizations (IGOs). Some NGOs argue that health is a human right and that pharmaceutical companies should provide that right to countries free of charge; others insist that lower prices would improve the long-term health of people in poor countries without significantly affecting the industry's profitability, providing that certain safeguards are put in place. They claim that selected, one-off price reductions are not guaranteed in the long run and hence discourage long-term health planning in developing countries. Instead they are calling for a global approach to tiered pricing, which would incorporate 'pro-poor' policies, segregate the world's markets and bring lower long-term prices to all developing countries.

Very interestingly – and inconsistently with their desired outcome – none of the NGOs is purposefully targeting and arguing with generic drug manufacturers about the issue of access to healthcare.

Future outlook

The proportion of the global population living in developing parts of the world will continue to increase, so the problem of inadequate medical supplies and access to healthcare will worsen rather than disappear. The external pressure on companies will increase, requiring an *ad hoc*, reactive response by companies and a well-thought-out, proactive approach in the years to come. PPPs probably offer the most promising solution, since the price of drugs is but one of four factors in access to drugs. If companies do not want to be left alone on all four of these factors in the future, they will have to engage proactively or even create PPPs today.

Health economics in developed countries

What should pharmaceutical companies contribute to healthcare systems?

Access to an adequate healthcare system is seen as a basic right of citizens in all developed economies and affordable healthcare is a primary objective. However for governments across the world healthcare is a major concern because it is costly. The G7 countries spend between

6.8 per cent (UK) and 13.2 per cent (USA) of their gross domestic product on healthcare, with spending on drugs as a proportion of total health-care spending ranging from 8 per cent to 15 per cent. Although this is a relatively small proportion of total healthcare costs the amounts are large, for example the US drug budget amounted to $154 billion in 2001, a 17 per cent increase on spending in 2000. Since pharmaceuticals are produced by highly profitable organizations they are an easy target for governmental attempts to contain costs. High prices are preventing many senior citizens, even in developed countries and especially in the USA, from buying necessary drugs. And with the expected increase in the elderly population (rising to about 20 per cent of the US population by 2020, up from 12.5 per cent in 2003), healthcare expenditure will rise even further, placing a considerable strain on governmental and societal budgets.

Economic relevance

There are three major reasons for choosing a publicly accepted approach to the health economics issue, as described below.

Risk exposure   In the USA, Europe and Japan (which accounted for 92 per cent of pharmaceutical companies' revenue in 2002) the economic downturn has resulted in decreased tax revenues for governments but healthcare costs (especially the cost of drugs) have risen, as have the profits of the leading pharmaceutical companies. The latter have come under increasingly fierce attack by the press and the public, and govern-ments have proposed new legislation. If the industry continues on its current course there will be even more calls for generic products and parallel imports in order to reduce healthcare costs, thus reducing companies' profits. By choosing a publicly acceptable approach to the health economics issue and appealing more to patients as important healthcare purchasers, companies can minimize the risk of losing further influence and profits.

Customer retention   By excluding many senior and poor citizens from access to healthcare because of the high cost of drugs, companies are excluding a huge part of their customer base as many drugs are espe-cially developed for the elderly. Offering special prices to senior citizens would enable them to maximize their revenue streams.

Reputation   Pharmaceutical companies are generally the most prof-itable and visible part of the healthcare value chain. They are seen as the villains of the health economics problem, despite the fact that they are not entirely to blame. Polls have shown that their reputation has suffered huge damage. If research-based companies want to keep their licence to innovate and succeed in the battle with generic manufacturers they will have to restore their image as healers.

Industry and stakeholder perspectives

Many pharmaceutical companies argue that expenditure on drugs does not drive healthcare costs and that studies have shown that the quality-adjusted price of medicine has actually fallen over time, in contrast to rising prices for medical services. They insist that expenditure on drugs still only accounts for a fraction of total healthcare costs and that the increase in drug expenditure has less to do with price rises than with a rise in the prescription rate. Hence the industry does not see itself as responsible for the increase in healthcare costs. It argues that no one is looking at the consolidated income statements of doctors and pharmacies, just at pharmaceutical companies' income statements. The industry has failed to switch the focus of discussion from a purely cost-driven perspective on healthcare to a value-led focus by showing that the use of medicine can be cheaper, for example, than surgery.

At the same time as defending their situation in the healthcare market, pharmaceutical companies have been trying to prevent the market entry of generic manufacturers and to hinder parallel imports. At the moment a leading company is facing a huge wave of criticism and calls for the boycotting of its products because of its instruction to Canadian pharmacies (whose prices are lower than in the USA) not to sell to US citizens, thus halting cross-border sales. On the other hand companies are beginning to offer senior citizens discount cards, Medicaid rebates and access to other discount programmes.

Numerous stakeholder groups blame pharmaceutical companies for many of the world's health problems. NGOs claim that countless senior citizens and people with low incomes are being deprived of essential drugs. Meanwhile governments, in their desperate fight to reduce healthcare costs without restructuring their healthcare systems, are calling on doctors to prescribe more generic products. They are also allowing companies in Europe to reimport drugs and are even passing new laws, for example in Germany pharmaceutical companies are now required by law to give a fixed discount of 6 per cent on all their products.

Future outlook

With an ageing population in the developed world and falling tax revenues, the health economics problem will grow even worse as countries will not be able to continue to provide the current standard of healthcare to their citizens. Healthcare systems need to be revised, with all parts of the supply chain cooperating to find an acceptable solution. The fact that patients are willing to spend more money on over the counter drugs than on life-saving prescription drugs shows the need for a much broader discussion on health economics. Finally, it is necessary to adopt a global approach to healthcare economics and drug pricing in the face of growing public anger with the industry.

Table10.3   Current and potential sustainability issues

Current environmental issues

- Environmental footprint
- Biodiversity

Potential environmental issues

- Leaching of pharmaceuticals into the environment
- Exposure of healthcare personnel to the dangers of excessive exposure pharmaceuticals (hazardous and non-hazardous)
- Resistance to antibiotics

Current social issues

- Ethical clinical testing

- *Biocolonialism*, Developed countries benefiting from medicines originating from plants in under developed countries, biopiracy, patenting of biological entities

- Women's health issues
- Stem cell research

- Genetically modified organisms
- Prevention of incorrect medication

Potential social issues

- Marketing practices, advertising to consumers and/or doctors
- Human rights
- Access to other drugs (and not only Aids drugs) such as those for cancer
- Regulatory influence, relationship between companies and governments

- Disease prevention versus treatment of outbreaks
- Bioterrorism
- Product quality/liability
- Efficacy of drugs

- Relationship between pharmaceutical companies and generic manufacturers

Other current and future issues

The pharmaceutical industry faces a variety of other sustainability issues, as outlined in Table 10.3.

Learning from resolved sustainability issues

The pharmaceutical industry can learn much from sustainability issues resolved in the past, both environmental and social. Some of them were resolved proactively, but many were resolved reactively in response to increasing external pressure, especially in the case of environmental issues in the 1980s. Some caused serious damage to the industry's reputation. The industry's response to these issues was determined mainly by the degree of business risk involved and extent of public pressure. Two major issues were biotechnology research and animal testing (the latter is discussed in Box 10.1). Both were very publicly debated and widely criticized, and strong external pressure was put on pharmaceutical companies. Both constituted a business risk so it made economic sense for companies to resolve them. It appears that their actions were successful as none of the external stakeholders we interviewed cited animal testing or biotechnology research as matters of concern in the pharmaceutical industry today.

Box 10.1 Animal testing

In the mid 1990s pharmaceutical companies were strongly criticized for testing their products on animals and subjecting them to pain and intolerable conditions. Some radical protest groups even threatened the lives of pharmaceutical employees.

Animal testing is an expensive procedure, so it was in the industry's interest to cut down on the practice in order to reduce costs. Working in collaboration with the less radical protest groups, companies quickly reduced their amount of animal testing to that deemed acceptable by governments and regulators, and they also improved the conditions for animals in their laboratories.

Today, pharmaceutical companies and groups such as PETA (People for the Ethical Treatment of Animals) are jointly lobbying at the governmental level for a further reduction in the permissible level of animal testing.

Summary

This section has shown that environmental issues are less pressing than social ones in terms of confronting the pharmaceutical industry with challenging problems. The fact that there is still a dearth of middle and top managers to deal with these issues means that it is almost impossible for the industry to act proactively at the moment. Instead companies tend to react to external pressure only when it has reached a threatening level, for example in the face of financial pressure from capital markets or falling profits due to public dissatisfaction (Figure 10.2).

Some companies are reconsidering the way in which they handle sustainability issues. At the moment there is an emphasis on crisis management and measures to avoid further damage to their reputations, but they are also working on a proactive, value-based approach to issues. Switching from a cost perspective to a long-term value perspective on sustainability issues will automatically lead to a change in behaviour and a more structured approach to corporate sustainability management.

Corporate sustainability management

As sustainability issues are growing more complex and having an increasing impact on the pharmaceutical industry and society, and because public pressure is mounting, some companies are beginning to engage in corporate sustainability management (CSM) and others are redesigning their internal approach to it. The five predominant areas of CSM are:

- Awareness, vision and culture.
- Sustainability strategy design.
- Organization.
- Communication and stakeholder interaction.
- Issue management.

Awareness, vision and culture

Awareness of the topic of sustainability is seen in the industry as a crucial first step. While the sustainability officers in our study showed a sophisticated understanding of sustainability management and the current sustainability issues, general managers seemed less familiar with the concept. Moreover employees in operational and public affairs departments had greater awareness of the concept than employees in marketing and

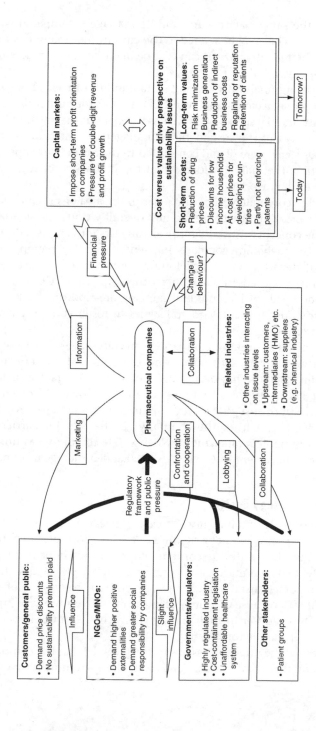

Figure 10.2 Pharmaceutical companies' responses to sustainability issues

finance, and the same was true for middle managers compared with junior managers. This may be related to the current method of creating awareness in the industry, which can best be described as a 'middle-up, top-down' approach.

There is a strong unanimity among sustainability officers about the necessity of top-management and even CEO support for further progress in sustainability and the spread of awareness throughout the organization. Approximately half of the sustainability managers in our study stated that their CEOs were aware of and committed to the further development of CSM, but the other half considered that top managers constituted a major barrier to their work.

With regard to corporate visions and goals in the area of sustainability, because of the broad nature of companies' overall visions and goals, in some cases the concept of sustainability already fits into and is reflected in the latter. Uniquely, one company has sent about 20 top employees from different departments to developing countries in Africa for six months (planned and coordinated in partnership with NGOs). These employees, equipped with laptops and cameras, are reporting back from the field to their departments and colleagues to foster cultural change and raise awareness.

The more forward-thinking companies strongly believe that ensuring their culture reflects their social and environmental responsibilities is one of the most important tasks of CSM. Others are unsure whether it is necessary for all employees to be involved in or know about the concept of sustainable development, but our study revealed that knowledge gaps within the company can be a major barrier to progress in sustainable management. Not a single company has linked salaries to the achievement of CSM goals or included such goals in their incentive systems.

Sustainability strategy design

There are two types of sustainability strategy: an overall corporate strategy and the formulation of strategy at the issue level. Both are obviously interrelated, but they differ in content, duration and impact. At the moment only two pharmaceutical companies from one sample have designed a corporate sustainability strategy and are convinced of the need for it not least because CSM may offer a competitive advantage in the near future. Others differ in their thoughts on whether a CSM strategy is needed or even can be formulated.

Nevertheless all the interviewees in our study agreed that the corporate strategy of a company can influence and create the environment for CSM, and 64 per cent of general managers and sustainability officers said that their companies had integrated environmental and social criteria into their strategies and operations.

Organization

Organizational structure

In general the topic of sustainability and CSM in pharmaceutical companies was first brought up by environmental health and safety departments, which were among the first to realize that public criticism of the broad lack of corporate ecological and social responsibility represented a potential threat to the industry. Today they are still the standard bearers in many companies, and some have established cross-functional teams, sustainability councils or sustainability departments. At the board level it is usually the chief operating officer (COO) who takes responsibility.

The tasks of sustainability officers are very broad and vary slightly between companies. Crisis management of the most crucial issues and designing a structured approach to CSM are two of the most prevalent tasks. In addition, interacting and communicating with stakeholders and spreading the concept of sustainability through the organization are regarded by sustainability officers as top priorities.

In the course of their work sustainability officers face a number of barriers to progress. The principal barriers are listed below, with the three most significant ones at the top:

- Opposition or lack of interest from investors: the majority of investors question the need for and economic relevance of sustainable development.
- Managerial thinking: managers mainly have a short-term profit orientation, which goes against the time required for sustainable development initiatives.
- Lack of interest from customers: customers are not willing to pay a sustainability premium.
- Lack of appropriate tools and processes: sustainability officers lack the tools and processes needed to advance CSM, especially control and monitoring tools.
- Managers' lack of knowledge/expertise: within companies there are huge knowledge gaps about and lack of understanding of the concept of sustainable development, sometimes even within the designated committee.

- Lack of economic reasoning: understanding of the economic benefits of CSM is still poor, so sustainability officers cannot draw on their strongest argument.
- Lack of support from top management: some sustainability officers still lack the support of top management, which makes it difficult for them to argue internally about the importance of the concept of CSM.

Besides the work of the sustainability units, 53.6 per cent of the general managers surveyed thought that corporate and R&D staff could effectively promote social progress and improve environmental performance. Conversely 76.1 per cent considered that marketing/sales and finance staff provide the strongest opposition to the concept of sustainable development, and typically only interact with the sustainability unit on an irregular basis. Fifty-five per cent believed to varying degrees that more extensive collaboration between their departments and the sustainability unit or standard bearer would help to promote sustainable business practices.

Organizational processes, systems and tools

The executive managers who participated in the discussions agreed that few of the current organizational processes reflect sustainability criteria, and that so far no specific sustainability processes or systems for overall sustainability management have been set up, although an eco-management and audit schemes for environmental health and safety (EHS) management exists in most of the companies studied.

Sustainability officers consider that organizational decision-making, budgeting, incentive systems, monitoring and controlling, and feedback/adjustment processes should pay attention to sustainability issues. Because of the long history of EHS, many of these processes already reflect specific EHS criteria, but for many companies the relationship between sustainability management and organizational processes remains a grey area.

Nevertheless many companies explicitly or implicitly use tools that relate to implementing, measuring, monitoring or promoting the concept of sustainable development. The majority of these tools are used only for environmental purposes, but many have the potential to be used to improve social responsibility.

Communication and stakeholder interactions

Internal communication – selling the business case

The aim of internal communications about CSM is to sell the business case for sustainability by increasing awareness and understanding of the concept. Responsibility for the process varies among companies, but usually the tasks are split between the sustainability unit and the corporate communications department. In most of the companies in our study the sustainability unit drafts the content and decides on the target group, and communications personnel handle the actual communications.

Communications are usually tailored to upper and top management on the one hand and to everyone else in the organization on the other. In order to gain the support of top management, sustainability officers use economic reasoning and focus on the long-term benefits of including sustainability issues in the pharmaceutical business model. Communication is interactive and takes the form of discussion papers, speeches, presentations, cost–benefit analysis and scenario planning. Communications to all other employees are one-way and aimed at raising awareness by providing information and best practice examples in sustainability/environmental reports, newsletters and so on.

Stakeholder interactions

Interacting with stakeholders, or external communication, is regarded as essential by the majority of sustainability officers, but the degree to which this takes place varies greatly between the more and less advanced pharmaceutical companies. The two main tools are sustainability reporting and stakeholder dialogue.

The majority of companies have a history of two to ten years of EHS reporting, and some American companies issue reports on corporate philanthropy. Some of the companies that publish an EHS report are currently working on a sustainability report, while others have given their EHS reports titles such as 'EHS Report: On the Path towards Sustainability', indicating a change in thinking on the issue. Only two or three companies have published reports with titles such as 'Corporate Citizenship Report' or 'Sustainability Report'. The responsibility for such reports rests mostly with the sustainability unit, although in some companies it is a joint effort by the sustainability unit and the corporate communications department.

Although dialogue is the most effective way of interacting with stakeholders and it is regarded as a top priority for sustainability management, only a few companies engage in it. The pharmaceutical industry has a history of hiding behind opaque corporate walls and defending itself against stakeholders. Nonetheless 53 per cent of the general managers in our study ranked 'listening more to stakeholders' ideas and feedback' and 'greater transparency' as the most effective ways to improve relations with stakeholders.

The prevailing tactic in the industry is to detect potential sustainability issues early on in order to reduce the risk of being publicly accused by NGOs or other stakeholders of bad practices. Most NGOs are open to dialogue to achieve their aim of increasing the social and environmental responsibility of the industry, but radical NGOs tend to base their campaigns on rather emotional/ideological arguments rather than on scientific facts.

The financial markets are always open to dialogue on sustainability, but do not actively seek information on the concept of sustainable development, for example at company road shows. They treat sustainable development initiatives as a niche investment market, with only slowly growing interest to mainstream markets. In essence they restrict their interactions with pharmaceutical companies to exchanging information on social and environmental performance (sustainability reports) and pointing out potential sustainability crises.

In general, managers seem to be very open to and motivated by industry initiatives and PPPs. The latter are seen by more or less all parties involved as being the only means of addressing the most pressing health issues. Pharmaceutical companies are increasingly engaging in PPPs with bodies such as IGOs, NGOs and governments by contributing knowledge, capital and drugs.

Governments and other regulatory authorities have only a limited interest in comprehensive sustainable development efforts by the industry. Instead their focus is mainly on health economics and product-related legislation. Regulators (for example drug approval agencies such as the US Food and Drug Administration) work closely with individual companies and regard the pharmaceutical industry as a trusted and credible partner.

Issue management

The approach of most companies to managing crucial sustainability issues can best be described as muddling through, and only one or two have adopted a structured and comprehensive approach. Issue management is more akin to crisis management than an ongoing process, and no one is made to take ownership of a specific issue. Issues are often detected too late because tracking or early-awareness systems are absent. Companies usually have no procedures to evaluate the economic significance of issues and options for action. In the worst cases they react unprofessionally to external pressure and cause further damage to their image.

Summary

The pharmaceutical industry's progress in CSM compared with other industries is low to moderate. In general sustainability managers are struggling both to obtain the necessary support of top management and to raise awareness throughout their companies. Only a few companies have formulated a sustainability strategy; most are still pondering the link between sustainability management and corporate strategy/culture. The companies that participated in our study have chosen different organizational set-ups for CSM, but none has established a comprehensive organizational process. The main challenge of internal communication efforts is to sell the business case for sustainability, while external relations departments are in the process of setting up stakeholder dialogues. Issue management can be characterized as reactive, more a case of muddling through than well-thought-out.

Assessment of the business case for sustainability, its potential and exploitation

Value drivers

As discussed earlier, there are two general perspectives on dealing with social and environmental responsibility. First, the cost perspective focuses on the cost of all activities in the field of CSM (for example investment in new technology, managerial costs, taxes and fines, costs related to law suits, and so on). Second, the value perspective focuses on the potential value creation offered by CSM. In general value added falls into one or more of the following categories: revenue increase, cost reduction and intangible values (licence to operate). In essence the value perspective defines the business case for sustainability.

All of the sustainability officers and some of the general managers we interviewed were convinced that there are good business reasons for social and environmental responsibility. The three most important value drivers for sustainability officers were licence to operate (46.6 per cent), improved brand value and reputation (60 per cent) and attracting talent and increasing employee satisfaction (93.3 per cent). Reputation is important or very important to the companies, as 94.8 per cent of the general managers confirmed. Our survey revealed that 67.2 per cent of the companies had experienced varying degrees of brand damage in the previous three years, mainly through media campaigns (35 per cent) or conflicts with the authorities (37.5 per cent).

In the hierarchy of value drivers (Figure 10.3) the top two are revenue increase and cost reduction. As many of the participating companies confirmed, these are influenced by a variety of value drivers at different levels in the hierarchy, such as increased eco-efficiency, risk reduction and so on. The value drivers have different time horizons, as indicated in the figure by t = 1 (companies that have already achieved some cost reductions) and so on.

Many sustainability officers in the pharmaceutical industry believe that with a structured and comprehensive approach to corporate social and environmental responsibility by means of CSM, a competitive advantage can be gained, as long as other companies are struggling with their CSM approach.

Establishment and future potential of the business case

The business case for sustainability is only to a minor extent established in the pharmaceutical industry, for two reasons. First, in general companies' approach to crucial sustainability issues is marked by a high degree of vagueness and uncertainty, reflecting the lack of a sophisticated CSM system. Second, the average pharmaceutical company views sustainability and the management of corporate social and environmental responsibility from a cost perspective. Though companies see CSM as a means of reducing costs in some areas, for example through increased eco-efficiency, in other areas, they mainly view it as a cause of increased costs (or in other words, reduced revenues).

The majority of companies do not recognize the economic potential of CSM, despite the efforts of sustainability officers to foster a change in thinking by pointing out the positive effects that CSM would have on their companies' value drivers. The industry's strong progress with environmental matters explains their relatively high achievement with the 'eco-efficiency' value driver. However with all the other value drivers there is a significantly lower level of achievement, resulting in only average success with the top value drivers 'revenue increase' and 'cost reduction'.

There are two main reasons for the lack of progress with CSM: the large number of internal barriers that have to be removed, including management resistance, and the time needed to develop a suitable CSM process. The pharmaceutical industry started this process later than other industries. There are few factors that could help sustainability units to promote the business case for sustainability, the most promising being public and NGO pressure, and peer group pressure, that is, increased competition on environmental and social issues within the industry.

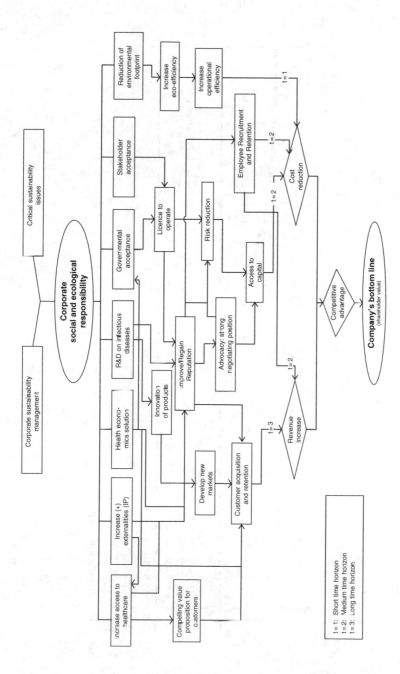

Figure 10.3 The effect of corporate social and ecological responsibility on a company's value drivers and bottom line

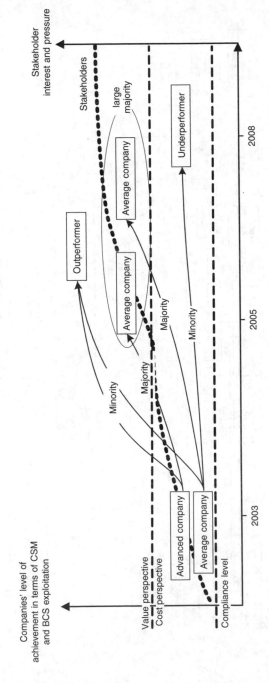

Figure 10.4 Sustainability roadmap

The draft roadmap presented in Figure 10.4 is based on the conclusions we have drawn on sustainability issues, the current status of CSM in the industry and the value drivers that define the business case. The further development of CSM will rely heavily on joint efforts by companies and stakeholders and a switch of focus from a cost perspective to a value-driver perspective. While it is already possible to identify companies that are more advanced, average or underperforming in terms of CSM, they are relatively close together and focus on costs. In the medium term increased differentiation is likely, with some companies changing to a value-driver perspective. In the long-term it can be predicted that the industry will split into (1) a minority group of underperformers that still focus on costs, (2) a majority group of average performers and (3) a minority group that has caught up with today's advanced companies to form a group of outperformers. Finally, stakeholder interest in the concept of sustainable development (mainly financial markets) and pressure from NGOs is likely to increase in the coming years.

Notes

1. For the complete empirical findings see http://www.imd.ch/research/projects/bcs.
2. For a more detailed discussion of all four sustainability issues see http://www.imd.ch/ research/projects/bcs.

Appendix 1: Environmental Issues (SO Survey)

Category	Individual item indicated by respondents
Environment in general (10)	Environment (5) Environmental footprint (3) Environmental performance of products (1) Conservation* (1)
Impact on biological environment (10)	Biotechnology (1) Agricultural practices (1) Biodiversity (3) Biodegradation of products (1) Pesticides (2) Natural pest control* (1) Organic farming, sustainable agriculture (1)
Soil (3)	Erosion (1) Degradation (1) Contamination (1)
Air/atmosphere (46)	Climate change and CO_2 emissions (34) Odors (2) Hazardous air pollutants (1) Ozone depletion (1) Emissions (3) Improving local air quality (2) Reduce emissions (2) Climate change strategy (1)
Noise (3)	Not further specified
Waste (12)	Waste incineration (1) Packaging (1) Waste disposal (1) Recycling/waste management (8) Minimizing landfill (1)
Long-term impact of discharges into environment (7)	Chemicals (2) Toxic substances (2) Antibiotics (1) Pharmaceuticals (2)

Category	Individual item indicated by respondents
Radiation (5)	Radio frequency (1) Nuclear power and waste (3) Radioactive discharges (1)
Resources (20)	Energy consumption (7) Water consumption (3) Raw materials (1) Long-term supply (1) Paper use (1) Energy management* (1) Sourcing of wood* (1) Renewable energy* (3) Energy efficiency (2)
Transportation, spatial issues (5)	Transportation (1) Access to remote sites (1) Congestion (2) Development of rural areas (1)

* Managerial responses to issues rather than issues as such. Absolute frequencies of occurrence are parenthesized.

Appendix 2: Social Issues (SO Survey)

Category	Individual item indicated by respondents
Ethics (10)	Bribery (1)
	Child labor (2)
	Money laundering and tax evasion (1)
	Corruption (1)
	Ethics (1)
	Human rights (3)
	Cultural diversity (1)
Globalization (10)	Social dimension of globalization (1)
	Education (2)
	Nutrition (1)
	NGO activism (1)
	Security (1)
	Poverty (1)
	Insurability of global risks (1)
	"Uncontrolled" globalization (1)
	Role as a supplier of much needed employment (1)*
Developing countries (10)	Environmental and social dumping (1)
	Digital divide (2)
	Indigenous people, local culture (1)
	Lack of environmental infrastructure (1)
	Social welfare (1)
	Access to drugs the developing world (2)
	Development of small local businesses (1)*
	Support health care and infrastructure (1)*
Health (32)	Alcoholism (3)
N.B. Occupational health & safety are excluded	AIDS (2)
	Food safety (1)
	Health in the developed world (4)
	Obesity (1)
	Safety (2)
	Access to drugs, healthcare, adequate pricing (10)
	Tobacco (1)
	Malaria and other tropical diseases (3)

Category	Individual item indicated by respondents
	Children's health (1) Rising cost of healthcare (1) Supplying milk to schools* (1)
Working conditions in the supply chain (9)	Work-related accidents & illnesses (1) Occupational health & safety (7) Suppliers' working conditions (1)
Social issues (in general, also including communities) (9)	Social issues (5) Residential and recreational areas increasingly closer to industrial sites (1) Access to remote areas (1) Community development* (1) Recruiting locals* (1)
Human Resources (also in a global context) (14)	Equal opportunities and rights (2) Human resources (1) Job scarcity, workforce reduction (1) Finding new corporate culture (after merger) (1) Labor relations (1) Well being of employees, employee loyalty (2) Diversity (1) Recruiting disabled personnel (1) Corporate HR policy and standards (2) Participative engagement of employees (1) Educating multicultural workforce and staff (1)

* Managerial responses to issues rather than issues as such. Absolute frequencies of occurrence are parenthesized.

Appendix 3: Key Terms and Management Issues (SO Survey)

Category	Individual item indicated by respondents
Term used for corporate sustainability (7)	Corporate social responsibility (2)
	Responsible Care (1)
	Corporate responsibility (1)
	Business ethics (1)
	Sustainable development (1)
	Sustainability (1)
Stakeholders (11)	Community relations (4)
	Stakeholder relationship (2)
	Public acceptance in general (2)
	Manage opposition to fossil fuels (1)
	Public acceptance of waste in the environment (1)
	Stakeholders' perception of current performance (1)
Awareness (4)	Awareness and expertise of entire workforce (3)
	Awareness of senior management (1)
Goals (13)	Eco-efficiency (2)
	Sustainability-driven innovation (2)
	Develop new technologies (1)
	Develop sustainable products (1)
	Socially responsible marketing (1)
	Continuous improvement (2)
	Transparency of revenues (1)
	Recruit and retain talent (1)
	Compliance with UN Global Compact (2)
Upstream (4)	Supply chain management (2)
	Social and environmental performance of suppliers (1)
	Cooperation with suppliers (1)
Production (4)	Safety (2)
	Quality (1)
	Social issues (1)
Downstream (9)	Product stewardship (2)
	Product design (3)

Category	Individual item indicated by respondents
	Traceability of products (2) Support customers (1) Environmental and social impact (1)
Communication	Reporting (2) Communication on chemical/sustainable products (2) Communication on environmental, health and safety practices (1) Building a sustainable brand (1) Marketing practices (1)
Tools and systems (13)	Integrating sustainability into business processes (2) Measuring and reporting performance (2) Environmental management system (2) Risk management (1) Target setting (1) Exchanging best practices between divisions (1) Full cost accounting (1) New corporate vision (1) Development of tools and methodologies (1) Social performance management (1)
Environmental regulation and compliance (13)	Regulation on climate change (1) Remediation costs (1) Tightening regulation on emissions to air (1) EU policy on chemicals (1) Cost of waste disposal, environmental legislation (2) Energy policy (1) Requirements for productions and products (1) Lack of uniform legislation (1) Compliance with environmental legislation (1) Eco-taxes (1) Weakening pressure from environmental legislators and regulators (2)

Note: absolute frequencies of occurrence are parenthesized.

Index